George Formby

An Intimate Biography Of The Troubled Genius

*

David Bret

Copyright © David Bret 2014

David Bret has asserted his moral right to be identified as the Author of this Work in accordance with the Copyright Designs and Patents Act 1988. All rights reserved. No part of this publication may be reproduced or transmitted in any form or by any means, electronic or mechanical, including photocopying, recording or any information storage or retrieval system without the permission in writing from David Bret.

A catalogue record for this book is available from the British Library.

ISBN: 978-1-291-87220-0

George Formby

An Intimate Biography Of The Troubled Genius

David Bret

Acknowledgements

Writing this book would not have been possible had it not been for the inspiration, criticisms and love of that select group of individuals who, whether they be in this world or the next, I will always regard as my true family and *autre coeur*: Barbara, Irene Bevan, Marlene Dietrich, René Chevalier, Axel Dotti, Dorothy Squires, Anne Taylor and Roger Normand, David Bolt, *que vous dormez en paix*, Lucette Chevalier, Jacqueline Danno, Hélène Delavault, Betty and Gérard Gamain, Annick Roux,Taylor, Terry Sanderson, Charley Marouani, Dennis Taylor, Dorothy Cottrell-Johnson, Simon Blumenfeld, Charlotte Bush, Irene Handl, Dorothy Hyson, Kate Mills, Dinah Sheridan, Pat Taylor, Morrissey, Dennis Poulter, Peter Pollard and Jacky Morley. Also a very special mention for Amália Rodrigues, Peter Burton, Joey Stefano, those *hiboux, fadistas* and *amis de foutre* who happened along the way, and *mes enfants perdus*. Thanks too to my agent Guy Rose and his lovely wife, Alex; and also my wife, Jeanne, for putting up with my bad moods and for still being the keeper of my soul!

N'oublie pas….La vie sans amis c'est
Comme un jardin sans fleurs

Introduction

The actress Thora Hird declared that he had been sent by God. Such was the devotion of his fans that over 100,000 of them turned up at his funeral. His record compilations, though dated and with many songs over-released, still outsell those of any other nostalgia artiste. His films, complete with their poor continuity and corny dialogue, represent the very best of British family humour.

George Formby successfully transcended every class barrier and was equally at home entertaining royalty in the most opulent surroundings as crawling through the mire, risking life and limb to cheer the lads at the Front. He brought joy to millions worldwide, yet never achieved lasting personal happiness. Throughout his career his loyalties were tested and torn between a grasping family he had been conditioned into respecting—but which he only ended up loathing—and a near-psychotic wife who made much of his private life a misery, yet without whose nagging and shrewd business sense he almost certainly would not have made it to the top.

On stage and screen, George Formby rapidly established himself as the seemingly inarticulate little man who nevertheless triumphs over adversity to ultimately prove that he is by no means as gormless as one has assumed—armed with the weapons of his particular trade: a clutch of catchy songs, a huge toothy grin, and a charisma which unequivocally placed him above all his contemporaries.

"I wasn't very good, but I had something the public seemed to want," he once said of himself. He was, of course, selling himself short. George Formby remains the ultimate all-round genius, a blazing lodestar of talent which will never be replaced.

One:
A Chip Off The Old Block

"I don't think anybody understood him. I don't know whether he understood himself." Irene Handl, co-star.

His father, George Formby Sr, known in music-hall circles at the beginning of the century as "The Wigan Nightingale", had the most inauspicious start in life. James Lawler Booth, born in Ashton-under-Lyme on 4 October 1875, was the illegitimate son of Sarah Jane Booth, a Lancashire prostitute who, in the space of ten years, was convicted 140 times for offences which included theft, vagrancy, brawling, and most frequently drunkenness.

In a thoroughly unfortunate childhood, James would find himself shunned by his mother, and shut out of the house whenever she was entertaining a man—which was often. Despite the fact that she was just four-feet tall and decidedly unattractive, there was never any shortage of clients. The youngster was beaten by his numerous "foster fathers", such as the Frank Lawler who probably fathered him and whom Sarah Jane married when James was six months old. It is not known if his name was actually *changed* to Lawler at this time, or whether this was simply his middle name. Lawler certainly was no less cruel towards the boy than his mother, shutting him out of the house for hours and sometimes nights on end, allowing him in again only when he had earned enough coppers from singing in the streets to pay for their tobacco and Sarah's gin. It is not surprising, therefore, that by the age of ten—through sleeping rough and not eating properly—James had already developed severe chest trouble and acquired the "graveyard" cough which would later form an essential component of his stage act.

By the time he was twelve—and his mother had been imprisoned for the umpteenth time—James had finally left home to work in a Todmorden cotton-mill. Show business, however, was his only interest, albeit that he had never set foot in a music-hall, and he had supplemented his poor wages by singing in local pubs. It was here that he had been "discovered" by an unscrupulous impresario and teamed up with another boy as the Glen Ray Brothers.

For several years, executing a badly-choreographed song and dance routine—like his more famous son, spontaneity would provide James with that integral element of magic, as opposed to organised patter—the Glen Ray Brothers had toured the provinces. According to the generally accepted story, it was whilst they were passing through a Northern railway station and James observed a number of coal-wagons destined for Formby—a small town between Ormskirk and the coastal area perhaps appropriately known as Mad Wharf—that he hit upon the idea of re-baptising himself George Formby.

Bearing in mind that Formby Sr was unable to read and write until he was well into his teens, this seems extremely unlikely. According to the records of Birkenhead's Argyle Theatre, the entertained was still being engaged as J H (never J L) Booth until 1897. When he was about twenty the theatre *manager*, Daniel Clarke, suggested that he change his name to Formby after *he* had observed the lettering on the coal-wagons. The George, again according to Clarke, was chosen in honour of the great comic, George Robey.

As a solo entertainer, Formby Sr had slowly but surely amassed a following in his native Lancashire. Despite its limitations, his act had achieved immense popularity nationwide, a success which had begun with a gimmick—an on-stage alter-ego, John Willie, whose catchphrase—"I'm coughing better tonight!"—accompanied by his rattling cough and droll repartee, would have them rolling in the aisles, even when audiences were well-aware that he was terminally ill.

For two decades, John Willie represented the then archetypal Lancashire lad: gormless but not *entirely* stupid, dry-humoured, inarticulate and well-intentioned, the sort of character working-class people adored and readily identified with, because this odd little man with the cut-down bowler, shoes on the wrong feet, and his pre-Chaplinesque antics always found a way of seeing the funny side of misery and destitution. In this respect, in years to come Formby's example would be followed by the likes of Little Tich, Jimmy James, Rob Wilton and Beryl Reid. His songs, on the other hand—numbers such as "Since I Parted My Hair In The Middle" and "I'm Such A Hit With The Girls"—were decidedly light-hearted and closely resembled the work of his Gallic counterparts, Dranem and Mayol, and the Anglo-French chansonnier Harry Fragson. Formby Sr was also credited with "inventing" Wigan Pier—when he confided to audiences that this was his favourite bathing spot, the less knowledgeable would rush off with their buckets and spades, only to discover that the "pier" was actually a landing-stage of the Leeds-Liverpool Ship Canal connecting Wigan to Warrington!

It was in Wigan, in 1898, that Formby Sr met the woman who would become his wife. At the time he was involved with Ivy Caston, a music-hall hoofer of whom almost nothing is known. Caston was staying at a lodging-house in Marsh lane run by a couple named Hoy…but when Formby called on her one evening and found she was not in, he promptly fell for the Hoys' feisty twenty-one-year-old daughter, Eliza.

Eliza's parents, devout Catholics, were horrified to learn that their daughter had been asked out by a music-hall turn, and forbade her to have anything to do with him. When she found out that she had been seeing Formby behind her back, Eliza's mother accused her of being "loose", and she received a thrashing from her father. Even so, the couple continued courting, and on 11 August 1899 they were married at Wigan Registry office. Theirs would prove a happy, fruitful union. Possessed of a staggering consumptive virility, Formby is reputed to have sired several children on the wrong side of the blanket. He had thirteen children with Eliza, six of whom did not survive infancy, while their fourth child would one day achieve the international fame his father had only ever dreamed of.

Despite their initial dislike of their son-in-law, it did not take the Hoys long to accept him, particularly when his young wife persuaded Formby to convert to Catholicism, and over the next few months Hoy taught him another skill—equestrianism. In his younger days in his native Newmarket, Hoy had worked as a jockey, and he was currently employed as an undertaker's "horse-breaker", prior to the evolution of the motor-driven hearse.

Hoy rather hoped that the exercise, combined with plenty of good food and fresh air, would put a little colour into Formby's dreadfully pasty cheeks. What no one knew at the time, however, was that the 24-year-old entertainer was already in an advances stage of phthisis, or pulmonary tuberculosis, an incurable progressive wasting disease brought about by his childhood years of neglect. Indeed, Formby's condition was *so* critical that as early as 1900, two years after their marriage, Eliza began insisting that oxygen cylinders be installed in the wings, wherever he was appearing.

After their wedding, the Formbys—they never called themselves Booth, and Eliza never addressed her husband as anything but George—lived with Eliza's parents. Their first three short-lived daughters were born here, but it was at their first home, 3 Westminster Street, on 26 May 1904, that George Hoy Booth, the future George Formby, came into the world. Over the course of the next fourteen years he would be followed by Louisa, Frances, Ella, Mary, Frank, Ethel and Edward. Two more babies are thought to have been stillborn.

He was born blind, on account of a caul, or membrane, enclosing his head, and was unable to see for several months. In August 1939 the star took great pleasure in revealing to the *Daily Mirror* that he owed the miracle of regaining his sight to a simple sneeze:

> *Every time I sneeze now I think what a miracle it was. One day my mother took me across from Liverpool to New Brighton on the ferry boat. A gust of wind, or summat, made me sneeze. I sneezed so hard that the shock opened my eyes for the first time. Mother took me to the doctor's and he bathed my eyes. From that day to this I've never had any trouble with my eyesight. Even those big arc-lamps in the film studios don't affect me. A Manchester specialist is so interested in my case that I visit him every year for an examination. There's an old superstition which says a person born with a caul will never be drowned—the wife has it now, so it'll be handed down through the family as an heirloom. Ee, lad, I'll always have a soft spot in my heart for the blind!*

Young George did not have to suffer the hardships which had been imposed on his father. At the time of his son's birth, Formby Sr was earning £35 a week in pantomime, and as much as £15 a week in the legitimate music-hall—a phenomenal sum at the time—and had progressed far and beyond his native Lancashire, following a comment in a London newspaper by Marie Lloyd, the undisputed Queen of British Music-Hall, that in her estimation only two variety acts were worth seeing besides herself: Dan Leno and The Wigan Nightingale.

George was enrolled at the prestigious Notre Dame private school close to the family's new home in the more opulent Dickenson Street.

The arrangement would prove but temporary. A nervous, underweight child, George was inattentive in class. The nuns both terrified and intimidated him, particularly Sister Veronica, a sadistic individual who, he later claimed, never missed an opportunity to rap him over the knuckles with a ruler over the slightest misdemeanour. Sister Veronica was Notre Dame's music teacher, and it was probably on account of her that Formby Sr took his son away from the school when he was seven and doing *well* in music—the only subject that had ever interested him—though only through fear. The apprehension instilled in him by this woman would never leave him and, for the rest of his life, despite having the most astonishing sense timing an ear for rhythm, George Formby would never learn how to read or write music.

From the summer of 1911, "school" for George would be a succession of racing stables. Unable to forget his own appalling childhood, Formby Sr—who by this time owned several fillies—needed to give his son and heir a more privileged start in life. George was taken on as a stable-boy, firstly at Bishop's Cannings in Wiltshire, then by Jack Drake, at Middleham's Warwick House Stables. His father had every confidence that George would one day make the grade as a jockey.

The regime at Warwick House, however, was far harsher than it had been at the Catholic school. George had to be up at four every morning to clean out the horses, the other stable-boys bullied him on account of his puny size—at the age of eight he weighed just 55 pounds and fell victim to every childhood ailment. Subsequently, every time he received a beating he would abscond and make his own way back to Wigan, only to be escorted back to Middleham the next day by his mother.

Whether George actually *wanted* to follow in his father's footsteps at this time is not known. He had successfully mastered the art of playing the Jew's harp and the mouth-organ, and he *is* known to have had a passable singing voice. Formby Sr, however, was virulently against George having anything to do with the stage. Indeed, he would not allow him to see his *own* act, not even when he appeared in the Royal Variety Show in July 1913.

George stuck it out at Middleham for another year until, weary of all the absconding, Formby Sr apprenticed him to Thomas Scourfield, at Epsom. His racing career would prove decidedly unenterprising. His first mount was in the Apprentice Plate at Lingfield Park—on Formby Sr's Eliza, named after his wife. The weather was atrocious, and George was suffering from mumps but insisted on competing with a field which comprised thirty-five runners. He came last. Over the next few years he would ride seven seconds, more than twenty thirds, but not one winner.

In April 1915, Formby Sr *was* persuaded to lift hiss embargo when a producer friend, Will Barker, asked him to "loan" him for George to appear in his latest film, a five-reeler entitled *By The Shortest Of Heads*. The stars were Violet Hobson and Sidney Blackmer, a 20-year-old hopeful who had just enlisted to serve in Europe with the American Expeditionary Forces. Another star was Moore Marriott, what later achieved notoriety as Will Hay's sidekick, Harbottle, in his famous comedies.

Sidney Blackmer, whose successful film and stage career would continue well into the Sixties, later dismissed this effort as "goddam trash". Few Formby fans have been able to form their own opinion, since only one complete print of the film is thought to have survived, and this remains locked in a London archive. Blackmer, however, appears to have judged it accordingly—the film *is* dire, with the exception of the final racing sequence.

George also appeared in another film at around this time—*No Fool Like An Old Fool*—of which absolutely nothing is known, and from which not even the stills survive.

By The Shortest Of Heads was shot at Epsom, and upon Formby Sr's insistence George was paid the princely sum of one-pound for his appearance. He also demanded that his son be put through his paces for the film's gripping final race by the legendary Steve Donoghue, the Warrington-born jockey who had won that year's Derby and who would do so a record-breaking six times over the next decade. In addition, Formby Sr arranged for the *Daily Mirror* to do a photo-shoot, which appeared in the newspaper on 19 April under the heading: GEORGE FORMBY'S LITTLE JOCKEY SON WHO WEIGHS ONLY THREE STONE 13 LB.

In the film, George played a stable-boy who, adopted by a trainer, outwits a bunch of criminals—setting a precedent for almost *all* of his future films—then wins £10,000 for his benefactor in a race. The film was not successful, though it did warrant a brief mention in *Bioscope* upon its re-release, during the summer of 1918:

> *It is an exciting photoplay of love and sport, capitally acted and redolent of the real turf atmosphere [though] it is the race itself which lifts the film above the ordinary, and the sight of the tiny jockey (George Formby Jr) gradually drawing away from his rival will raise the most phlegmatic audience to enthusiasm.*

Immediately after completing the film, which everyone expected to be a one-off, George's father secured him another position with a stables—this time in County Kildare, near the Curragh. Since there was virtually no racing in England during the war years, most owners—including Formby Sr—had transferred their horses to Ireland, and George was assigned to a trainer named Johnny Burns. In August 1915 he was enrolled at the school in Athgarvan, his first full-time education in four years, and that same week he rode a horse named Halfcast in Ireland's first ever apprentice race and came second. On account of the hectic work schedule doled out by Burns, he very rarely made it to class before lunchtime, and was frequently caned by the headmaster.

As had happened in England, George made innumerable attempts to run away from the stables, largely because of the unsociable hours and the bullying of the other stable-boys. The latter nicknamed him Cloggy, because he came from the same place as the much-lampooned footwear. Once, accompanied by another boy George named as Hamilton, he got as far as Dublin, only to be picked up by the police and locked in a cell for the night—such was the extent of his homesickness. On 10 October 1918, he sneaked away from a race-meeting at Baldoyle and, booking his passage on the *Leinster*, he sent a telegram to his father, asking him to meet him at Holyhead Docks.

When George had last seen them, his parents had been living at Hindley House, a large detached residence at Stockton Heath which Formby Sr had converted into a smallholding. In 1917, however, the family had moved to Hillcrest, a slightly larger house in Warrington's London Road, which George had yet to see. Fortunately, he never made the journey. Burns had reported him missing, and he was apprehended thirty minutes before the ship set sail. A little over two hours later, the *Leinster*, with its 510 passengers and crew, was torpedoed by a German U-Boat and sunk. There were no survivors.

The incident had given Formby Sr a scare he could well have done without, and in November 1918 George was sent back to Middleham, this time to the stables owned by Dobson Peacock. His second period in the village, far happier than the first, was recalled by Dennis Poulter, the son of the local craftsman who, a few weeks after he arrived in Middleham, presented George with his very first musical instrument, a harmonica. He told me:

> *George was befriended by three people: Jane and Violet Parish, and my father Herbert Poulter. Jane, affectionately known as Aunt Jin, was the eldest of a fairly large family, and when orphaned at the age of fourteen she had decided to care for the other children herself. By the time George came to Middleham, she was also the stable lads' housekeeper. Her sister, Violet, was in service at a town in the village and my father was the local shoemaker. Every year at Middleham, on Whit Sunday, there would be a fancy-dress parade, and in 1920 my father, accompanied by Violet, wheeled him through the streets in a barrow. All three were very fond of him—he was very small for sixteen, very nervous, didn't see much of his family, and this adopted family protected him from the other boys' bullying.*

George remained at Middleham until the end of 1920, travelling occasionally to Newmarket to race for Formby Sr's friend, Lord Derby, who owned a stable there. Exactly why he decided to return to Ireland at a time when he was blissfully happy and spending more time at Aunt Jin's cottage, adjacent to the castle, than he did at the actual manor house, is not known. He had only been in County Kildare a few weeks, however, when on 8 February 1921 he received a telegram from Eliza, bearing the sad news that his father had passed away. Formby Sr had collapsed in the wings of the Newcastle Empire, where he had been appearing in pantomime, following a violent coughing fit which had ruptured the blood vessels in his larynx, causing a haemorrhage. He was just forty-five.

It had taken George Formby Sr a good ten years to die, yet his doctors had advised him that with proper medical attention—by cutting down on his appearances in some of the smokier flea-pit theatres, and by taking an occasional respite at a Swiss sanatorium which, as one of the highest-paid acts in England, he could easily afford—he might have lived a little longer. His excuse had always been that he needed to provide for his wife and seven children, though young George was of course providing for himself.

Towards the end of his life, many of Formby Sr's performances had been curtailed, or cancelled altogether by Eliza, a fiercely protective woman who only ever had her husband's best interests at heart. In the Spring of 1917 her overtly caring nature had resulted in the couple being served a writ by the Southport Palladium, when Formby Sr had failed to turn up for a show there, only to perform in London a few days later. Eliza had defended him by providing the London High Court with a doctor's certificate—and by giving the judge a piece of her mind—and the Formbys' lawyer had pleaded for clemency, describing his client as "having one foot in the grave". However, Formby Sr had lost his case and had been ordered to pay the manager of the Palladium £175 in damages.

George's father was interred in the Catholic section of Warrington's Manchester Road cemetery—newsreel footage of the event has survived—and his grave was marked by an ornate marble tomb, embellished with an alleged replica of Manchester Hippodrome's proscenium arch within which there is a chiseled relief portrait and the inscription, "After Life's Fitful Fever He Sleeps Well". And as if aware that he would one day be almost forgotten—having been majestically overshadowed by his son—Eliza had the word "comedian" inscribed beneath his name.

After the funeral, leaving her other children to be looked after by relatives, Eliza took George on his first trip to London, hoping the bright lights might help him through his grief. At the Victoria

Palace, the scene of so many Formby triumphs, they happened upon a comedian named Tommy Dixon who, not content with purloining his material, had already begun styling himself "The New George Formby". George was appalled, and though he was totally unfamiliar with his father's patter, he made up his mind there and then that he *would* follow in his footsteps.

Eliza Booth, bereft of her anchor, approved wholeheartedly of George's decision and over the next few months devoted herself to launching him on the stage. In his later years George insisted that he had never wanted to cash in on his father's name, but this was not true. Although he refused to perform under the name Formby—choosing his first names, George Hoy—he did not argue when Eliza opted to use him as an excuse for "resurrecting" her husband and put her son in his father's John Willie garb: the jacket which was several sizes too small, the concertina-bottomed trousers, the shoes which Formby Sr had always worn on the wrong feet, the cut-down bowler. Even the thick pancake make-up was copied...and so were the songs.

George Hoy's debut performance—he was sub-billed George Formby's son, just in case anyone did not know—took place between features at Harrison's Picture House (subsequently the Hippodrome) Earlstown, between Warrington and St Helens, in April 1921—just ten weeks after his father's death. He was accompanied by Harry Duckenfield, Formby Sr's pianist and arranger, and halfway through his first number dried up due to stage fright. He would have given up completely had not several of his father's more ardent admirers yelled encouragement, though George himself would always be the first to admit that as a "green" sixteen-year-old, his John Willie interpretation left a great deal to be desired.

This apparently third-rate performance had its compensation, for also in the audience was Daniel Clarke, the manager of the Argyle Theatre, Birkenhead. This was the man who had supplied his father with his stage-name. Invited to the show by Eliza Booth—"out of respect for the lad's much-missed old man—he offered George a one-week engagement at his notoriously difficult establishment…a ten-minute spot on a very full bill which was completely drowned by the hissing and booing from the galleries.

For the next two years, billed as George Hoy and engaged as a warm-up act—poorly-paid, but supported financially by his mother—George toured the Northern halls and cinemas, always emulating his father. Then, quite unexpectedly in 1923, his whole life dramatically changed, on account of two impromptu "acquisitions". One was a musical instrument, the other a woman!

Exactly *where* George bought his first ukulele (technically a banjo-ukulele) is not known. The star himself claimed that he had paid fifty-shillings for it from a hard-up comic, whilst his brother Frank maintained that it had come from a Manchester second-hand shop. What is certain is that George first introduced it into his act during a week-long engagement at the Barnsley Alhambra because, he said, he had never known what to do with his hands. Accompanying himself to "Going Back To Tennessee", not a *deliberately* tuneless rendition of the classic, he received a standing ovation!

Afterwards, George would try to convince himself that such over-zealousness had been a mere fluke. The theatre's manager, Charles Lawson, had heard him plucking the instrument in his dressing room. While standing in the wings, waiting to announce the next act, he had observed that George was clearly on the verge of drying up. Therefore, to save his embarrassment, and to stave off a possible dilemma—if the warm-up was booed, the other acts on the bill frequently had a hard time calming the audience down—Lawson had sent on one of the stagehands with George's ukulele, and the young man had turned to the audience, and quipped something along the lines of, "Here, see of you can play this!" When he received *another* standing ovation the next evening, however, prompting Lawson to move him further up the bill, George knew that he was on to a surefire winner. Dispensing with his John Willie get-up, though not for the moment his father's songs, he announced that henceforth he would be known as George Formby.

George (centre) during a Whit Monday fancy-dress parade circa 1920 (Dennis Poulter)

George, aged 18 and on the threshold of fame, shortly after his father's death (GFS)

Two:
Count Your Blessings!

"Wherever George had to go, Beryl had to go too. I just used to say all the time, 'If you want George, you've got to have me.' They always wanted George, so they had to put up with me!"
Beryl Formby, wife.

Beryl Ingham, a 23-year-old Accrington-born clog-dancer, had formed a variety act known as The Two Violets with her sister, May. Attractive, blonde—and feisty—she met George in 1923 when they were appearing on the same bill in Castleford, West Yorkshire.

It was hardly an auspicious occasion, for when George tried to show a little courtesy by asking the pretty blonde how she was, she snarled at him to mind his own business. She excused herself by declaring that her father had warned her never to talk to strangers. Commenting on George's act—for which he was now blacking his face, spouting an endless tirade of parrot jokes *and* singing his father's songs—she declared, "If I'd have had a bag of rotten tomatoes, I'd have thrown them at him!"

A more sensible man might have given such a seemingly arrogant, outspoken creature a suitably wide berth. In retrospect, however, despite her domineering, conniving ways, Beryl would prove the best thing that had ever happened to him as far as his career was concerned. On the personal level, however, this bossy, surrogate-mother figure was probably the personification of his very worst nightmares.

George, buck-toothed and loveable, and wholly unaware of his unexplored, indeed immeasurable talent, was immediately attracted to Beryl, but terrified of making an initial approach. He was by no means a virgin, having enjoyed any number of one-night stands, mostly with dancers or chorus-girls. Beryl, however, was no woman of easy virtue. In the days when show business was not generally regarded as an acceptable profession for young ladies, the Ingham sisters were chaperoned virtually everywhere by one or both of their parents—an obstacle which George soon overcame when he learnt that Beryl's father was the landlord of a pub, the Black Bull in Darwen. With his natural wit and charm he very quickly befriended Ingham, and in next to no time was invited to the family home for Sunday tea. However, during this and his subsequent visits to the house, Beryl still looked down her nose at him every time he turned up on his newly-acquired motorcycle.

Their seemingly one-sided courtship dragged on for over a year, with George pestering Beryl to marry him—always receiving the same snappy negative response, usually in front of her family and friends in an attempt to humiliate him. Finally, in August 1924, he decided that he had had enough, that an ultimatum would provide the only solution. Any more rational man would have given up on her, of course, but Beryl had set his senses reeling, even though she would never see *him* even remotely as an object of desire. Therefore, borrowing his mother's car—a spanking new Rover which was the envy and talk of Wigan—he set off for Darwen, in the middle of the night, and in true "Lancashire Romeo" fashion positioned himself under Beryl's window and began crooning, or so he later claimed:

> *How I love these Darwen girls,*
> *With their bright and sunny curls…*
> *From their red and ruby lips…*
> *I get the taste of fish and chips!*

The noise is said to have roused half the neighbourhood although

George stuck to his guns, shouting that he would *only* go away once Beryl had agreed to become his wife. Desperate to shut him up, now that the tables had been turned and *she* was the one feeling embarrassed, Beryl agreed.

George was nevertheless so convinced that Beryl had accepted a marriage proposal *only* to get rid of him, and that the next time she saw him, she would not mince her words in telling him so, that he said nothing to his mother. The proposal coincided with Beryl's acceptance, on his behalf, of a week-long engagement at the Alhambra, in London's Leicester Square. George was once more the warm-up act—the part of the bill that all artistes loathed, but in the days when entertainers were more or less *compelled* to work their way to the top via the ranks, an integral part of the music-hall regime.

The manager at the Alhambra had never heard of George Formby Jr, but had included him on the bill because his father's pianist, Harry Duckenfield, was accompanying one of the other acts and had recommended him, even offering to pay George's fee out of his own pocket, just to give him a break at one of the most prestigious music-halls in Europe. The Alhambra had been the first establishment to introduce a chorus-line, in the 1860s, and had been used as a model for the more famous Folies-Bergere, in Paris. George Formby Sr had regularly topped the bill, and though he too was unfamiliar with his son the orchestra leader, a snobbish individual named George Saker who rarely made an appearance on the podium before the interval—preferring to leave the "amateurs and other riff-raff" to his deputy—actually *insisted* on conducting the young man billed as "A Chip Off The Old Block" as a tribute to George's father.

George and Beryl's wedding took place a few weeks after the Alhambra season—on 13 September 1924, a Saturday, though he often joked that it had been an "unlucky" Friday. They married at Wigan Registry Office, with an aunt and uncle stepping in at the last moment as witnesses—and to vouch for George because he was still legally a minor. Indeed, Eliza did not find out that her son was married until the couple were due home from their honeymoon. To Eliza's way of thinking, Beryl was already a "scarlet woman" who had lured her son to London—it did not matter that they had slept in separate rooms. Additionally, any marriage which had not been blessed by the Church was, she declared, invalid. Therefore, whilst he was living in "open sin" with his "floosy", neither of them would be welcome in her house. Clearly, George's mother was forgetting that she and his father had also been married at the same registry office.

Beryl had anticipated such a reaction, which was why she elected to stay in the car, outside Hillcrest, whilst George was facing the music—and she readily agreed to the church ceremony which took place two months later, in spite of being fiercely agnostic. To a certain extent, Eliza was pacified by this, though she is said never to have liked the women who, in her eyes, not content with leading her "Georgie" astray, had now taken over the development of his career.

Beryl's apparent psychosis almost certainly stems from the fact that in the days when wives were only too frequently regarded as subservient—particularly in Northern England, where traditionally the man worked to support his family, and the wife stayed at home to look after it—*she* had given up her own career to manage his. Just how far Beryl would have developed as an all-round entertainer as opposed to George's sometime stooge in pantomimes and stage-revues, is not difficult to ascertain. Clog-dancers were already going out of fashion when she met George, and though undeniably very pretty and an above average hoofer, she possessed neither the talent nor the temperament to progress beyond her own limited sphere. In contrast, George was blessed with a *natural* presence and personality, and would have made it to the top on these strengths alone. Mistinguett, Chevalier, his own father and even Marie Lloyd had already proved that one did not necessarily require the vocal ability of a Melba or Caruso, or the dancing skills of a Duncan or Nijinsky, to fill theatres.

Beryl, however, would always appear to resent what she had given up for her husband, and their marriage began with her effectively holding the upper hand, a position she retained. *She* had paid for the honeymoon, and when George informed her that he was in the red to the tune of £70—most of this was money he owed on his motorcycle—Beryl dipped into her savings and cleared his debts. It is no secret that he would spend another thirty-six years paying her back.

Beryl told George that they would never have children—not that she disliked them, but that they would end up getting in the way of his career if *she* spent time away from him bringing them up. George tried to argue but Beryl would not be swayed, and in a rare fit of pique he headed for the nearest dog-pound, where for a few shillings he bought a brown and white mongrel which had been about to be put down. Beryl took to the dog at once—the first of many—and baptised him Mickey Dripping!

Neither was Beryl pleased when, early in October, George signed for a series of third-on engagements at a small Morecambe theatre, aware that The Two Violets had been booked with the Newcastle Empire for the whole of that week. Beryl was earning £10 a week in those days—twice as much as George—and, suspecting that he might start "fooling around" so soon after their marriage, she tried to force the manager of the Empire to take George on too. He may have agreed, had she not tried to dupe him into paying George the same salary as herself, claiming that he never worked for less on account of his always being inundated with offers.

The manager, Thomas Convery, had been a close friend of George's father, and prided himself on the somewhat morbid fact that the great man had died only hours after his final performance at the Newcastle Empire. Convery checked George out, and when he realised that beryl had tried to con him, he came close to firing her. She, however, refused to be thwarted: having recognised her husband's enormous potential—something his peers have said *he* would not have done without her constant harping on and pushing—Beryl had taken George in hand. She taught him how to dress, stressing the fact that a Lancashireman would not be regarded as vulgar by Southern audiences if he abandoned the stereotyped flat-cap image and appeared on stage in a tuxedo. She taught him what to sing, how to use his hands when he was not playing his ukulele, what jokes to tell, and how to monitor audience reaction by playing mostly to the galleries, which contained the genuine fans, those working-class men and women who recognised within him so much of themselves.

Some years later, Beryl would offer a legitimate excuse for her frequently insufferable presence and behaviour, blaming this on her husband's tiresome indolence, and intimating that George actually gleaned pleasure from her incessant nagging:

> *George is hopeless when I not with him and is as miserable as sin. I always have to be in the wings when I'm not acting with him. I appear with him on the stage and in his comedy act, but he does his famous ukulele act alone—when I have to be all the time in the wings, or anyway within hearing. And believe me, if I leave George alone for a minute he goes off and buys a new car or a new jumper...*

It was Beryl, too, who insisted that George stop "plonking" his ukulele and learn how to play it properly. And ironically, his first major engagement—a six-month contract at £15 a week—was with the Newcastle Empire. Here he was a hit with the instrument though at some venues, such as the Oldham Palace, he was requested *not* to play it. In this part of the country, his father's records were still selling and some theatre managers were receiving pay-offs from Formby Sr's record company to continue promoting his name. And what better way of doing this than to employ his sound-alike son to perform his songs?

The Palace revue, Thomas Convery's and Arthur Merts' *Formby Seeing Life*—subtitled *A Merrygoround of Laughter and Melody*—which opened on 2 November 1925, also saw George resurrecting his father's John Willie, complete with his graveyard cough, and was basically a hastily thrown together rehash of Formby Srs sketches from the war years: "The Wigan Railway Line", "Mugs For Luck", "Formby On The Boulevards", and a farce entitled "The Interrupted Song", where George desperately tried to complete with a heckler.

For many, the highlight of the Palace revue was a sketch entitled "Prisonville", which featured George's dog. Since acquiring Mickey Dripping, George had taken him everywhere and after each show the little mutt trotted on to the stage to take a final bow with his owner. Now, in this highly emotive—some might say most un-Formby-like tableau—Mickey Dripping would jump on to the prisoner's lap and be sung to sleep with a tender ballad, "Goodnight, Little Fellow, Goodnight".

George's co-stars in *Formby Seeing Life* were husband and wife team Jenny Howard and Percy King, whilst Beryl and her sister May emerged from "The Clog-Dancers' Retirement Home". The critics, many of whom had turned up at the first night expecting to be disappointed, loved it. One anonymous scribe enthused on the *Oldham Chronicle*:

> *The name of George Formby has for years attracted all theatre-goers and it is well to know that, in all probability, George Formby Jr will prove just as popular*

> *as his father—the revue presented at the Palace last night is as funny as the name led us to expect it would be. George Formby is the drollest comedian we have heard for a long time, and his apparent simplicity, while always coming out on top, was obviously to the liking of the audience. At every appearance he was greeted with roars of laughter. With Formby in it, any revue is to be assured of success.*

Despite the sterling reviews, George could continue emulating his father for several more years, partly because this was all the theatre manager expected of him, but largely because he was naturally indolent. As long as he could eat well, provide for himself and his wife and keep sending a little money home to his mother, and of course tinker around with his motorcycle, it did not matter much to him whether he became as famous as his father or not.

In February 1924, George and his mother had visited the His Master's Voice studios at Hayes, Middlesex, where Eliza had persuaded him to make a test-recording of Formby Sr's 1916 song, "Rolling Around Piccadilly", though this had never been issued commercially. The pianist had been Madame Adani. Despite her exotic-sounding name she was a Cockney who, when not accompanying hopefuls for auditions, worked as a cook in the studio canteen! The previous year, Madame Adani had played on Gracie Fields' very first 78rpm recording, "Romany Love", which like George's first effort ever saw the light of day.

During the spring of 1926, Beryl Formby negotiated—with a great deal of tolerant wrangling—a one-off deal with the Edison-Bell Winner Record Company for George to cut six sides. Released that autumn, all were Formby Sr songs, with George sounding *so* like his father that it is often difficult to tell them apart. With the exception of "John Willie's Jazz Band", all were acoustic recordings done in a single take—and for good measure, George re-cut "Rolling Around Piccadilly". None of them sold well, however: the few fans who bought them were again interested only in the artiste whose work was being covered, and some critics found them in very poor taste. One even accused George of "digging up the dead", completely ignoring his own admission that he had not recorded them for financial gain, but to pay tribute to his father in this the fifth anniversary year of his death.

The advance on royalties paid by Edison-Bell Winner in 1926 was almost negligible—around £50—but George was not allowed to do with it as *he* liked. Setting a precedent which would last another thirty years, Beryl placed £49 in the bank, and gave the remaining £1 to her husband for spending money. He used some of this to buy cigarettes, and when Beryl saw him passing these around to friends, she told him in front of everyone that if they *wanted* to smoke, then they could smoke their own cigarettes and not his!

For the time being, Beryl was only being cautious. Though George *was* getting plenty of work—enough for the couple to purchase their first home, a semi-detached house at 836 Lancaster Road, Barton, near Preston, *and* a small flat in London's Great Portland Street—public opinion had become divided between the ones who liked to hear him "honouring" his father, and those who reproached him for earning an easy living *off* Formby Sr's success. Therefore it was impossible to gauge audience reaction in some towns until the actual playbills had been posted. This meant that he could alternate between playing to two-thousand spectators one evening, and a near-empty theatre the next. The latter reaction often caused the management to cancel the rest of the week's performances, forcing the Formbys out of their hotel or guest-house into seedy digs. The couple's over-fondness for frugality when times were far from lean would almost take on an art-form, and within a few years George Formby would be regarded as one of the most tight-fisted entertainers on the tour-circuit, some said second only to Maurice Chevalier.

At the end of May 1926, coinciding with the Edison-Bell Winner recording session, George opened at London's Shepherd's Bush Empire in Thomas Convery's revue, *Formby's Good Deed*. The week-long season was the end result of an almighty struggle, and a final heated row, between beryl and a man named Gillespie—assistant to Sir Oswald Stoll, the head of one of the most important theatrical emporiums in Britain at the time.

Three years previously, Gillespie had had a run-in with Archie Pitt, Gracie Fields' entrepreneur husband, over his comment, "There's nothing quite so common, Mr Pitt, as a Northern turn on the London stage!" During negotiations with Beryl, who had recently completed an elocution course, Gillespie repeated this in reference to George, and she understandably hit the roof, calling Stoll personally and reminding him of her husband's earlier appearances at the Alhambra. Stoll, however, was less impressed by minor achievement than he had been after reading the reviews for the Convery revue in Oldham, and Gillespie's vow "never to put on a Formby farce in a million years" was overruled.

Again, George placed the emphasis on imitating his father, performing all the Formby Sr songs and recreating his "John Willie At Home" sketch, though tableaux such as "The Palace", The Jamboree" and "The Golf Links At Sunnydale" were original creations, and saw him dressing as a knock-kneed boy scout. His co-stars were Harry Brento, June Stirling—and Mickey Dripping—whilst at the eleventh hour Beryl was persuaded to put in an appearance. However, following a snide remark from Gillespie that one Formby on the bill was sufficient, she insisted upon being billed as Winnie Hardy.

Having witness several rehearsals for the show—and complained to Beryl that his stomach had ached through laughing so much—Sir Oswald Stoll wrote the press-release himself, part of which read:

> *George Formby in shorts, complete with pole and whistle, is a sight for the "gods"—and for other parts of the house as well. "Be prepared" is the excellent motto of this splendid [Scouts] movement of which Our George is the latest member...a magnificent combination of hilarious ad original comedy, superb vocalism, attractive dancing, tuneful melodies and acrobatic novelties, one of the greatest and merriest entertainments EVER seen on the music-hall stage. So rare is it that the son of a stage favourite achieves the dizzy eminence of his father that the tremendous success of George Formby ranks as one of the most remarkable in music-hall history.*

The London critics, of course, would always be greatly divided in their opinion of George. Even when he became a megastar many of them would still look upon him—along with almost every one of his Northern colleagues—with a certain disdain, and regard him as vulgar, and on stage or screen he would rarely make an appearance in the all-important West End.

As far as the recording studio was concerned, however, Beryl's avaricious demands would prevent any serious contract from coming George's way for another six years. In September 1929 he cut two sides for the Dominion label: "In The Congo" and the self-composed "All Going back". There should have been six more, but the managing director did not feel that he was worth the money Beryl was asking for a carbon-copy of the man he had admired—and for the sarcastic reviews he was attracting, such as the one which appeared in the November edition of *Sound Wave*:

> *This record gave us quite a shock. George Formby, the famous Lancashire comedian "passed on" some considerable time ago, yet here he is once more, as large as life—speaking gramophonically—and his thousands of admirers should give him or rather his voice a warm welcome. How he "came back" we confess we don't know.*

It was not until the spring of 1932 that the great Formby recording boom was launched, when George signed a three-year deal with Decca. This got off to a shaky start on 10 June when two acetates were completed at the company's small Chenil Galleries studio: "Our House Is Haunted" and "I Told My Baby With My Ukulele". Despite the latter's title, George was too nervous to play his ukulele and had to be accompanied by a poor session-audition pianist. The recordings were subsequently rejected. The original pressing of "Our House Is Haunted"—retitled "The Ghost" because Gracie Fields was singing a song at the time called "The House Is Haunted"—did eventually resurface. It is more impressive than the later recording, because in this version George sounds *exactly* like his father, a comparison which is better appreciated today than it was back then. George positively drawls the tale of the "ghost" who, were the narrator not quite so dim-witted, he would realise was no spook, but his wife's lover:

> *I used to have three sets of clothes once to wear,*
> *But now I can find only one,*
> *I said to my wife, "Where's me clothes?"*
> *She said, "I'll see if the ghost has 'em on,"...*

Each night I can hear him below,
And the wife knows I'm frightened the most,
She gets up and leaves me in bed pale with fright,
Whilst downstairs she hunts him for hours left and right,
I haven't seen her since eleven last night...
Oh, I wish we were rid of the ghost!

George fared slightly better a few weeks later when he recorded "Chinese Laundry Blues" and "Do De O Do" with the Jack Hylton Band—the latter an inferior umber which is only memorable on account of Nat Gonella's superb trumpet solo—though there had to be several takes for both because George kept missing his cue. This made him so despondent that Beryl cancelled two further sessions which had been booked for that summer, and George did not enter the studio again until towards the end of the year.

"Chinese Blues" had first been offered to George by its composer, Jack Cottrell, in 1922, at which point he had turned the song down, claiming that it was too jazz-orientated. Later, he said he would not have recorded it at all had it not been for Jack Hylton, who heard him singing it at a party—and even then he only agreed to do the two takes providing Hylton accompanied him. Its title was subsequently changed to "Chinese Laundry Blues", and though George had no intention of ever recording a sequel, it would prove the first in a long-running saga about the ubiquitous proprietor of the Limehouse Laundry, a stereotyping which is today regarded as most politically incorrect. Indeed, in 1995 when celebrations were being prepared for the 50th anniversary of World War II, the BBC were specifically requested *not* to broadcast any of George's Mr Wu songs.

Born in Oldham in 1892, Jack Cottrell had tried his hand at any number of jobs before turning to the stage. He later formed the comedy duo, Sid and Billy, with Dorothy Sheepwash (aka the singer, Billy Morton) whom he married. Some time during 1931, when the pair had starred in Thomas Convery's revue, *Just Plain Folk*, at the Oldham Palace, George had been signed up to make a guest appearance. Cotterell's widow, a still vivacious octogenarian when I interviewed her, told me:

> *Jack was writing material for Sandy Powell at the time. He would often wake up in the middle of the night with a tune in his head ad wouldn't be able to sleep again until it had been written down—later he would have our daughter's little toy piano next to the bed, ready for those flashes of inspiration. That's how most of his Formby songs came about. And of course, Beryl did her utmost to stop Jack earning any royalties by offering to buy the songs outright for a fiver apiece. Jack always took her money, but he also made sure that he got the royalties as well. With several small children to clothe and feed we needed the money! But the most important thing Jack ever did for George Formby was never made public. Years before he persuaded him to record "Chinese Blues" it was Jack Cottrell who got him to revert to the name Formby, no one else.*

Jack Cottrell supplied George with twenty-two songs over the next few years, fourteen of which were recorded. The composer's personal favourite was "Levi's Monkey Mike", inspired by a visit to the Hampstead home of Gracie Fields and her then husband, Archie Pitt, when he had been entertained by the couple's pet marmoset. The antics of Mike, the Tipperary anthropoid who is so bright that he plays "The Wedding march", sneaks into an old maid's bedroom and ends up being elected Chancellor of the Exchequer, show the workings of a decidedly surrealist imagination:

> *He taxed the laces in our boots,*
> *And taxed our Christmas pudding…*
> *Now, working men just give an ear,*
> *We're all right now, so never fear,*
> *Who's going to take the tax off beer?*
> *Levi's monkey, Mike!*

Cottrell's steadfast refusal to recognise George's "composing" talents by allowing his name to be added to the credits infuriated Beryl and brought out her barely concealed mean streak, as Dorothy Cottrell recalled:

> *Beryl Formby was an extremely nasty woman towards just about everybody who came into contact with her husband. I don't know why she hated me. Maybe it was because Jack was quite a bit older than me, or because I was just as glamorous as she was. Even so, Jack and I were blissfully happy together and I certainly wasn't amorously interested in George Formby! When we were appearing in the Convery revue our dressing-rooms were connected by a swing-door. Beryl would hold it for me, then let it smack into my face. But she was at her most cruel when we were all appearing a few years later in a show in Blackpool. My little daughter, June, was admitted to hospital with a tubercular abscess. Jack would sneak in to see her whenever he could—the doctors had told us that it was touch and go, and they were convinced that she was only clinging to life because of her daddy's visits. When Beryl found out, she stopped him from going—it was either that or he would never work for Formby again. Fortunately, June didn't die, though Jack was never the same again.*

Beryl's insensitivity resulted in there being no more Cottrell songs for George, and started off this tremendously nice, much-respected man's slow, tortuous decline. By 1936, when Cottrell was still only forty-four, he would be bedridden and virtually penniless, supported largely by a doting wife who had taken employment as a dance-teacher and relocated her family to Upton, near Pontefract in West Yorkshire. Yet even weighed down by illness and near-destitution Cottrell put others before himself, raising a large amount of money for the dependents of miners killed in the Upton Pit Disaster through sheet-music sales of one of his last works, "Song Of The Pit". And when Cottrell finally succumbed to cancer in 1947, for all the wealth and success he had brought George's way, Beryl would not allow her husband to send flowers to the funeral, claiming that these would only be a waste of money seeing as how Cottrell would not be able to see them!

Unlike many "visual" artistes, George soon grew accustomed to working in the studio, and even his most hilarious performances here do not suffer when deprived of an audience. Jack Hylton had been suitably impressed to *demand* to work him again, though not so much, it would seem, to allow George's name to appear on the record labels. Of the three numbers he recorded with Hylton on 13 October, for "The Old Kitchen Kettle" George is referred to simply as "vocal refrain". To be fair, he could hardly complain, for he had insisted upon leaving his name off the label of "Chinese Blues".

From this session came the side-splitting "I Told My Baby With My Ukulele", an exercise in pure, unadulterated ragtime which is almost as appealing for its sizzling instrumentals as it is for George's uncompromising put-down of his latest flame:

> *Her hair was brunette type.*
> *It had pretty wrinkles like you see in tripe…*

> *Her face it is so bright,*
> *You can't see a blemish on a foggy night,*
> *And when she smiles of her own accord,*
> *Her face lights up 'cause she's lantern-jawed!*
> *Her teeth they are divine,*
> *All the colours of the rainbow there you'll find,*
> *Black, blue, green and red, you bet,*
> *She only wants a white 'un for a snooker set!*

This little ditty ends with George complimenting his sweetheart on her lovely neck—by buying her soap and a sponge to wash it—before bashing her over the head with his beloved instrument!

The song was the first of over two-hundred written by Harry Gifford and Fred E Cliffe, as a team, separately, or in collaboration with other composers. Half of these were issued on 78rpm recordings, whilst the others were either just performed on stage, or put on to acetates and consigned to vaults. Cliffe (Clifford Howcchin) was a stalwart Liverpudlian, forty-seven when he began working with Gifford (Henry Folkard), a middle-aged Devonian who had enjoyed a minor success with a revue, *Reflections,* which had toured London and the provinces in 1931. How these two vastly different men met is not known, though when George recorded "I Told My Baby With My Ukulele" they were working in a tiny office in Streatham. Much of the time Cliffe would write the lyrics, which Gifford would set to music using basic melodies which rested easily on the ear, adhering to the music-hall adage that a song should stay in the memory after three airings. Astonishingly, despite the phenomenal success of their work, they would hardly ever see George save in the recording studio. Cliffe could not stand Beryl, and she was unable to tolerate Gifford whom she often dismissed as "one of them" on account of his single status.

The BBC played "I Told My Baby With My Ukulele" and its flipside, "If You Don't Want The Goods Don't Maul 'Em" to death—though they frowned on its "companion-piece", Jack Cottrell's "With My Little Ukulele In My Hand" when it was released the following summer.

The song was peppered with double-entendres, though fairly tame in comparison with other material George would perform in the not too distant future, setting a precedent which would largely be responsible for his becoming without any doubt the most feted British male entertainer of his generation. Whereas Gracie Fields, his nearest female counterpart, provided an anodyne to the slight suggestiveness of some of her comedy numbers by offering audiences works of a romantic or religious persuasion, George hardly ever ventured far from his bouncy style and pulled few punches once he realised that he could get away with it. "Bugger the critics and the snobs," he once said. "So long as the audiences like what I do and *they're* not offended, I don't care what anybody else thinks!"

Review copies of "With My Little Ukulele In My Hand", coupled with "As The Hours And The Days", were sent to the BBC and several music publications within days of its release, and a few hundred copies—subsequently to become much sought-after collectors' items—found their way into the shops. Decca received so many complaints that the record was quickly withdrawn and instructions were given for the A-side to be replaced with the less risqué "Sunbathing In The Park".

The two stanzas of the song which caused the most offence, according to the moral watchdogs at the BBC, alluded to "Mr Formby' preoccupation that his musical instrument represents for him a substitute phallus." George has taken his lady-love, Jane, for a stroll along the sands. However:

> *I felt so shy and bashful, sitting there,*
> *'Cause the things she said I didn't understand,*
> *She said, "Your love just turns me dizzy,*
> *Come on, big boy, get busy!"*
> *But I kept my ukulele in my hand!*

And, the subsequent birth of their baby:

> *My heart did jump with joy,*
> *I could see he was a boy,*
> *For he had a ukulele in his hand!*

During the autumn on 1932, Beryl decided that it was time to find George a manservant—to take care of his clothes, clean his cars, make sure his ukuleles were set out correctly in the wings, and answer the telephone and his less important correspondence. Advertisements were placed in several local newspapers and there were dozens of applicants, though the man Beryl eventually settled upon would prove considerably more than a general factotum. Over the next twenty-nine years he would be regarded by George as a trusted servant and friend, a surrogate brother and soul mate all rolled into one efficient, patient and loyal package. His name was Harry Scott, and many years later he would recount his stylised, albeit sometimes overbearingly sycophantic account of his life with Britain's top show business couple in *The Vellum*, the official magazine of the George Formby Society:

> *My first week's wages with the Formbys was £5. It was still £5 a week nearly thirty years later when George died. George could be tight with his money when he wanted...in fact, I cannot honestly remember George buying a drink for anyone on more than two or three occasions all the time I was with him. I was rarely out of*

> *their sight. I went with them everywhere, and I enjoyed every single moment. Yet even though we did have our disagreements—I actually walked out on them more than once—I would do it all again, even for a fiver a week!*

There seems little doubt, however, upon studying Scott's *The Fabulous Formbys* and reading between the lines—the story ran consecutively over fourteen issues of *The Vellum*—that whilst he nurtured an innate respect and admiration for George, for three more decades Harry Scott would carry a torch for Beryl, in spite of his own happy marriage—the only thing, some sources have said, which prevented their relationship from progressing perilously beyond the platonic:

> *Beryl was always full of generosity...She called me her brother. She was more a friend of mine than George was throughout most of the long time that I was with them. When I had a row with her—and that can happen with the best pals in show business—stage hands could ask her two minutes later, "Is that your brother, Mrs Formby?" She would answer, "Yes, that's my brother, Harry." A marvellous woman, was Beryl Formby. She was the best!*

On 26 December 1932, George and Beryl opened in their very first pantomime, *The Babes In The Wood*, at Bolton's Grand Theatre. She had insisted on adding the "the" to the title because, she declared, this would distinguish it from the inferior productions being staged up and down the country! Sitting in the audience during this performance was Bert Loman, one of the North's most eminent impresarios, a man who, like Beryl, never minced words. When Beryl asked Loman for an honest appraisal of her husband's pantomime skills, he told her, "Not much."

Beryl's response to this—"Can *you* do any better?" was met with a tarty, "Much better, Mrs Formby, so long as you have the brass!" A contract was drawn up there and then: Loman would "mortgage" out his services for £300, to be spread evenly over thirty-six monthly payments, after which—providing George made the grade, which of course he did—he would be offered pantomime seasons in Loman's theatres.

It was public pressure—the fact that his records were getting a lot of airplay, or being noticed one way or another and selling well, and that now, whenever he was playing it did not take long for the HOUSE FULL signs to go up—which led Beryl into deciding that George was ready to begin making films. It did not matter that he was initially uninterested in the medium. From Beryl's viewpoint, anything Gracie Fields could do, *her* husband could do infinitely better...or so she thought.

Initially, Beryl approached Basil Dean, the head of ATP—Associated Talking Pictures, later to become Ealing Studios. Dean had recently produced Gracie's immensely successful *Looking On The Bright Side*, and had just contracted her for *Sing As We Go*. Over the telephone he had snarled at Beryl, "George Formby? What are you planning on doing, dear, digging him up?" *She* had not seen the funny side of this, but before she had had time to give him a piece of her mind, Dean had begrudgingly arranged a meeting.

Gracie Fields' stepdaughter, Irene Bevan, recalled the outcome of this:

> *Basil Dean was a miserable bastard. There's absolutely no other way of describing him. He was thoroughly disliked in the business because he could be so nasty and spiteful. And George's wife was almost as bad, so you can imagine all the fireworks when those two met, all the demands she spouted for someone who was, after all, a*

novice so far as films were concerned. Dean told her, "I'm certainly interested in having Formby on my books, but I sure as hell don't want his fucking wife. Just make sure you trap your tongue in the door on your way out!" And that was that, at least for a couple of years...

Beryl was knocked back by virtually every studio in and around London, but this only fired her determination. Irving Asher, the British representative for Warner Brothers who soon afterwards would discover Errol Flynn, granted her an interview at Warner's Teddington Lock studios. Asher's speciality was "quota quickies"—these were the cheaply made, usually direly scripted and acted B-movies which were churned out like factory products to compete with the big American productions being imported into Britain. He told Beryl that although he had seen and appreciated her husband's act, there was no question of George ever making the transition from stage to screen because he was "too stupid to play the bad guy and too ugly to play the hero". Beryl left Asher's office in tears—but only because she had wanted to throttle the man!

A few weeks after Asher's rebuff, George was in his dressing-room after his show in Warrington when he was approached by John Blakeley (1888-1958), the director of Mancunian Films, a small company which did not have a great deal of money, but which *was* interested in giving George a fair crack of the whip. In 1953, Blakeley's final film would be the tremendously successful *It's A Grand Life*, the Frank Randle vehicle which helped make Diana Dors a household name.

George's response—"It's got nothing to do with me, lad. You'd better go see the wife!"—did not fill Blakeley with terror, as had happened with some of the others. The director was holding all the trumps, and told her that his terms were non-negotiable: a fifteen-day shooting schedule, with a budget of just £3,000 which would include a £200 salary for George, and ten per cent of the profits for the star. The contract was signed at once, and to save money—and to keep an eye on George—Beryl announced that *she* would be playing his leading lady!

The result of George's first thrown together enterprise with John Blakeley was *Boots! Boots*! Even before the film went into production, there were problems with Beryl, as Dorothy Cottrell explained:

> *The songs and the entire script for* Boots! Boots! *were written by Jack Cottrell, though Beryl tried to claim all the credit for George by saying he had written it—you know, so he could rake in the profits, if there were to be any, Well, this time Jack was wise to her, though I was very angry with him for allowing George to sing "Baby" to that horrible woman, particularly as he had written the song for me!*

Boots! Boots! Was shot in a disused warehouse above an Albany Street garage, just off London's Regent Street. Initially, this presented problems with the skeleton crew, headed by director Bert Tracey, who also appeared in the film which had to be shot over the clamour emanating from the workmen below...until Tracey installed a bell, which was rung each time a scene had to be shot. Then the men would disappear to the nearest pub, frequently with George in tow, which of course defeated the director's objective, resulting in much of the film being completed after the workmen had clocked off, when the pub was shut!

Boots! Boots! has a very basic storyline, Roy Fogwell's camera-work is amateur—fixed position, with the actors walking in and out of the frame as if attending a badly-organised audition. The acting is appalling—only George and Beryl stand out, giving some indication of how scintillating their stage performances must have been, even in these, their formative years—in particular displaying how much Beryl had to offer, and how much she had given up to manage her husband. "Shades of Libby Holman and a second-rate Mistinguett," was how she was described by Irene Bevan—not by any means a back-handed compliment.

The dialogue, too, in parts smacks of the later Formby genius. John Willie is the cynical, inefficient "boots" or factotum at a provincial hotel. Picked upon by the manager and the chef (Bert Tracey), he in turn intimidates the scullery-maid, Snooky (Beryl). Given his limited intellect this is the only way he thinks he can woo her, until he is taught the rudimentaries of seduction by the flighty chambermaid, Marie, who is having an affair with her boss. Marie encourages the intensely shy John Willie to put his arm around her and pretend that *she* is Snooky, though the outcome is not what she is expecting:

M: Can you feel a strange sensation, a peculiar feeling within you?

JW: Yes I can, them pork pies I've had for me dinner!

M: Oh, John Willie. I'm bursting with love!

JW: Oh, don't burst. Undo something...

M: John Willie, look into my eyes. Don't you know that the eyes are the windows of the soul?

JW: Well, your windows want washing. But those eyes, like twin stars. Those nostrils, like twin cylinders. Those ears, like twin petals.

M: Petals? What kind of petals?

JW: Bicycle petals…

Elsewhere in the scenario, John Willie confronts an effeminate client who, three decades prior to gay liberation, demands a pink room. "Oh, fairies!" he exclaims. Then after they have pranced around to "Here We Go Gathering Nuts In May", John Willie flattens him. After another altercation, he throws the chef out of the window. For the lovebirds, however, all ends well when the manager becomes aware of their talent—the factotum's singing, and Snooky's tap-dancing, which John Willie gets her to speed up by standing her on top of the kitchen stove!

The manager engages the pair for a cabaret spot when the billed artistes fail to appear, and the transformation is remarkable as the characters become the actors portraying them: George in his dinner suit, singing two numbers with the Harry Hudson Band; Beryl, debagged of her dreary uniform and bottle-bottom glasses, a vision of loveliness and grace. The film ends with them in one another's arms, crooning a delightful little love-song:

> *Although the skies be dreary and grey,*
> *Promise me that you'll never stray away,*
> *My baby, baby,*
> *You're my sweetheart…*

During the shooting of *Boots! Boots!*, Beryl would set a precedent for being inexcusably catty towards George's co-stars, male and female. In theatres she had always done her utmost to discourage him from "having a jar with the lads", and a murderous stare had kept chorus girls well at bay, but on the set her jealousy was taken to the extreme when she observed him chatting to a young actress named Betty Driver (1920-2011), who had appeared with Gracie Fields and Archie Pitt on their revue, *Mr Tower Of London*. Three decades on she would portray one of

Britain's best-loved television barmaids in *Coronation Street*. It mattered little to Beryl that Betty was only thirteen—the fact that she was pretty, and had an infectious smile, was enough for Beryl to put her foot down once shooting had wrapped and demand that Betty's scene in the film—performing a music-hall ditty during the cabaret sequence—be removed from the finished print. John Blakeley reluctantly did this, but left Betty's name in the credits. This too was removed when the film was re-released in 1938, but when the film eventually emerged on DVD, many years after Beryl's death, it had been put back in.

"I don't care is she *was* only thirteen," Irene Bevan recalled Beryl saying about Betty Driver. "She behaved like a floosy, and I wasn't having any of it!"

George and Beryl in *Boots! Boots!* (1934)

Three:
I'm Hitting The High Spots, Now!

"What a life George had with Beryl. There was no doubt as to who was boss. Almost the same situation as poor Arthur Lucan with the harridan Kitty McShane, though not quite as physical." Arthur Askey, comedian.

Between the completion of *Boots! Boots!* and its release, George made two visits to the Chenil Galleries, where besides "Baby" he recorded several of his most roguish songs. "The Wedding Of Mr Wu" was the second instalment of the Chinese sage and saw the church on Limehouse Way decorated with washing from the laundry, whilst the guests attempted to Anglicise themselves by using their chopsticks to eat peas, and a jazz-band replaced the ukulele interlude. And in "Swimmin' With Women", George tells us what happened during a visit to the local swimming baths on a mixed-session day: the low point when a large woman he saves from drowning only turns out to be his wife—and the joy of being with his sweetheart, Adeline:

> *You ought to see her latest bathing costume,*
> *It's nothing but a little piece of trimmin'.*
> *And what I took to be her face,*
> *Turned out to be a different place,*
> *When I went swimmin' with the women!*

This was one of the numbers George performed in *The Babes In The Wood*, which played the New Theatre, Ashton-under-Lyme, in January 1934. He clomped on to the stage, wearing an old pair of canvas boots two sized too big for him. "These belonged to my old man," he told the audience, earning himself a standing ovation before the fun began. Formby Sr's boots would make an appearance in every pantomime until George's very last one in 1960—he would baptise them "The Boot Repairer's Despair", and in 1940 pay as much to have them preserved and encased in leather as it would have cost to buy another ten pairs. He often said that they were his only superstition. "A grand man wore them first, ma'am, and I'm proud to be wearing them now," he would later tell the future Queen Elizabeth.

A few weeks later, the Formbys attended the London opening of *Boots! Boots!* Southern cinemagoers, however, who had raved over Gracie Fields' screwball comedies, did not know what to make of this one, though it was *so* successful in the North of England that John Blakeley immediately contacted George to make another film—and this time the budget was increased to £8,000.

Off The Dole was adapted from a music-hall revue, one which had starred George's younger brother, Frank. Unfortunately, it will go down in history as one of the worst British films ever made. It begins well. John Willie is thrown off the dole because he is too lazy to look for work, but is saved when an uncle asks him to take over his private detective agency. After the first ten minutes, the plot runs haywire. No one seems to have a clue as to what they are supposed to be doing, and one gets the impression that no matter how the mostly fixed-frame tableaux *could* have been edited and arranged, the film still would not have made much sense. Even more astonishing was the fact that this little horror was even *more* popular in the North of England than its predecessor—grossing some £40,000 at the box-office—whilst everywhere else it was deservedly ignored and assigned to obscurity.

The sections of the film with George's and Beryl's songs were another matter—even the bungling John Blakeley had been unable to ruin these—and resulted in George being courted by Ben Henry, Basil Dean's Northern representative, who in time would become the Formbys' agent. Now, though, when Beryl learned *whom* he was working for, he was sent packing. Blakeley, meanwhile, upon hearing that Dean had attempted to poach "his" star, decided to capitalise on George's success whilst he had the chance. Piecing together the songs from their two films, and supplementing them with a couple of atrociously edited sketches, he came up with *George Formby Cavalcade*, which starts off with the opening credit, "Hear Again The Songs That Made George Formby The Idol Of The People!"

The ruse made Blakeley a tidy sum, but ended his partnership with the Formbys. As soon as Basil Dean realised that George was wasting his talents with a "two-bob outfit", he moved in on Beryl with an offer which quickly enabled her to swallow her pride *and* put up with the man's arrogance and rudeness.

Gracie Fields' stepdaughter, Irene, was at the studios when the Formby's arrived for their first meeting with Basil Dean:

> *Beryl barged in, dressed and acting like Lady Muck, with her poor little husband lagging behind like the lackey. She told him, "Remember what I said. You speak only when you're spoken to, and you leave all the negotiating to me." Gracie had just had a huge success with* Look Up And Laugh *and was then shooting* Queen Of hearts, *a wonderful piece of slapstick being directed by her [second, but not until 1940] husband, Monty Banks, and Dean thought he would be the ideal director for his first film with George. He and Monty were such dear, funny men that any collaboration between those two would have to be a riot, so long as we all managed to keep Beryl and Dean from going for one another's throats...*

The film was *No Limit*, the first of eleven George would make under his five-year contract with ATP, starting out with a budget of £30,000. Dean, however, made it very clear from the signing of the document that Beryl would *not* be appearing in the production...indeed, that she would only be tolerated on the set in her capacity as "Mr Formby's adviser" providing she kept her mouth shut and her opinions to herself. Unfortunately, Monty Banks' choice of Florence Desmond (1905-93) for George's leading lady did not go down at all well with Beryl.

One year George's junior, Desmond's career had constituted one triumph after another. Having studied ballet since the age of ten, in 1926 she had augmented C D Cochran's dancing troupe and had appeared I several of his famous annual revues, holding audiences spellbound not just with her nifty footwork and fine singing voice, but with her startlingly accurate impersonations of Jimmy Durante, Ethel Barrymore and Tallulah Bankhead. Since then she had toured Britain on numerous occasions, appeared on the cabaret circuit and starred opposite Gracie Fields in *Sally In Our Alley*, produced by Basil Dean in 1931.

After witnessing Desmond's performance in the 1934 Cochran revue, *Streamline*, James Agate, one of Britain's sharpest critics, had observed, "She has not only a white-hot sense of the ridiculous, but can present it in a dozen different disguises." But if the media adored her, many of those who worked with her had a different tale to tell. Desmond, a Londoner by birth, had made it quite clear what *she* thought of Northerners whilst working with Gracie Fields, as Irene Bevan explained:

> *Gracie condemned Florence Desmond for being such an out-and-out snob. Their antagonism began one day when the studio provided everyone with afternoon tea which they ate on their lap. Florence asked them to take the bread and butter back, saying she only ate brown bread.*

That stuck in Gracie's gullet. It was something quite silly, but it gives a good insight into her weird outlook on life, and the way she had been brought up. "Stuck up little so-and-so. White bread's not good enough for her. Who does she think she is?" Eventually, Gracie and Florence did become friends, but Florence always loathed George Formby. "That dreadful, slobbering little oaf," she called him, whilst he always referred to him as, "That snotty-nosed little minx," and completely ignored her every time she threw a tantrum. The first of those occurred when Beryl warned her to keep her hands off her husband—not that she'd even tried such a thing. Florence screamed at her that she wouldn't be amorously interested in him, not if he was the last man on earth. And absolutely everyone at the studio detested Beryl. Poor George couldn't speak to anyone without her giving him the third degree. And if that someone happened to be a woman—even if she only smiled or said Hello—Beryl would accuse him on front of everyone of wanting to sleep with her.

Neither did Beryl see eye to eye with those running the studio canteen, in particular the French chef whom she accused of patronising them when he decided to surprise the Formbys by serving them his interpretation of Lancashire hot-pot. Beryl told him that she could not possible eat such "muck", to which the chef replied that if she could do better, then she would be welcome to have his job! The pair found themselves getting on like a house on fire, however, when Beryl barged into his kitchen and gave him an impromptu cookery lesson—the next time hot-pot showed up on the menu, the Frenchman received nothing but praise, though he flatly refused to have anything to do with the couple's other favourite "delicacy"…beef-dripping toast!

No Limit was filmed mostly on location on the Isle of Man, in the summer of 1935 during the actual TT (Tourist Races) Races week. This enabled Monty Banks to hire several of the riders, who were paid £75 a week for their services whether they worked or not, *and* ensconced at the Plush Majestic Hotel. The other "riders", the studio stuntmen, received just £5 for each day they were called to the set and were expected to find their own accommodation. This resulted in the stuntmen going on strike for several days, until Banks capitulated—he saved the extra money he was compelled to pay the stuntmen by placing an advertisement on local cinema screens for crowd extras, most of whose only remuneration was the hope of seeing fleeting glimpses of themselves in a George Formby movie. Only the ones who appeared on the grandstand during the race scenes were paid the going rate.

George was firmly against the studio providing *him* with a stunt-double, though Beryl had insisted that he should—just about the only detail she and Monty Banks agreed upon all through shooting the film. George duped them both, however, during the scene where he rides his machine at break-neck speed, jumping clear a split-second before it somersaults over the edge of a cliff. Beryl had gone off to the studio canteen, and Banks had assumed the man on the bike to be a stunt-double…until a grinning George pulled off the helmet and goggles.

The director was suitably impressed with George's performance not to re-shoot the scene with a stuntman, though he was obliged to report the matter to Basil Dean. George was not insured to take such inordinate risks, and had things gone wrong claims for damages at his level could easily have put ATP out of business. Beryl later said that she had only found out about the incident four months afterwards, when George confessed all at the film's premiere. This was not true: Dean had contacted her at once, in her official capacity as George's manager, and Beryl had shared his concern. Between them they decided that his future contracts should include a clause stipulating that he should never again be allowed to ride a motorcycle in any of his films...one which George would, as will be seen, promptly ignore.

As this was the middle of the tourist season, Beryl, completely disregarding Basil Dean's warning that she should take a back seat in the production, ensured that she milked the publicity for all it was worth. "It's *his* film," she told the press, whom she encouraged to photograph George acting the fool or chatting to the holiday crowds. "And as you can see, the people are *only* interested in him, not his so-called screen love-interest!"

This was very true, but the tension between George and Florence Desmond, which was bad enough *before* filming began, escalated shy-high when Beryl arranged for bills to be posted on the sides of the equipment vans which proclaimed, "Associated Pictures Now Filming *No Limit* With GEORGE FORMBY".

Desmond saw red. She had already had a ferocious row with Basil Dean because George was being paid more for the film than she was, telling the producer, "The man's as thick as two very short planks. It wouldn't surprise me if he can't *read* his lines, let alone remember them!" Dean had refused to give her a rise in salary, but he had been unable to ignore the terms of her contract, the fact that she *was* George's co-star, and entitled to equal publicity. She therefore told Dean that unless these posters came down immediately, *she* would walk off the set, and sue. Beryl merely scoffed at this, declaring that leading ladies were two-a-penny, which brought the most vociferous outcry from Monty Banks, a chirpy little Italian who hardly ever quarreled with anyone, but who nevertheless tore a strip off Desmond for going over his head, and even threatened to fire her from the production. The situation was saved by George, who—waiting until his wife had gone off to the hairdressers—personally removed the "offending" posters, well aware that the public knew *exactly* who was the star of the film, and also aware that his actions would get him into hot water with Beryl.

One word describes *No Limit*—sublime! Indeed, it is virtually inconceivable that it is separated from the trashy Blakeley production by less than a year—or that, for such a bubbling, optimistic film, there was so much behind-the-scenes misery, for this certainly does not transpose itself on to the screen. George Shuttleworth, a mother's boy chimney-sweep's assistant from Flagdyke, adapts a 1928 Rainbow motorcycle in the hope that he might be able to enter the TT Races. Then, financed by his mother—who steals the money from her skinflint father's stash, which he has hidden in the sofa—George sets off for the Isle of Man. "With my gears in reverse—the other way round, I'll finish first," he sings on the train, to a collection of characters straight from a *Punch* cartoon.

Aboard the ship—in a woeful continuity error this starts off as the *Mona's Queen*, but changed while mid-ocean into the *Manxman*!—George meets Florrie (Desmond), the secretary for Rainbow Motorcycles with whom he has been corresponding for a while, sending her photographs of "George Shuttleworth, Speed Demon", in the hope that he company might sponsor him. Neither knows who the other is until George abseils down the side of the ship to retrieve Florrie's hat. He plunges into the sea, tears his suit, and she recognises him from the photograph she finds in his pocket whilst repairing his jacket. She then falls for the gentle, shy underdog, whilst spurning the advances of Rainbow's boorish ace-rider, Bert Tyldesley (Jack Hobbs).

As George's champion, Florrie helps out when his money is stolen: blacking his face with soot, she parades him on the beach, where he entertains the crowds until sprung by his landlady, who concludes that he may not be able to pay his bill. No problem, here—George is not really hard-up, just collecting for charity! He enters the TT Trials—breaking the speed record when his brakes fail and the throttle jams wide open, but ending up with the shakes and vowing never to ride another bike—a vow he is persuaded to keep when a rival company sends a pair of thugs to pay him not to participate in the main event, and to smash up his bike by riding it over the edge of a cliff. The machine takes George with it: he grabs an overhanging branch and backflips on to the cliff top, offering one of the film's few moments of slapstick. He then uses his bribe money to offer his sweetheart a good time.

Meanwhile, George's mother and grandfather (Edward Rigby) arrive on the Isle of Man. The old man, who has always dismissed George as useless, changes his mind now that the lad has made good. He pays off George's rivals, whilst Florrie presents him with a prototype machine on behalf of Rainbow, who have nominated him their official rider. This incurs Tyldesley's wrath—henceforth, he is the enemy engaged by another rival manufacturer.

The big race is tremendously exciting, with George doing almost all of his own stunts. Before the start, the two men fight—stepping out of character, George bashes Tyldesley. From here on the hero comes up against every obstacle, crashing through fences and gates, several times falling off his machine, always neck-and-neck with the foe, whilst around them the other competitors drop like flies—until the last lap, when Florrie spurs him on by holding up a sign, "I Love You". "Must have been a summons—he shot away like a bullet!" observes the commentator. Then, five-hundred yards from the finish, George runs out of petrol and has to push, collapsing as he passes the post—authentically so, on account of the heat and the fifteen takes demanded by Monty Banks—just seconds before his rival screams past.

The songs in this film are arguably the best performed in any of George's Ealing comedies. From the zippy "Riding In The TT

Races" to Florence Desmond's "Riding Around On A Rainbow"—which has everyone joining in aboard the ship and which is made all the more effective by Roy Fogwell's curious camera angles. And from George's and Desmond's romantic little *chanson*, "Your Way Is My Way", to the comic-strip humour of "In A Little Wigan Garden", these musical delights represented a sparkling antidote to the dark days of the Depression:

> *Crocuses croak with the frog and the smoke,*
> *From the gas-works near,*
> *The one thing that only grows*
> *Is the wart on my sweetheart's nose...*
> *'Neath the Wigan water-lilies,*
> *Where the drainpipe overflows,*
> *There's my girl and me,*
> *She'll sit on my knee and watch how the rhubarb grows!*

It was during the shooting of this film that George substituted his John Willie bowler with his infamous grey felt trilby—which subsequently became a fixture in almost every one of his celluloid appearances. Beryl bought it for ten shillings, and after each day's work it would be locked away in a steel box in the studio props department. No one but Beryl and George were ever allowed to touch it, it had its own chair in the studio canteen, and always occupied the seat between the Formbys when they were in the cutting or projection room—giving way to rumours that they hardly every spoke to each other whilst they were on the set, which of course *was* partly true.

No Limit was released in March 1936, and despite being awarded a thumbs-down by the London critics was a huge success nationwide, finally bringing George the recognition he deserved, though not yet putting him on a par with Gracie Fields.

Basil Dean, however, knew that he was on to a winner, and therefore decided to stick to the tried-and-tested formula with George's next film—using the same director, scriptwriter *and* leading lady as before, and as many songs as George's team could come up with at such short notice.

George and Beryl were not told that Florence Desmond was going to be in his film until Desmond had been sweet-talked into doing so by Basil Dean. This was not an easy task, for the actress was still of the opinion that George was a "dirty little man", an "amateur" who had no interest whatsoever in acting or trying to remember even the simplest parts of the script, preferring to improvise as he went along. Desmond told Dean that if she *did* sign the contract, he would have to swear that Beryl would ever be allowed on to the set. Dean did so with his fingers crossed behind his back, though he did worm his way into Desmond's good books by offering her the same (undisclosed) salary as George, for which she signed a pledge that this would never be made public.

Having secured Desmond, Dean went to see the Formbys. Beryl called him all the names under the sun, but instructed George to sign the contract all the same, and George reiterated that he did not mind *who* his co-star was so long as he was getting his "brass", and so long as his "management team"—in other words, Beryl—had access to the studio and set at all times. Dean attempted to take him to one side and explain that this might prove difficult, for Monty Banks and some of the other actors had petitioned Dean, begging him to banish this troublesome woman. Beryl, however, got the first word in: unless Dean and everyone else agreed to her terms, she would go looking for another producer.

Technically, as George was contracted to ATP until at least the summer of 1941, Beryl could not do this. He had, however, already been courted by several top producers—including Elstree

Studios' John Maxwell—and it would not have been impossible for one of these to buy him out of his contract with Dean. He therefore decided not to take any chances, though such was the tension during shooting—with George and Desmond not exchanging a single word unless it was part of the script and the cameras were rolling—that Dean gave his own studios wide berth for almost a month.

Keep Your Seats Please was based on the Petrov play, *Twelve Chairs*—though in this particular instance their number had been reduced to seven—and also featured that fine character actor, Alastair Sim, portraying a creepy, over-the-top lawyer. An elderly millionairess, Georgina Withers, bequeaths her fortune to charity to prevent her greedy relatives from getting their hands on it—anyone who wants a memento of her, she declares in her will, will have to buy one!—but she had concealed £90,000 in jewellery and bonds in the seat of an antique dining chair, one of a set which is about to be auctioned. In view of this, she has left a letter at the lodging house where her favourite nephew, George, the family black sheep resides, urging him to purchase them so that his other relatives will not be suspicious.

The action cuts to George, an out of work concert-party artiste, plucking his uke in a pawn-shop. He tried to pawn his instrument to raise the money to pay for his room, but is unable to do so and when he gets back to the lodging house he discovers that the landlady has rented it to Florrie (Florence Desmond). She is being pursued by welfare officers who are trying to take away Binkie (Fiona Stuart), her dead sister's child whom she has promised to look after. When it emerges that she too cannot afford to pay for her room, both are evicted and set off for the auction rooms. What George does not know is that one of the chairs has already been sold to a drunken sailor. He therefore buys the six under the hammer, holding up the proceedings by informing the auctioneer that he has no money—no problem, he says, for he will borrow this from his aunt's lawyer, Drayton (Sim). Drayton, however, knows what is inside one of the chairs, and wants them for himself. He burns George's letter of proof, though their subsequent conversation is overheard by conman Max (Gus McNaughton), who agrees to help George and Florrie in exchange for a percentage of the booty, which increases with each step of the search.

By now, all the chairs have been sold and the trio set off on a quest to recover George's inheritance. The first has been bought by Madame Louise, the celebrated voice coach—a visit which ends up with George and Max being suspected of being her lovers, and manhandled out of her house by an irate husband—though not before George has serenaded her with "When I'm Cleaning Windows", the most accomplished song in the film. Elsewhere, Florence Desmond emulates Tallulah Bankhead and Gracie Fields when she duets with Fiona Stuart in "Standing On The Tip Of My Toes", and she and George sing to the child, harmonising beautifully in "Goodnight Binkie", though the film's title-track is far less memorable.

With Drayton and the welfare workers still in hot pursuit, the trio also draw a blank with the next purchasers—an incompetent doctor with a buxom nurse who attempts to undress George for his examination, with hilarious slapstick consequences, and a bungling magician who has acquired three of the chairs. George and Florrie are invited on to the stage to participate in his latest illusion, and George slashes the chairs—from which emerge a psychotic duck which attacks him, a mischievous monkey, and a flock of doves...but still no valuables.

Convinced that his legacy must be concealed in the sixth—and he thinks final—chair, the friends head for the home of a pair of eccentric sisters, only to discover that the contents of its seat have been devoured by the pet goat. They kidnap the goat and rush it to the hospital—on a crowded bus. The goat is disguised as a dog and wears a mask which George has produced out of nowhere along with his uke, with which he accompanies himself whilst entertaining the passengers with a few couplets from "Keep Your Seats Please." "It's a hippopotapig," he tells the conductor. The goat, however, had merely scoffed a number of metal objects.

George then learns that a *seventh* chair was snapped up by the drunken sailor, who is about to set sail on his ship, *The Bumblebee*. The final pursuit ends with George and Florrie missing the ship, though Max gets there before it leaves, beaming triumphantly because he believes he has duped the other two. The sailor, however, has pawned the chair, enabling George and Florrie buy it back—once he has pawned his ukulele, and all their clothes! And of course he finds what they have been looking for, and asks his sweetheart to marry him.

This time, the London critics *did* sit up and take notice of a Formby film. "Wigan's George Formby is now funny enough to take on the West End," quipped one, though virtually *no* cinemas in this part of town were interested in screening his films, with 75 per cent of their profits still coming from the North.

"When I'm Cleaning Windows" remains one of a select handful of "property" songs which, his most ardent admirers believe, may not justifiably performed by anyone but George Formby. In her biography of sorts—*My George* was written for the George Formby Fan Club at the end of 1938—Beryl states that George himself had composed the song during a very short break on the set of *Keep Your Seats Please*, and that she had helped him. This, of course, was pure invention. Fred E Cliffe had written the lyric early in 1936, and Harry Gifford had set them to music. George had simply "kited" the credits, as usual, to get a third-share of the royalties which he was legally not entitled to—something the pair had "consented" to when informed by Beryl that to refuse would result in her husband not performing any more of their songs.

George recorded the first version of the song—a saucy series of Peeping Tom anecdotes, set to ragtime—along with three other songs on 27 September 1936, at Blackpool's Feldman Theatre. The unusual location gives each performance a "bouncy" feel which might not have been achieved in the caustic confines of the studio. It proved his biggest success to date, selling 150,000 copies within a month of its release and earning George his first silver disc. Like the earlier "With A Little Ukulele In My Hand", however, it attracted media condemnation on account of its "prurient" lyrics—offering some critics proof, they alleged, to add to the rumours being circulated by the likes of Florence Desmond, that George really was "a dirty little Northern would-be Casanova".

> *Now there's a famous talkie queen,*
> *She looks a flapper on the screen,*
> *She's more like eighty than eighteen...*
> *She pulls her hair all down behind,*
> *Then pulls down her—never mind,*
> *Then after that pulls down the blind,*
> *When I'm cleaning windows!*

The lyrics were *intended* as considerably more than innuendo, though George would argue that since *he* never let on exactly *what* the talkie queen was pulling down in front of the window, any "filth" came from the listener's mind. Since 1932, however, when he had begun performing his own material, each number had been gauged by audience reaction, and for most fans—as with Frank Randle and Max Miller—there appeared to be no limit as to how far he could go without actually offending *them*:

> *The blushing bride she looks divine,*
> *The bridegroom he is doing fine,*

> *I'd rather have his job than mine…*
> *Pyjamas lying side by side,*
> *Ladies' nighties I have spied,*
> *I've often seen what goes inside,*
> *When I'm cleaning windows!*

It was this last stanza which resulted in the recording of "When I'm Cleaning Windows" being assigned to a drawer at the BBC—in those days controlled by the puritanical John Reith—and marked NTBB…Not To Be Broadcast. "If the public wants to listen to Formby singing his disgusting little ditty, they'll have to be content to hear it in the cinemas, not over the nation's airwaves," Reith declared. Strangely enough, none of the cinemas screening *Keep Your Seats Please* received a single complaint, for the footage containing the "naughty" bits had ended up on the cutting-room floor. And the record *was* broadcast, infrequently and late at night, for the mere fact that some announcers persisted in referring to "the banned Formby song" which only stimulated listeners' interests, resulting in the record selling more copies than it might have done otherwise. "The windows are not yet *clean* enough," quipped one snooty request-programme host—the day after which shops reported running out of copies of *all* Formby recordings and sheet-music. And the windows would get even dirtier! Six months after cutting the original version, George recorded "The Window Cleaner Number Two", and this one included several stanzas which upset the usually unshakeable Beryl:

> *To overcrowded flats I've been,*
> *Sixteen in one bed I've seen,*
> *With the lodger tucked up in between…*
> *Now lots of girls I've had to jilt,*
> *For they admire the way I'm built,*

> *It's a good job I don't wear a kilt,*
> *When I'm cleaning windows!*

There was a "gay" version of the song, popular among the "Dilly Boys"—the rent-boys who hung around Piccadilly Station:

> *The milkman is a randy swine,*
> *He's got eight inches, maybe nine,*
> *And up my flue it feels divine,*
> *When I've been cleaning windows*

George himself found it hard to comprehend what the fuss was about. As the product of a Wigan backstreet, he had been raised on what he took to be harmless innuendo. In his part of the country the predominant interest among the locals had always been whatever the other locals were getting up to. This and the and the "front parlour gossip" which children were not supposed to hear provided George with a rich array of source material for his work, and was a sound excuse for his name to be included amongst the song-writing credits, though his *actual* contribution as a composer as opposed to a "supplier of ideas" has been much overestimated. The ideas for some songs are said to have come from Beryl—her expression, when bored, "I'm sitting pretty with my fingers crossed", being an example. The broadcaster Peter Clayton, writing in the *Sunday Telegraph* in 1974 on the occasion of the publication on a book of Formby lyrics, made another interesting comparison:

> *Possession of a book of George Formby songs is roughly the equivalent of having your own rotating wire stand full of seaside comic postcards. "When I'm Cleaning Windows" is pure Donald McGill set to music, an aria about honeymoon couples, bathrooms, underwear....and*

> old maids. Verses about Blackpool rock, flannelette nightshirts, violin bows and the prowess of the handyman constitute a crescendo of innuendo in song after song. As you read through them you see why adults would exchange significant glances over your then innocent head when George Formby records were plonked on the wind-up gramophones of your childhood.

Donald McGill [1875-1962] remains the most popular post-card artist ever, drawing some 20,000 cards in a 50-year career, renowned for their double-entendres. George's favourite postcard is said to have been the one depicting an agonised casualty patient, and a bungling nurse being told by her superior, "No, nurse. I said *prick* his boil!" McGill's speciality, outsized women strolling alongside feeble, henpecked husbands, would remind many of the Formbys, later in life.

Beryl was incensed at the BBC's suggestion that George's work was apparently unfit for human consumption. Marching into John Reith's office, she gave him such a piece of her mind that he personally read out an apology that evening before the 9 o'clock news. The ban on the song, however, was not lifted.

The media were so busy attacking "When I'm Cleaning Windows" that they overlooked an equally "vulgar" little gem from the same session. "Sitting On The Sands All Night" was written by Jack Cottrell and told of what happens on the beach after dark, where the police "perve" on courting couples, where girls shine electric torches up Scotsmen's kilts, and where blisters appear where they should not. And where ultimately:

> *You start feeling rather stiff,*
> *Then you find that you're stuck right,*
> *With a boat-hook sticking in your Westward Ho!*
> *Through sitting on the sands all night!*

Over the years, the BBC would ban around forty Formby songs—not just those appertaining to "Mr Wu" and "Fanny", and without always having listened to them. Sometimes, a very good number never progressed beyond the acetate solely on account of the title, which the composers steadfastly refused to change. Reading some of these, one is hardly surprised: even today, titles such as "Cucumber Time At Kew" and "I Was Waggling My Magic Wand" would be hard put to get past the censor. One regarded as particularly lewd was "I Was Touching My Lucky Charm", whose title *was* changed—to the even worse, "I Was Touching My Wishbone." There was also a "gay" song, "Antonio My Romeo".

George began work on his next film, *Feather Your Nest*, at the Ealing Studios during the summer of 1936. He and Beryl were now living in London—and apparently hating every moment of it—but driving back to Barton on Friday evenings when the set had closed down for the weekend. Here, on 18 July, they were interviewed for the women's page of the *Blackpool Gazette & Herald* and photographed with their Alsatian, Peter, who George said was training to become a postman! The young woman, who signed her feature only as Sylvia, observed:

> *Whenever Mr and Mrs Formby are away, Mrs Formby's father re-addresses the letters, and Peter takes them to the village post office some distance away and posts them. He has never been known to drop one. And when meals are ready, he trots up the garden to find Mrs Formby's father and gently lifts that gentleman's hat off!*

During the interview, which barely touched on his career, George managed to get the date of his marriage wrong, declaring that he and Beryl had tied the knot in August 1925. Sylvia was then shown around the house, and marvelled at the costly features: the glass panels of the sun porch which contained reproductions of Formby Sr's tomb design, the Tudor panelling in the dining room into which was set his father's portrait, the inch-thick velvet curtains emblazoned with the arms of Lancaster, the metallic wallpaper in the bedrooms, and the Chinese box-room which was there just for show—and whose ceiling slanted, George cracked in the days when political correctness did not exist, like Mr Wu's eyes.

George's new film was less troublesome than the last two. Now that he was a household name, Beryl was more or less able to dictate her own terms, and she had given Basil Dean *orders* that this time there should be "no Eye-Ties and stuck up little trollops"—she was of course referring to Monty Banks and Florence Desmond.

Dean agreed wholeheartedly. He too had grown weary of all the on-set squabbles, so he brought in the less-excitable—and less amenable—William Beaudine to direct, and the little-known Polly Ward was engaged as George's leading lady. This resulted in a film which was nowhere near as funny as its predecessor, with a lack-lustre script by Austin Melford and Val Valentine, and a clutch of songs which—with the exception of the one which would become immortal—were comparatively bland.

Willie Piper works as a technician for a record company, along with his fiancée, Mary (Ward). The couple have secretly bought a house which they plan to move into after their wedding, which will take place once the hyper-nervous Willie has been given a pay-rise. Unfortunately, this may never happen on account of his tendency to drop and break something every time the factory whistle blows, and because of his disrespect for his boss, Mr Murgatroyd, whom he dismisses as a "bow-legged, bandy-legged, knock-kneed old stingy tight-wad". Mary, however, has such faith in her bungling young man that she filled their house with furniture, all purchased on credit.

Enter Rex Randall, the famous crooner—and utter pain—who after umpteen takes completes a wax of "Leaning On A Lamp Post" in Willie's studio. Randall was played by Val Rosling (1910) the resident artiste with the BBC's Henry Hall Orchestra and a very *good* singer—it is he who sings in the famous version of "Teddy Bears Picnic"—who willingly agreed to sing badly on purpose for the privilege of starring in a Formby film! Willie drops the wax, then he and Mary set about tracking down Randall to cut another whilst the studio is closed. Their trail leads them to the Turkish baths. "You can't go in there—it's full of Turks with nothing on," he tells Mary. Inside, he is mistaken for an overweight boxer and given the works by two burly masseurs. Eventually he emerges from his ordeal looking a wreck, having missed the crooner, who has left the baths for Brighton. Mary tells him not to worry. She has had a brainwave: she and Willie will break into the studio, and *he* will cut the recording!

Willie Piper's version of "Leaning On A Lamp Post" proves a hit, by which time Murgatroyd has sacked him. Randall threatens to sue the company, but they do not know who the mysterious singer is. Finally, Willie comes clean…after a frantic race against time, with his sweetheart on the pillion of a purloined motorcycle, to prevent their house and furniture from being repossessed. *He* then signs the contract the arrogant Randall only ever dreamed of, and he and Mary are married. In the final scene, Willie is about to carry his bride over the threshold when the factory whistle blows and he drops her—into a muddy puddle!

At the beginning of October 1936, George found himself in hot water with Basil Dean when he made a £5 wager with a producer pal, Jack Taylor, that he would climb Blackpool Tower by way of its intricate inner network of staircases and ladders. Taylor announced this in the *Blackpool Gazette*, and on the morning of the climb George and Beryl arrived to find 6,000 fans clustered in front of the 500-foot structure. By this time, however, he had received a telegram from Ben Henry, his manager as well as the general manager of ATP. Henry stated that if he went ahead with this madness, his contract with Dean would be terminated forthwith. Clutching his ukulele case—it had been his intention to sing "When I'm Cleaning Windows" when he reached the summit of the tower—George shrugged his shoulders and told reporters, "Ah, well. I suppose even I can't lose £50,000 for a five-quid bet. But don't worry. Both our wagers have been given to the hospital. The sad thing, of course, is that I could have done it!"

Having failed to "ascend" in the world, so to speak, George was allowed to travel in the opposite direction when, on 18 October, he and Beryl were invited to appear at the venue where he had first plucked his ukulele—the Barnsley Alhambra. The occasion was a benefit concert in aid of the 58 miners who had been recently killed in the Wharncliffe Woodmoor Pit Disaster. Beryl had initially been against the idea of George's fee being handed over to charity, so she "hyped" up the event by arranging for George to address the Alhambra's audiences, by way of a link-up from the Blackpool Opera House, on three consecutive evenings prior to the concert. This way, she reasoned, their arrival in Barnsley, a town she loathed, would take on all the proportions of a royal visit and allow her to demand—and receive—almost as much in expenses as George's fee would have been, had this been a regular show!

The ploy worked. The Formbys were greeted at the railway station by 5,000 fans, and escorted to their hotel by the Dodworth Colliery Band. For a "small fee", in the event of getting her clothes ruined, Beryl consented to an underground visit to the recently repaired coalmine a few hours before the show.

Feather Your Nest premiered in the spring of 1937, and was another smash hit. It also provided George with the number most

most associated with him...a rare love-song, one of the few entirely void of innuendo, and one which did not come from the "Gifford-Cliffe Smut Factory", as the BBC had dismissed his current songwriting team.

Noel Gay's sublime "Leaning On A Lamp Post" was first recorded in September 1937. From its first public airing, until almost the day of his death, George would never be permitted to leave the stage without performing what the *Sunday Times'* Harold Hobson applauded as, "The true theatre, the real thing, the golden coin and the gates of pearl".

> *There's no other girl I'd wait for,*
> *But this one I'd break any date for,*
> *I won't have to ask what she's late for,*
> *She wouldn't leave me flat,*
> *She's not a girl like that...*
> *I'm leaning on a lamp-post at the corner of the street,*
> *In case a certain little lady walks by!*

Beryl had been firmly *against* her husband recording the song. The more famous became, the more grasping *she* became—in this instance arguing with Noel gay that, as George had created the song, *his* name should be added to the writing credits as had happened with Gifford and Cliffe and several others. Beryl was unable to blackmail Gay by threatening to "take her business elsewhere". For a start, he was not a regular Formby composer. Also, as he already owned copyright on the song *before* the public had even heard it—when *Feather Your Nest* was released in the summer of 1937, though the trade-show screening had taken place five months previously—George had to ask Gay's *permission* to record it. By this time, there were plenty of other artistes waiting in the wings, so to speak, to record cover-versions.

Beryl tried to twist Noel Gay's arm by declaring that no other singer would be able to get away with performing a song which by now was George Formby's signature tune...that if Gay *allowed* anyone else to record it, or refused to include George's name in the credits, she would sue him. Gay declared that if this happened, he would let the media in on Formby's most guarded secret—that *such* were his musical talents that he was not even capable of tuning his own ukuleles. Gay was referring to the fact that there would always be several pre-tuned instruments ready for George in the wings, each set in a different key to save time and not affect the continuity of his performances. One must assume though that he always pre-tuned them personally, for on some of his live recordings George can actually be heard tweaking his ukes between songs. All the same, Beryl conceded defeat and Noel Gay's name was added to her list of enemies, which is a great shame...Gay later confessed that he would have liked to have composed more for Formby than he did. His only other contributions to the Formby repertoire would be "The Left Hand Side Of Egypt" and "Who Are You A-Shoving Of" in 1941, neither of which were written especially for him.

Neither did Beryl approve of George's choice of B-side for "Leaning On A Lamp-Post". "Hi-Tiddley-Hi-Ti Island" was a 1922 number he had been singing for some time, again not written for him. Beryl objected to the stanza which, she declared, would give people the impression that the Formby marriage, now in its fourteenth year, was not the rock-solid institution they liked to present to the world. George told her she was being "just daft". In years to come comics such as Tommy Cooper and Les Dawson would get away with "slagging off" the wives they otherwise adored, though George *was* having personal problems with Beryl, not that this was the reason for insisting that the "offending" verse stay put. He was simply in his Donald McGill mode once more.

On this particular surrealist, cannibal isle, everyone lives in style, nude bathing abounds, and cows chew pins to enable the milk to come out in shilling tins. But this is not all...

> *The girls out there are full of sport,*
> *And wear their frocks a trifle short,*
> *Some are simply wrapped in thought...*
> *The life's so fast and swift and gay,*
> *You live two weeks, then fade away.*
> *I'm taking the wife for a fortnight's stay*
> *On Hi-Tiddley-Hi-Ti Isle!*

George with Florence Desmond, his co-star in *No Limit* (1935).They did not get along.

Four:
The Fiddler Kept On Fiddling

"There was nothing gormless about George, although he appeared so in his films. He was just a hard-headed Lancashire lad!" Eddie Latta, songwriter-mortician.

Beryl had certainly cause for concern when George began shooting his next film for Basil Dean. *Keep Fit* was a send-up of the craze sweeping Britain at the time, spurred on by the League of Health and Beauty. His co-star, Kay Walsh (1911-2005), was *the* perfect specimen of womanhood and unlike most of the others did not mind George's wink-and-nudge flirting technique while they were on the set. The young actress also took pleasure from the effect she was having on George—detected by Beryl's stern, ever-watchful gaze—and made it patently clear from Day One that she was a star in her own right and not about to be bullied by this "snooty little hoofer". The director, Anthony Kimmins, was so terrified of George's wife that he neither questioned or reproached her when she barged on to the set—most often when the red NO ENTRY sign was lit—too bawl him out in front of the actors and crew for what she declared was incompetence. Walsh had, in fact, wanted her friend Monty Banks to direct the film, but the otherwise placid little Italian had told Basil Dean, "The only time you'll even get me directing anything where that fucking Formby woman is concerned will be when she's playing the murder victim, and the scene's for real!" Monty was able to offer Walsh a little moral support, however, for he had persuaded Kimmins to give him a bit-part.

Needless to say, the tension was almost unbearable. Beryl tried her utmost to get Jay Walsh fired from the production, threatening Basil Dean that she would "persuade" George to break his contract unless Walsh was replaced with a less attractive actress, or "de-beautified" by being put into ugly clothes and by having a less feminine hairstyle! During the subsequent showdown in the producer's office, to which George was not invited, Beryl was told that, not only was Walsh going to complete *this* film, she had also been contracted to appear in George's next one, *I See Ice*, which would begin shooting as soon as *Keep Fit* had been edited. Beryl tried to argue, but Dean silenced her for the time being by informing her that George's salary for the new film would be £25,000.

Keep Fit was not quite as witty or well-scripted as George's previous Ealing films. Most of the "fringe" characters were bland, as were the songs, aside from the whimsical "I Don't Like". This was no doubt because the ever-meticulous Basil Dean had objected to George's non-existent songwriting skills being feted in the opening credits. Fearful of being dropped by George, Fred E Cliffe and Harry Gifford had offered the excuse that, given the tight shooting schedule, they had been unable to come up with any big production numbers, the likes of which had made George's first two Ealing films sparkle. Even so, this one was just as hugely successful, though today it rarely shows up in television and cinema retrospectives.

The storyline was pure escapist fantasy, and centered around the circulation war between two rival newspapers, the *Gazette* and the *Country Echo*. When the former poaches readers with its cookery competition, the *Echo* decides to organise a keep-fit contest part-sponsored by the local department store. Enter George Green, a timid gentleman's barber whose love for a pretty manicurist, Joan Allen (Walsh), has thus far been unreciprocated because she is attracted to the store's resident slab of beefcake, Hector Kent (Guy Middleton). Now enter Ernie (George Benson), George's gay "nervous Nellie" pal from the menswear department, whose task it is to deliver the sports kit samples to the gymnasium, but who is pressed for time because he has to attend an amateur dramatics rehearsal. George offers to go in his place, and the man whose sole claim to athletic prowess is that he once came second in a two-contestant egg-and-spoon race finds himself mistaken for one of the competitors. "If that's the result of physical exercise, thank heavens I had a mis-spent youth," observes one of the adjudicators after George has tackled the horizontal bar, only to fall off and end up dangling upside-down from a trapeze.

George is championed by a crooked photographer (Gus McNaughton) who gets him to pose for a picture which George naively assumes will be published in the newspaper...it is for the "before" half of a before-and-after fitness poster, with Kent taking up the other half as the preening, musclebound hero. We then learn that Kent has a criminal record and that, with his cronies, he is intent on creaming off funds from the sponsors.

When Kent has to postpone taking Joan for a trip on the river—he is about to pull off a heist—George takes her instead. Kent likes rowing, George can only punt. Even so, when Ernie secures him an Avon Rowing Club blazer and boater from his department, the pair set up a scam: in order for George to impress Joan and sweep her off her feet, Ernest will turn up disguised as an elderly toff and recognise George as the man who once saved him from drowning! Joan, however, realises that she has been set up when both men fall into the water and have to be rescued by Kent, who just happens to be passing. George than attempts a hasty exit, and he leaps over a hedge and is carried off on the back of a broncoing bull!

As happens in all Formby films, of course, the underdog comes out on top. Joan falls out with Kent when she discovers he has rifled the store's till and pinned the blame on George—who resigns—whilst the doting Ernie is given the sack for procuring him the Avon Club uniform. This results in a confrontation with the enemy, who accidentally knocks himself out by stepping on a broom. Arrested, George is hauled before a judge who berates him for being a bully, and unaware of his own strength!

Ernie, meanwhile, genuinely believing that *George* has knocked out the other man, suggests that the two should settle their differences at the keep-fit contest's boxing finale. Kent agrees, but because everyone assumes that it will be a walkover, no bets are laid. Kent then hits upon the idea of sending a couple of sparring-partners across to the "Battling Barber" training-camp—a farm—to feign being knocked out, thus giving the punters a misguided notion that George really is as dangerous as the judge made out. He is, but only on account of his lucky mascot—a lock of Joan's hair, which Ernie has concealed inside his glove. "Get up, I want to do it again," he exclaims to his barnyard audience, after felling Kent's henchmen and the referee. "I'm a killer and didn't know about it!"

Finally, the big fight takes place, with George—having had his mascot stolen by the referee—almost getting annihilated in the first round. He picks up, however, when Joan snips off another lock of hair, only to be floored again when Kent cheats by sprinkling pepper on his gloves. This calls for drastic action from George's sweetheart—in the form of a kiss, whilst he is in his corner seeing stars. Completely revitalised, he knocks out Kent in the final round, and as the lovers are jubilantly "stretchered" out of the arena, the crowd bursts into a chorus of "Keep Fit".

According to Irene Bevan and a number of others, it was Fate which enabled George to have a fling with Kay Walsh. On 18 June, just before shooting wrapped, Beryl was admitted to a private clinic in London to undergo an operation for appendicitis

—or so the press were led to believe—following a fall from a horse when she and George had been judging a gymkhana event. The clinic in fact specialised in gynaecological treatment, and the real reason for Beryl's departure from the set was to book into the clinic—under an assumed name—for a hysterectomy. As Irene explained:

> *As George was Catholic, he naturally wasn't supposed to be practising birth-control, but religion didn't prevent beryl from making sure they would ever have children. It was a well-known fact at the time that the Formbys had hardly ever slept together—and she often used to say that as she wasn't even remotely interested in having sex with him, no one else would look at him twice. But with all those pretty girls hanging around the studio she was convinced that he would stray sooner than later, so she "had everything taken away", as they say, so that hopefully George wouldn't go looking elsewhere for what she'd never given him. The ruse worked for a little while—until she started telling everyone about his shortcomings in the boudoir. And who wouldn't have had problems, having to put up with that sort of thing?*

Beryl would always rue her decision not to have children, as the ever-doting Harry Scott intimated in *The Fabulous Formby*:

> *Years later, George and Beryl realised as thousands of other self-centred, ambitious couples have realised, that wealth and fame are no substitute for the love and trust of a child of your own. All of her creative and physical energy was spent in driving the Formby fortune up to a staggering figure. George and his career were her babies. Yet it was Beryl who, most of all, regretted that they had a room which was never turned into a nursery.*

There was considerable behind-the-scenes speculation that Beryl also "misbehaved" whilst George was making *I See Ice*. "There's absolutely no doubt about that," Irene Bevan told me. "Beryl was absolutely besotted with Gavin Gordon, a young actor who starred in the film, so she allowed George to sew a few wild oats for once whilst she went off and did the same. After all, it wasn't often that a woman like her had the opportunity to sleep with a man who'd bedded Garbo and Dietrich!"

Though it seems almost certain that he *did* sleep with Beryl and a string of other famous women, Gavin Gordon (1901-83), a strapping six-footer who had appeared as a virgin priest opposite Garbo in *Romance* (1930) was the long-term partner of the actor, Edward Everett Horton. Even so, it must have been gratifying for Beryl to learn that other men found her attractive, and that some would-be suitors were not deterred by George's super-star status. Gordon may have been the first. He was by no means be the last.

I See Ice was again written and directed by Anthony Kimmins, and besides Kay Walsh co-starred Betty Stockfield and Garry Marsh. The latter (Leslie Marsh Geraghty, 1902-81) had actually had a part in a 1920 Formby Sr revue, and until the mid-thirties had featured in dozens of B-movies, mostly thrillers. Marsh later confessed that he had only agreed to appear in a Formby film because Basil Dean—never the most tactful of men—had told him that with his rapidly receding hairline he would make the perfect Formby comedian-villain-stooge. Dean was proved right, but though he enjoyed countless such roles until he retired in 1967, there would only be three more films with George.

The story was more convoluted than ever and contained several sub-plots which were removed from some prints when the film was re-released as part of a Formby double-bill during the fifties. He played George Bright, a photographer's apprentice who invents a tiny camera which he conceals in his bow-tie. Assigned to a job in Birmingham, George is befriended by Judy, a pretty young skater (Walsh), after he has saved her from a pile of luggage at the railway station. She and her partner Paul Martine (Cyril Ritchard) are on their way to London to participate in an ice-show, after which Martine is to play in the London Cyclones-Canada Buffaloes ice-hockey final at the Imperial Rink. All travel on the same train, though what George does not know is that the vehicle is scheduled to divide at Birmingham.

"I'm told I look pretty good with my skates on," Judy tells him, whilst George offers to share his sandwiches and a pig's trotter—and innocently replies, "Ee, you'd look good with nothing on!" Then she is dragged off by the toffee-nosed Martine, as the train splits and George finds himself in the wrong half and on his way to London. In panic he pulls the communication cord and is nabbed by the guard and given an option: an on the spot £5 penalty, which he cannot afford, or two weeks in prison. This leads to the film's first mad-cap chase: George wrecks the dining car, gets menaced by an ugly dog, and hides in Judy's carriage. Sprung by Martine, he is saved by the Judy, who persuades her partner to take him on as their property man. The police, however, are waiting for him at Euston, so he leaves the train disguised as a woman—the script called for a Sybil Thorndike lookalike. "I'm a Tiller Girl," he coos, sparking off another chase wherein he again evades his pursuers.

  Judy has developed a soft spot for George, and she coaxes him into putting his camera to good use. Burmanov, the famous explorer, has just returned from the North Pole and is tetchy about being photographed. George snaps him at the rink where Judy and Martine are about to perform, but is caught out. Harried into one of the dressing-rooms, he emerges clad as one of the Cossacks who are about to assist in Martine's spectacular ice-jump over the backs of eight men. George, naturally, ends up as the eighth man. Ordered to kneel, his false beard becomes frozen to the ice. Judy's and Martine's act is ruined, and they are fired, whence Martine exacts his revenge by shopping George to the police.

Nonplussed, Judy helps George to develop his film. The picture, however, reveals more than the burly explorer. In the background George has inadvertently snapped the editor of a leading newspaper, Galloway (Garry Marsh) canoodling with the wife of an influential sports supremo. Initially, George does not cotton on to this...or the fact that Galloway thinks he is blackmailing him by trying to enforce him to buy the picture. More mayhem ensues when George announces that he does not want *money* for the snap and the negative—just an assurance that Galloway will print another photograph which he has taken, of Judy, on the front page of his newspaper in the hope of someone offering her a lucky break.

George, meanwhile, is hired to take sneak-shots of the ice-hockey final, an event from which photographers are barred, by a rival paper. He is still being pursued by the police, and by Galloway's henchmen, who believe he has the negative. The editor has paid for them to dine at the plush Lotus Club, where salmon is on the menu. "Ask him to open a fresh tin," George tells the waiter, before the slapstick resumes. This time, the police apprehend him and he is thrown into jail and gets out just in time for the big match, in which Martine is the Cyclones' star player.

Judy has been engaged as the pre-tournament entertainment, and George is sneaked into the referee's box so that he can get good shots. He is, of course, called to referee, causing pandemonium on the ice and getting rumbled by the players, who scramble all over him to get at his camera...which he has tied around his leg. George therefore gets his pictures, and with them the position of ace reporter from the rival editor. More importantly, he ends up with the girl!

For *I See Ice*, Anthony Kimmins commissioned *two* endings—one to please Beryl, in which George and Kay Walsh are left sitting on the ice and merely appear to be *about* to kiss, and another, the one most commonly seen, where their lips actually meet not once, but twice. There were also three fine songs: "Mother What'll I Do Now?", "Noughts And Crosses", and Harry Parr-Davies' "In My Little Snapshot Album…which Gracie Fields' arranger and personal composer had written for her, only to be told, "Better give that one to Formby, love. It's a bit too rude for me!"

> *Now I've got a picture of the vicar's wife,*
> *Chasing the curate with a carving-knife,*
> *Now what he did was all in fun,*
> *But that's not the kind of thing that's done,*
> *I could see he'd pinched her hot-cross bun....*

George was visited I the set of *I See Ice* by *Film Weekly's* Leonard Wallace, who had arranged to interview him some weeks previously. Beryl quickly put the dampers on this, however, when she asked Wallace for a list of the questions he was going to ask—a common prerequisite, so that she could "guide" George through his responses. Wallace had scribbled the heading, "Introducing George Formby—Next Year's Comedy King", across the top of his pad, ad as in her estimation George was definitely the flavour of the moment who needed absolutely *no* introduction, the interview was scrapped and Wallace warned to watch his step. His feature, published in the 6 November 1937 issue of the magazine, was nevertheless amongst the most praiseworthy ever written about George. It certainly offered his career, "South of Birmingham", a tremendous boost:

> *Unknown to half of England a couple of years ago, I doubt if any other star, with the possible exception of Gracie Fields, has made such a quick climb into the favour of British filmgoers. I'll give him another year, and I'll bet he'll be running level with Gracie for the honour of being Britain's most popular film star. George has buck teeth and a feckless grin. He is a broad comedian, a knockabout clown, a ukulele strummer, a comic-song singer, and still half a variety artist in a strange element. He also has that spark of personality that breeds universal appeal and commands universal affection. The teeth and the dumb grin are his properties, like the clown's red nose and white diamond patch. But the spirit of Formby is in his eyes. There is a smile in them that can turn to the most touching pathos, like the eyes of a spaniel. There is also in them an unquenchable optimism that sums up the very essence of his character, that of the good-natured simpleton who is put upon and badgered, but who always comes back smiling. He is the perfect pattern of all the timid men, the dunderheads, the bullied, pushed around underdogs. In his ultimate triumphs all these little men triumph also, and as most of us have a streak at least of that sort of thing, we get a vicarious pleasure in a vicarious victory. With his honest broad appeal, and his closeness to the hearts and psychology of the ordinary person, he is one of the most important discoveries British studios have made for years.*

At the end of June, days after finishing the film—and for the first time in thirteen years without Beryl—George opened at Blackpool Opera House in *King Cheer*, Jack Taylor's latest revue. Sylvia, who edited the *Blackpool Gazette*'s women's page, was allowed to sit in on rehearsals and told George that in her humble opinion the revue's best songs were "The Lancashire Toreador", "With My Little Stick Of Blackpool Rock", "Hindoo Man", and "Sitting On The Sands All Night". This pleased him. "I'm writing most of my own melodies today," he said. "I strum out the tune on my uke, and a couple of lads I have jot it down as music. *I* don't know a thing about music—and there you are!"

The revue kept George occupied for the rest of the summer, during which time the house at Barton was sold, and he bought a five-bedroomed property at Little Singleton, five miles from the centre of Blackpool. "Garthallen" was set in four acres of landscaped gardens and woodland, and boasted a full-sized tennis court which, George joked, would be handy for keeping chickens in! The couple moved in on 9 September, Beryl's thirty-seventh birthday...by which time the house, like all the others, had been rebaptised "Beryldene".

On 15 November 1937, George appeared in his first Royal Variety Show, alongside fellow Lancastrians Gracie Fields and Norman Evans. On the morning prior to this, he succumbed to a colossal attack of nerves. Beryl later said that she had helped him through one crisis by instigating another. "A moment's serious thought told me that there was no time for half measures," she recalled. "George was a bad case, so we had a row—and row we did, as we had never done since we'd been married. I told him off left and right. He'd been so nervous he hadn't wanted to get out of bed, but when I began rowing at him he was *glad* to get out!"

According to Beryl, the couple had kept at it, hammer and tong, until late in the afternoon, when they had gone off on a shopping spree and George had bought a chromium sports cycle. After riding around the store to the amazement of the other shoppers, he had taken it for a "test-drive" up and down Oxford Street before finally setting off, nerves-free, for the Palladium:

> *By then George was so exhausted with the day's row and the excitement about the new bike that he hadn't a trace of stage nerves! I do believe that he was one of the calmest people backstage during those antagonising seconds before the first curtain. I was in my usual position in the wings when George went on with his ukulele. I'd pinned on him the tie-pin which King George had given his father...and I gave him a kiss as he went on, just to show him once more that the row had been a fake!*

The Royal Variety Show set another precedent as far as Beryl's impeccably organised routine was concerned. George had been told that his spot would amount to twelve minutes exactly—not a second more. Beryl therefore went out and bought a stopwatch to augment an already-present notebook and clipboard which were used to keep a record of the songs George performed in every show, along with a number-coded record of his self-confessed abysmal jokes. Like Tommy Cooper after him, only George could have an audience in stitches with such deliberately dire patter. The idea behind this was that Beryl was able to gauge the public's reaction to George's work, enabling songs which had not gone down particularly well to be revamped or even removed from his repertoire—there were always dozens more ready to take their place, many of which he never got around to airing. And now she began timing them, bringing the comment from the stridently acerbic critic, Hannen Swaffer, "Not content with keeping her husband on a leash like a pet monkey, Mrs Formby has now taken to *clocking* his every movement."

In the spring of 1938, with war-clouds gathering on the horizon, Basil Dean's morale-boosting crusade saw him putting his biggest star, Gracie Fields, into *Keep Smiling*, an optimistic vehicle directed by Monty Banks...who Dean also assigned to the next Formby film, *George Takes The Air*, with shooting scheduled to begin as soon as the Gracie film had been completed. Beryl, however, objected to Banks *and* the title, but especially Dean's decision to hire Kay Walsh as George's co-star for a *third* time. Subsequently, Anthony Kimmins was brought in to direct, Walsh was dropped and replaced by Polly Ward—who was read the "keep-your-hands-off-my-husband" riot-act by Beryl, and the title was changed to *It's In The Air*.

The storyline was extremely improbable, but the slapstick remains amongst the most perfectly-times and side-splitting that George ever performed. The big production number in the middle of the film, where George and the entire military cast mince and sing the title-track, is pure high-camp—so perfectly over the top that only a Liberace precursor and a few drag-queens are missing to complete the line-up. He played George Brown, a would-be recruit who is rejected by the RAF for being too gormless. Not only is he unable to distinguish his left from his right, when he turns up for enrolment with his dog, Scruffy, but without the obligatory gas-mask, he remarks that he has only been provided with one…which he has given to the dog. He then wanders into the communications room where, filling in for the operator whilst he takes a break, he serenades a couple of pilots over the air with "They Can't Fool Me", before pulling the wrong lever and blowing up the set—causing Scruffy to put on his own gas-mask, a masterpiece of bungled editing!

Disappointed, George returns home, where he cannot resist trying on his sister's boyfriend's uniform when he goes on leave, and in the pocket he finds a letter addressed to an RAF official, which he delivers to the HQ in his motorbike and sidecar. Here the CO (Garry Marsh) mistakes him for a dispatch rider and orders him to drive to the Glenbridge airbase—ploughing through farmyards, gates, road-works and fords. Here he is mocked by the other recruits—on account of his Northern accent

—bullied by the sergeant major, and befriended by his pretty daughter, Peggy (Ward). Initially, she dismisses him as a "headquarters nitwit", but she and the others warm to him after he sings a song berating the sergeant major, a man who is so hard, George declares, that he would strangle his own mother:

> *His medals break our hearts,*
> *He won them playing darts…*
> *His feet fill up the road,*
> *Knock-kneed and pigeon-toed,*
> *We'd sooner shoot him than salute him,*
> *Our Sergeant Major!*

George is tricked by a snooty officer with designs on Peggy into billeting in the sergeant major's quarters and, after a hilarious Faydeau-type routine, wakes up next to him in bed. For this he is brought before the CO and made to perform the offending song again. And of course, he has changed the words:

> *He's as generous as can be,*
> *So sentimental, kind and gentle…*
> *He's got a heart of gold,*
> *So fearless and bold!*
> *He's like Samson—strong and handsome!*
> *Our Sergeant Major!*

After this episode, the sergeant major rumbles George's identity and enlists him for flight-training, where a pilot about to fly a prototype plane mistakes him for an engineer and asks him to "run up" the engine. Still confusing left and right, he execute a series of aerial loops and death-defying stunts—at one stage switching off the engine! Scoring a perfect hit whilst accidentally dropping a bomb, he impresses his superiors, and is elevated to a fully-fledged pilot. The film ends with George performing the film's show-stopper title-song...on stage in a revue, in a model plane which subsequently drops to bits!

Though they did not work together as frequently as George would have liked—on account being more or less tied to Gracie Fields—George enjoyed Harry Parr Davies' company. "A cheerful antidote to that fucking viper," was how Monty Banks described the on-set presence of the man who supplied Gracie with some of her most celebrated songs—"Wish Me Luck As You Wave Me Goodbye" and "Pedro The Fisherman" were but two—though there would never be any really big songs for George.

A moody, totally unpredictable Welshman, Parr-Davies was just twenty when he wrote his first song for George, "Your Way Is My Way", in 1935. He was the perfect foil for George's decidedly off-beat sense of fun, and the only person who could call Beryl a "miserable bleeder" to her face and get away with it. Effeminate, thin, pasty-faced and unable to see a thing without his trademark bottle-bottom spectacles, he and George spent a lot of time together whilst shooting *It's In The Air*—mostly at the pub near the studio, and with Beryl's blessing. Her naivety stretched to a point where she thought her husband would be safer in the company of a "grumpy Nancy-boy" than being pestered by the likes of Polly Ward. She had lately revised her opinion that Polly was only slightly less promiscuous than Kay Walsh or Florence Desmond—an opinion nurtured by her own paranoia. Snooty they may have been, but thus far *all* of George's co-stars had been respectable young women.

"It was Harry's constipation that always made him grumpy," Irene Bevan said. "That troubled him more than anything. He used to come down to breakfast on a morning and say, 'The Chooser's been!' We all knew then that he'd been to the lavatory and that he would be in a good mood!"

Another drinking partner—and gay to boot, though also married—who could not stand Beryl was Garry Marsh, who genuinely believed that her domineering was becoming detrimental to George's health. Marsh, however, preferred a more salubrious kind of entertainment to smoky pubs, as he explained during a 1967 interview:

> *One day I said to George, "Let's go out to the Café Royal for a few drinks and a bit of grub." He said, "Ee, I'd love to!" And suddenly I noticed that his face dropped. He said, "Beryl, she'd never wear it. Besides, I can't afford it!" I said, "What do you mean, you can't afford it? You're getting thirty-thousand a picture!" At that moment Beryl came across the set. I said, "Beryl, I'd like to take George out tonight, give him a few drinks. What about it? It'll do him good. He's been working very hard, it'll take his mind off things." She said, "Off what things? Off me? Do you know what would happen if he went out with you? He'd come home in the early hours of the morning, stinking drunk, and with lipstick all over his chops. No, he's coming home with me. Aren't you, George? And that was that!*

Whilst shooting *It's In The Air*, George took delivery of his first custom-built car—over the next twenty years there would be another 130!—a fabulous Rolls Royce. He still hung on to his six-cylinder SS1 Coupé, which he had purchased second-hand in 1933. Both cars were registered in Beryl's name, it was later claimed to prevent George from "fooling around". If he ever *did* decide to walk out on the wife who was so in name only, Beryl would at least be left with a small fortune in metal.

Why George continued to allow himself to be picked upon is not easy to understand. Maybe he was afraid of creating a scandal by leaving her—or perhaps he actually *enjoyed* being henpecked. His career would certainly have collapsed without her domineering spirit, for whist Beryl only *nagged* her husband, she could prove a veritable vixen where theatre managers, producers and songwriters were concerned. She demanded and got the very highest fees, argued "nit-picking" contractual details which anyone else might have ignored, and swelled the Formby coffers beyond even her own expectations. Yet though George was by this time the highest-paid male entertainer in Britain, it was common knowledge amongst the show business crowd that his wife allowed him just five-shillings a day pocket money—less, if he could get through the day without spending it all. Good friends such as the comic Tommy Trinder, whom Beryl just managed to tolerate, believed that George often used his wife's ruling as an excuse to get out of buying a round of drinks—or to rid himself of hangers-on and scroungers, such as certain members of his family who might have regarded him as a soft touch. "Beryl never missed a thing," Trinder said in a television interview shortly before his death, in 1989. "She always felt, 'Well, here's the goldmine and I'm not going to let anybody else take their pick and shovel there!' I'd say, 'Why don't you give him a couple of pounds and let him live it up?' Beryl would get very haughty at that!"

Beryl also accompanied George to his tailor's, bartering with the assistants for a bargain, and frequently not even paying for the finished suits, claiming that to boast the logo. FORMBY SHOPS HERE, would bring them all the business they could handle without having to charge her for her purchases!

For her own clothes, Beryl visited only the more exclusive fashion emporiums, causing a sensation whenever she turned up at a function clad in the finest silks and furs, wearing trademark bird-of-paradise hats, and dripping with diamonds. George invariably trailed behind, wearing his tuxedo, or nervously clung to her arm like he was escorting his mistress to some coy, adulterous rendezvous.

On 15 October 1938, as much for his personal pleasure and satisfaction as for the publicity stunt it really was, George returned to the racetrack for a single meeting, riding Luck Bert in the October Handicap Hurdle, at Northolt Park. The horse was the 6-4 favourite, and everyone at ATP had a bet on it—though the jockey, George, was given explicit instructions by Beryl not to waste his money. He risked one pound, the horse refused a fence and was disqualified. To teach him a lesson, Beryl yelled at him in the middle of the members' enclosure for spending money they could "ill afford—at this time the couple had around £50,000 in the bank—and deducted the cash he had lost from his following week's allowance!

And George *was* making a lot of money. Between February 1938 and the end of 1939, Regal Zonophone, with whom he had signed a contract in the summer of 1935, released his records on average at the rate of one a month. Few would be regarded as Formby classics, but they sold extremely well and helped his bank balance to stay healthy. He also earned a great deal from radio appearances—firstly from his *A Lancashire Lad* series which began in January 1938 and ran for several months, followed by three *Formby Do* broadcasts during the summer, and ending with some thirty twice-weekly programmes on Radio Luxembourg, sponsored by Feenamint laxative. The signature tune for these, a parody of the theme-song from one of his films, had him warbling:

> *Keep fit and take a hint,*
> *It will give your eyes a glint,*
> *If you take Feenamint!*

In the autumn of 1938, George began shooting *Trouble Brewing*.

Anthony Kimmins again directed, though this time not under the auspicious gaze of Basil Dean who, having had enough of dealing with Beryl, had passed the reins to Jack Kitchin. George's leading lady was Googie Withers (1917-2011), then virtually unknown, and playing the chief crook was Ronald Shiner (1903-66), a beady-eyed, raucous-voiced Cockney comedian whose huge trademark nose had recently been insured for £20,000. "If he breaks his conk during the action sequences, he'll end up getting as much for the film as me," George told the press. He and Shiner got on very well, despite Beryl's interference, and they often went off to the pub together—they said to get away from the brewery in the film—during shooting. Shiner would become a Formby regular, appearing in six films.

George Gullip, who is described as "Sherlock Holmes and Sexton Blake rolled into one", is a print-room operator at a newspaper office. He invents an indelible ink finger-marking system which he puts to good use whilst tracking down a counterfeiting gang—known in the trade as "slushers"—assisted by his sidekick, Bill (Gus McNaughton) and Mary (Withers), the young secretary who has stolen his heart.

At the racetrack, George and Bill have won a tidy sum, backing an outsider which George—standing in for his newspaper's absent horoscope writer—has predicted will win. Bill—McNaughton in his usual role as con-man—has however take possession of the winnings, and offers drinks all around in the bar. The barmaid cannot change a £10 note, so up steps one of the counterfeiters who changes this and the others in Bill's hand for fivers—fake notes which are confiscated by a detective. The two friends then observe the crooks getting into a Blue Star Brewery wagon, and on hitching a ride end up not at the brewery, but at the swimming baths. Bill, the coward, purloins a bathing suit for George and sends him in after them—only this evening the baths are holding a free-for-all wrestling match. George ends up taking on the Terrible Tiger…and only he, of course, can win the bout aided by a hatpin, a bar of soap, and a lighted cigar which he shoves down his opponent's trunks, setting his posterior alight! The crooks get away!

Meanwhile, the newspaper's owner has offered a large reward for the apprehension of the criminals after finding fake notes in *his* winnings at the racetrack. Initially, George and Bill suspect the feisty opera star, Madame Berdi (Martita Hunt) to be the head of the operation because they have seen her speaking to one of the crooks at the afternoon meeting. They gain access to her house by masquerading as waiters at a party. George managed to get Madame Berdi to leave a fingerprint on a piece of paper, but she tucks it into the top of her stocking. He eventually retrieves it by crawling under the table and sticking his hand up her dress, a scene which had Beryl really hitting the roof—until the statuesque Miss Hunt threatened to *throw* her off the set unless she left of her own accord. The print on the singer's finger, however, fails to match the one found by Mary on her boss's banknote. Suspicion then falls on a certain Major Hopkins—though Mary and George do not at first know that the "slush" money he and Bill have seen in his apartment is there because Hopkins is the Chief of Police and examining the notes.

It is Mary who discovers the identity of the real culprit—the editor, Brady (Garry Marsh), who subsequently kidnaps he and incarcerates her in the brewery whilst arrangements are made to ship her out of the country to prevent her from blabbing. She manages to leave a message for the sleuths, who set off in hot pursuit. The film then ends up with the usual, frequently speeded-up mayhem, during which all the crooks end up being pushed into fermentation tanks and getting drunk. It also contains the most controversial scene in any Formby scene when George and his sweetheart topple backwards into one of the tanks, surfacing to enjoy a passionate mouth-to-mouth kiss!

This latter sequence—horror of horrors—caused a furore within the Formby household. Upon reading through the script, Beryl had ordered George to deliver a fleeting peck on his leading lady's cheek, and no more. Anthony Kimmins, however, had other ideas and told Googie Withers, "Make it a whopper!"—which she did, and though Beryl fumed for days afterwards, demanding twenty-three takes until she was certain that George's ardour for Withers had cooled, and choosing the least sensual one, it was the "whopper" which stayed in the finished print.

One of the songs pencilled in this film, "I Wonder Who's Under Her Balcony Now?"—George called it "a tale of lost love"—had been cut out during production because Anthony Kimmins had worried it might be misconstrued:

> *Will he kiss her under the nose,*
> *Or underneath the archway,*
> *Where her sweet william grows?*
> *If he's fresh and gets too free,*
> *I hope a bulldog bites him in the place it bit me...*
> *I hope he catches the lot,*
> *When she empties out her old geranium pot!*

One may assume what some of the snootier critics would have made of this one, had George performed it in the film. "Fanlight Fanny" *was* left in, resulting in a savage attack by *Picturegoer*'s Hubert Cole, though one fails to understand why, today:

> *She dances underneath a magic spell,*
> *She's full of charm and beer and stout as well...*
> *You can't tell if she's brunette or blonde,*
> *She's like something you drag out of a pond...*
> *She's a peach, but understand,*

> *She's called a peach because she's always canned!*
> *That's Fanlight Fanny, the frowsy nightclub queen!*

An influential but prudish individual, Cole had accused Gracie Fields of "inciting perversion" because she had used the Northern expression, "acting the goat"—a euphemism for clowning around and not, as Cole had concluded, one which alluded to oral sex! "You've got a dirty little mind," Gracie had told him angrily. Cole objected to the word "fanny"—in this instance, of course, a woman's name and not a slang word for vagina or buttocks, depending on which side of the Atlantic one happened to be on. In the magazine's 30 September 1939 issue, he admonished:

> *George caters for family audiences who don't want near-the-knuckle jokes. Yet when the latest Formby film came along a few weeks ago, I found that it contained two of three jokes in the worst possible taste. They were so "blue" that they staggered me. It may be true that George finds this type of joke popular on the music-hall stage. Music-hall audiences have a right to demand whatever humour they most prefer. But cinema audiences don't want that kind of stuff. The screen is too intimate a medium to be used for coarseness. "Blue" gags are not going to entertain George's millions of film-going admirers. They are going to embarrass and annoy them. He should give them up at once before they do him serious harm.*

The extraneous takes for the final scene in *Trouble Brewing* had pushed George to the limit. At the end of January—halfway through a season of *Dick Whittington* at the Manchester Palace, worried that the chill he had been suffering from for weeks was getting no better, Beryl took George to Harley Street—where he was diagnosed with an acute respiratory infection. He was told to stop smoking, and not to speak for a week: two things he later said he could not have done to *save* his life. He was, however, obliged to pull out of the pantomime—the couple were replaced by another popular duo, Billy Caryll and Hilda Mundy—and George agreed to take his first holiday in five years. In the middle of February, he and Beryl joined a five-week cruise to the West Indies.

The couple were accompanied by Beryl's parents who, George told the *Gazette*'s Sylvia shortly before leaving Blackpool, would be able to keep his wife company while he was catching up on his songwriting. "I've just completed five songs, including one called 'It's Turned Out Nice Again'," he added. "I got the inspiration for that one from the fact that I've been ill, and now I'm better." The song—its title referring to his famous catchphrase—had been sent to him a few days earlier by Fred Cliffe and Harry Gifford!

Gifford and Cliffe had also sent George two more instalments of the Mr Wu sage: "I'm The Husband Of The Wife Of Mr Wu", and the biting, "Mr Wu's Window Cleaner Now."

Next on the ATP production-line was *"Come On George"*, a horse-racing comedy perfectly suited for George who, having had first-hand experience of the sport, insisted upon doing most of his own stunts. For once, Beryl agreed with him, telling the press, "What George doesn't know about racing isn't *worth* knowing!" And this time there were two female co-stars: Meriel Forbes, and Pat Kirkwood, who played his love-interest.

The film opens at the racecourse, with the jockeys emerging one by one from behind a fence—followed by George, mounted on an ice-cream cart. The slapstick begins at once. Two pickpockets steal a wallet which ends up in his cart. The owner, a top trainer, spots it and sets the police on George, resulting in a wrecking chase, through the club house and on to a train—all the while, George is clutching his ukulele case. Here, he hides in the wagon transporting a psychotic horse named Maneater, which he manages to soothe. The stable are impressed, and hire him to ride Maneater in the forthcoming Bargrave Stakes, not telling him the truth about the horse's nasty temper—adopting the theory that the beast, rebaptised The Lamb, is only unmanageable when those around it show fear. "My Uncle Joe made *his* living following horses—with a bucket and shovel!" George quips.

George finds digs at the local police station where Anne, the sergeant's pretty daughter (Kirkwood), shows him to his room—a disused cell. When the police arrive looking for a pickpocket, he opens the door disguised as the maid. Then off he goes to serenade the horse:

> *I joined the gym for exercise,*
> *A lady instructor put me wise,*
> *She made my spare parts twice the size,*
> *I'm making headway now!*

Elsewhere in the song, George makes the obligatory reference to window cleaners, and has a sly crack at the BBC. Then, after singing the sergeant's obnoxious, catapult-wielding grandson, Squib, to sleep with "Goodnight, Little Fellow, Goodnight"—the number he had sung to Mickey Dripping in *Formby Seeing Life*—and crooning "Pardon Me" to Anne, he takes his sweetheart to the funfair, where the real hilarity begins.

In the flea-circus tent, Squib empties a tube of fleas inside the back of George's trousers, whilst the trainer pronounces, describing the insect battle taking place in an adjoining tank, "The troops are about to fall into no-man's land. Yes, they are now giving a stinging attack to the rear!" Later, when Anne comments on a troupe of scantilly-clad Parisian dancing girls, he tells her, "*You'd* look better than them with *nothing* on!"

The police-chase resumes—into a trailer from which he emerges in the guise of the world-famous acrobat, The Golden Phantom, creating yet more mayhem before making his way back to the stable, where he is told the truth about the horse he is about to ride. Terrified, George tries to back out of the race—a problem which is effectively solved by a visit to a brain-specialist who reveals that, whilst under hypnosis and barring any knocks to the head, our hero will remain fearless. En route to the racecourse, he is pursued by thugs sent by a rival stable, but outwits them by stealing their car. When he puts his foot down, however, mere minutes before the race is due to begin, the accelerator jams and he again ends up wrecking the clubhouse. *The* he is told that the race is a steeplechase, something he has no experience of riding!

Setting off at last, George is thrown at the water-jump and the horse continues without him. He whistles it back, it crouches for him to remount, and he tears past the post, emerging as the victor of nerve-racking photo-finish. And whilst the crowd is cheering, Maneater throws him the ten yards on to the trailer upon which is Anne is standing—which they both fall through. George finally gets to kiss his love *almost* on the lips, whilst his horse pokes his head through the flaps behind them. A masterpiece!

The climax to this film is *so* badly spliced—George actually changes direction, mid-air, in some prints!—that is has become legendary. In one of the earlier scenes, when George dashes on to the train after being chased through the club-house, it is being drawn by a LNER 4309 locomotive, though by the next scene this has been changed to a LMS *Dreadnought*. In addition, during this same sequence the editor has combined two vastly differing backdrops—the fabricated one of the Fells whilst George is running across the tops of the carriages, and the Kentish location which was used for the setting of the Avonbury Goods Yard! Later, when he is singing "I'm Making Headway Now" to the horse, he plays one ukulele for the song, and then walks off with another model, leaving his case behind, though by the next time he sings he has been reunited with the original. Finally, during the scene prior to the big race, George is speeding along a country lane when he almost runs into the back of a removal van—only when he overtakes this, he is suddenly careering along a triple-carriageway!

To the cinemagoer, *Come On George* may have appeared an over-frothy, light-hearted romp where no one takes anything seriously, and where even the crooks do not get their comeuppance. For the cast, however, shooting had been anything but pleasant. Neither George nor Beryl could stand the child actor, Ronald Stagg, who played Squib—nor Meriel Forbes (1913-2000), who soon afterwards married Ralph Richardson, and of whom George quipped, "When she talks, she sounds like she's got a gob full of marbles!" He also loathed Pat Kirkwood, a feeling which was mutual.

Eighteen when she appeared in *Come On George*, and with a few film credits already tucked under her belt, Pat Kirkwood (1921-2007) was first and foremost a singer-dancer who aspired towards a career in the West End. She was also very pretty and elegant, which to Beryl's way of thinking meant only one thing—George would immediately make a play for her. In her opinion, that would be even more likely if the director was able to get away with the scene he planned—pre-dating Marilyn Monroe—which would have a wind-machine blowing Kirkwood's skirt above her head, exposing her bloomers. Incensed, Beryl ordered a "deglamorisation" programme, informing Anthony Kimmins that unless the young actress was shorn of her lovely locks and put into dowdy clothes, George would not make the film.

Many years later, Kirkwood confessed how she had hated the whole experience of working in a Formby film, denouncing George as "cretinous and thick as pig-manure". "Try to converse with him and you'd find there was no one at home," she told one interviewer, adding somewhat smugly, "They wanted a plain, English rose, and I was never that!" Kirkwood was also disappointed that she was not allowed to duet with George on "Pardon Me", something which would have worked inordinately well. In fact, everyone connected with the film had *wanted* them to do the song together, and again Beryl had put her foot down. "Even serenading a girl on the screen was tantamount to his having sex with her, in Beryl's eyes, so George sang the number on his own," Irene Bevan said.

Another British actress who experienced problems with George—or so she claimed in a 1981 interview—as Phyllis Calvert (1915-2002), his co-star in *Let George Do It*. Calvert—born Phyllis Bickle, and referred to by George as "Phyllis Tickle", much to her annoyance—had recently appeared with Arthur Askey in *Charlie's Big-Hearted Aunt*. Confessing that George had always been the great hero of her childhood, though she had been twenty when she had first seen him—she explained what it had been like, working with him:

> *It's the highlights that remain in your memory, and meeting George Formby, there weren't many highlights...and like a lot of people you make films with, once you've met them they're just perfectly ordinary people. So he was a bit of a disappointment. I think the thing I admired most about him was his technique. He was a very dull man. I don't ever remember holding a conversation with him. But when you watched him doing his stuff on the floor, then he became a completely different person.*

Calvert then went on to explain how, before any Formby film got under way, the girls were forewarned of his reputation, though all the way through shooting he steered clear of her. She suspected this was because Beryl was watching his every move. Until the last day, that is:

> *It was quite extraordinary how he couldn't resist trying to make it with all his leading ladies. Beryl had to do some Christmas shopping, and I was in my dressing-room in the lunch-hour. A knock came at the door, and George stood there rather like a little boy and said, "Ee, I'm crazy about you!" And that was all!*

Beryl's absences from her husband's side were rare, but he took advantage of these occasions. Some sources have stated that no sooner was Beryl was out of sight than he would have a woman—more often than not a dancer or extra, but occasionally a co-star, such as Coral Browne, who was in *Let George Do It*—if not in his dressing room, then back at some discreet hotel, depending on the length of his "parole". Dorothy Hyson, who auditioned for the new film but failed to get the part, said:

> *George doted on his wife, there's absolutely no doubt about that. But he was even less interested in having sex with her now that she'd had the operation, not that he'd ever been passionate about her in that sense. Beryl was more like a nagging mother than a partner, yet he was so reliant on her for guidance, for handling the business side of things, that as much as she was starting to wear him down, he would never have been able to have coped without her.*

Let George Do It was a bubbly, hugely successful entertaining propaganda vehicle, rich with melodious tunes, possessed of a good script, and marred only by a silly ending. Much of the action takes place in Norway, during the early months of the war, where the eminent bandleader, Mark Mendez (Garry Marsh) is based and doubling as a Nazi agent, sending musically-coded messages over the air to German U-boats to that they can sink Allied shipping.

When one of Mendez's musicians—a ukulele player—is discovered to be spying for the British, he is disposed of…shot whilst the orchestra is playing "Oh, Don't The Wind Blow Cold", and whilst the audience's attention is diverted by the dancing of Mendez's partner, Iris (Coral Browne). A replacement is requisitioned from London, but unknown to Mendez this musician too works for British Intelligence. In Dover, however, there is a blackout, and Mendez is sent the wrong man—George Hepplewhite, a member of the Dinky-Do Concert Party which has just returned from France and who, instead of boarding the ship for Blackpool with his colleagues, ends up bound for Bergen.

Here, George meets his "contact"—Mary (Calvert), who leaves a note in his ukulele case instructing him to meet her for a briefing. This is signed "M", and when he shows this to Mendez's sidekick he is told that the bandleader always does this when discussing contracts. Mendez, meanwhile, sends along Iris to seduce George into giving himself away. She fails, of course, because he does not know that he is supposed to be a spy, though when he eventually meets Mary and she confides in him, he is only too willing to help. Sneaking into Mendez's room, he finds the code document and photographs it. Then he escapes out of the window, plunging through an adjacent bakery roof and dropping the camera. It, and George, end up in the flour-bin, then the dough-mixer, but he retrieves it and, in supplying Mary with the evidence she requires, wins her love.

The pair set up Mendez, sending a copy of the code to the Admiralty so that British destroyers can sail to the spot indicated by Mendez's message, and wait for the U-boat. "Wallop, Mrs Ducket—your mother's won a bucket!" George gleefully exclaims, and their mission succeeds when the British sink three enemy craft.

Mendez now suspects George of espionage and, whilst Mary—her task completed—prepares to leave for England on the *McCaulay*, he is administered a truth-drug, and confesses all before passing out. There then follows the most extraordinary dream-sequence, at that time the most powerful piece of anti-Nazi propaganda on British screens:

> *Mendez and his sidekick, wearing enemy uniforms from World War I—an allegory that the Germans were beaten then, and will be beaten again—try to capture George, informing him that he and Mary are about to be executed. Imitating James Cagney, George produces a machine-gun and shoots at them. Their trousers fall down, revealing Swastika undershorts, and George escapes to rescue Mary, whom they have imprisoned in the bakery. "George, I'm half-baked," she screams, about to be shoved into the oven. Together, they face the foe, throwing hand-grenades made of dough. George asks her to marry him: she responds that true marriages are made in heaven, and very soon they are following the sign marked PEARLY GATES. George is not permitted to enter paradise, however, until he has captured Hitler. He therefore embarks on his quest, riding a pallet-lift attached to a barrage balloon, and descends upon Hitler whilst he is addressing a rally. "You're my last territorial demand in Europe," George opines, bashing him senseless, whilst all the Nazis rush to congratulate each other...*

Mendez, meanwhile, now that his plan has been foiled, opts to deliver his next message to the U-boat in person, declaring that one of the next ships to be destroyed will be the *McCaulay*. Prior to this, during their broadcast the band plays "Oh, Don't The Wind Blow Cold", Mendez's cue to have George killed. He is tipped off, however, by another player (Ronald Shiner), and gets away, only to find that Mary's ship has set sail. Not to be beaten, he stows away on the motor-launch conveying Mendez to the U-boat.

The film ends with the usual free-for-all mayhem. George intercepts Mendez's message, contacts Mary of the *McCaulay*, and sends the U-boat's controls haywire so that its first torpedo goes off-course. The craft is then captured by the British, but before he is taken away, Mendez makes a last bid to sink the ship by firing another torpedo. George, however, has hidden in the chute so he and not the shell is shot into the air…to make a perfect landing on the deck of the *McCaulay*, with the quip, "Turned out nice again, hasn't it?"

The Formbys had wanted Anthony Kimmins to direct, despite their mutual dislike of each other. "Better the devil you know than the devil you don't," Beryl opined. Kimmins (1901-64) had served as a naval officer, aged just sixteen, in World War I, and now rejoined the Navy, where he would be very quickly elevated to Captain. His mission, serving on the *SS Nigeria* as part of Operation Pedestal—which prevented Germany from gaining control of Malta and the Mediterranean, and in turn the Middle East oil fields—is generally considered to have been a turning point in World War II. To replace Kimmins, ATP brought in Marcel Varnel (1892-1947), to fierce protests from the Formbys, who "did not want to take orders from a foreigner". Born Marcel Hyacinthe le Bozec, in Paris, Varnel had emigrated to New York in 1925 to direct operettas and revues on Broadway for the Schubert Brothers, and a few years later moved to Hollywood, to direct a trio of low-budget films. In 1934, having proclaimed his hatred of the American studio system, he had moved to England to work for British International, and then Gainsborough Pictures to work with the likes of The Crazy Gang, Arthur Askey, and Will Hay—his *Oh, Mr Porter!* with Hay was one of the most popular films of 1937. Despite their initial apprehension, the Formbys got along *so* well with him that henceforth they would be hard put to work with anyone else, and Varnel would direct eight of George's films.

The Americans were so impressed by this film, and in particular with the dream-sequence, that when it was released in the United States its title was changed to *To Hell With Hitler*. The biggest surprise of all was the film's success in Russia. Dubbed and retitled *Dinky Doo*, it opened at a small theatre in Murmansk—the country's most important fishing-port, in the north-west—primarily to entertain sailors stationed there who were then being fed a diet of Laurel and Hardy, Chaplin, and the Keystone Cops. Within weeks, it was transferred to Moscow, where for ten months it broke all cinema box-office records...resulting in a feature, published in *Russia Today*, which declared, it has to be said only half-seriously, that George Formby was fast becoming the most popular figure in the country after Stalin and Churchill! The publication's editor, Richard Bishop, concluded:

> *Mr Formby has kept the entire film industry of Moscow busy making copies of his films. And however our two ideologies might differ, we must have reciprocity and tolerance. The closer our two people can be brought together, the easier it would be to persuade the Russians to take from our way of life that which was best, while we, in turn, could take the best from their way of life.*

This may well have been true, but the publicity gimmick attached to the *Russia Today* spiel—that George, the "celluloid ambassador", had been awarded the country's highest honour, the Order of Lenin, was propaganda trash.

The film critic Leslie Halliwell, the greatest authority of the day, regarded *Let George Do It* as the finest of all the Formby films, and awarded especial praise to the song which tells of the family heirloom within which its narrator is baptised and wed:

> *In the train, my bride gave a shout,*
> *"Ee, what's that you're pulling out?"*
> *I said, "It's old-fashioned and it's tattered and torn,*
> *But I've brought it honeymooning with me, Gert!"*
> *When she said, "What is it, dear?"*
> *I whispered in her ear,*
> *"It's my grandad's flannelette nightshirt!"*

Another big hit from the film was the next instalment in the Limehouse saga. For the laundry has now gone bust, and our honourable Chinese friend has a new profession:

> *When he goes out working, interest he arouses,*
> *Polishing the windows with worn-out ladies' blouses…*
> *With a Hi-di-hi! and a long one-too!*
> *He's had his eyesight tested, a most important matter,*
> *Through a bedroom window, a lady he peeps at her,*
> *His eyesight's getting better.*
> *But his nose is getting flatter,*
> *'Cause Mr Wu's a window-cleaner now!*

With Enid Stamp-Taylor in *Keep Your Seats Please* (1936)

With Polly Ward in *It's In The Air* (1938)

Come On George! (1939)

With Formby stalwart Garry Marsh in *Let George Do It* (1942)

Five:
Swinging Along, Singing A Song!

"George has forgotten what it's like to have a bit of leisure, and apparently he's not likely to begin learning whilst our country is at war." Beryl Formby, wife.

Since the outbreak of war in September 1939, George had been begging Basil Dean—now the head of ENSA—to temporarily release him from his film contract and grant him a permit to entertain the troops in Europe. Dean had repeatedly refused, declaring that George would be better off touring English army camps and Navy bases. In the first week of February 1940, during a pre-trade screening of the rough print of *Let George Do It*, Beryl took Dean to one side and told him in no uncertain terms what she thought about his idea. Ten minutes later, the Formbys' names had been added to the ENSA list.

The couple were toldd that they would be sailing for France on 2 March. This came as a surprise to George, who had not expected to leave so soon. After her "ding-dong" with Dean, Beryl had assigned George to several shows, which she said could be cancelled owing to mitigating circumstances…including a marbles competition, in Castleford, in aid of Finnish refugees, which George said he would never postpone, not even if the instruction came from the King himself! Incredibly—which goes to prove *how* important George was in these days—the sailing was held up for four days until this engagement had been fulfilled. "It's not that I'm particularly fond of marbles," he told the *Blackpool Gazette*. "But it's for a good cause, and I've a sort of romantic attachment to Castleford because it's there that I first met a charming lady—my Beryl!" After the contest, which his team lost, George swiped all the marbles, signed them GF with the tip of a dart, and raffled them for charity!

Beryl, meanwhile, had set up a "Jump Fund"—so named after a Hertfordshire housewife who had sent her six woollen balaclavas which she had knitted herself, for Beryl to pass on to the soldiers in Europe. Beryl placed ads in all the local newspapers, urging female readers to follow Mrs Jump's example and supply her not just with headgear, but with scarves, socks and gloves. The response was quite unexpected: within three days Beryl received over a thousand articles of clothing, and others were sent to the local offices of the Thornton Home Guard, in which George and Harry Scott had enlisted as dispatch riders. This was more than a merely honorary gesture. Both took their duties seriously, and whenever George's tight schedule permitted they mucked in with everyone else. "It's a nice bit of twig, is this!" George cracked, whilst posing for photographs with his rifle—he was a crack shot, too—though most of his fans would have begged to differ, arguing that the only "weapon" they ever wanted to in his hand was his ukulele.

In Brest, on the coast of Brittany, George and Beryl were amongst the small pioneering concert-party which entertained the 40,000-strong British Expeditionary Force. For the first show of 26 March 1940, the couple improvised a hilarious "Dick Whittington" sketch, and George performed his most popular numbers, including "Imagine Me On The Maginot Line", which he had recorded the previous December. Parts of show were shown on cinema newsreels throughout Europe, and much of it was taped—however, though several acetates were pressed, the actual recordings would not be released during George's lifetime.

George's concert at Quimper, was heard on the radio by the *Blackpool Gazette*'s Sylvia, who became a close friend, and over the coming years acted as the Formbys' unofficial champion in the press. Their association got off to a bad start when Beryl took exception to the headline, "George Is Number 2", and Sylvia's opening comments:

> *I should rank George Formby as second to Gracie Fields in the affections of the B E F. Not since Gracie visited the B E F theatre have I heard such a hullabaloo on the air. George sang his new song. "Imagine Me On The Maginot Line", which, so he announced, his wife had written for him. Afterwards the audience was so excitable and undisciplined in its demands that George had to ask for order. Half of this young comedian's success can be ascribed to his unaffected intimacy with his audience. Las night he invited them to shout messages home. They nearly blew up the microphone. And when he invited them to tell the people in England if they were happy, their "Yes" could have been heard in Hamburg. No wonder they love George!*

George and a very apprehensive Beryl invited Sylvia to tea at their Singleton home on 5 May, a few days after their return from France—predictably enough, Beryl was terrified that this journalist had been worshipping her husband from afar for one reason only! In fact, she was pleasantly surprised: Sylvia was well into her fifties, plump and bespectacled, and had a husband and family. Beryl did, however, gently rebuke her for daring to suggest that Gracie Fields was a bigger star than George. After this, the two women got along like a house on fire, and Sylvia confessed that she too had put out an appeal for the Jump Fund during the Formbys' absence, one which had brought in dozens of sacks of knitwear.

Sitting in his living room, under the auspicious gaze of George

Formby Sr, whose portrait hung over the fireplace, George spoke of his experiences in "Garlicland". The looks on the men's faces, he said, would stay with him for ever, as would the stench of the converted fish-van which had been the company's only means of transport over the last five weeks. And only one thing had been worse than the dreadful seasickness he had endured each time he had stepped on to a boat—French food. "They were beginning to call me Tommy Tucker before we left," he grimaced. "I used to go along to the cookhouse and offer to give them three songs for a real English meal of bacon and eggs!"

Beryl also spoke of their "privileged" return journey from Honfleur, where their last show had taken place an hour before they were due to set sail. After the performance George had told an English admiral how he was dreading the overnight crossing because a storm was brewing and he had already left "half his insides" at the bottom of the Channel. The admiral had told him not to worry: an empty ship was scheduled to leave for England the next morning, and the 23-strong ENSA party would be welcome to travel on that. "George was very happy," Beryl concluded. "He said he could be ill in every room."

The next day—both suffering from a heavy cold—George and Beryl embarked on a four-week tour of munitions works in the North of England to raise money for the Fleetwood Fund, which aided families of killed or missing trawlermen. This constituted over a hundred 30-minute concerts, many taking place during the workers' lunch breaks which, the managers repeatedly informed ENSA, boosted output considerably more than any increase in wages would have done.

"Workers move about with a lighter step," Sylvia reported. "Smiles broaden on their earnest faces. They eat a bigger lunch—that's sure sign that they're feeling happy!" And at a gas-mask factory in Manchester, Basil Dean introduced his least-favourite "employee", swallowing hard when forced to read the brief speech prepared by the manager:

> *The North-West is a storehouse of rich things, of which the most prized, perhaps, is humour. And the leader of funsters is your own George Formby. He has carried his uke everywhere in the service of his country. In barn and cowshed, hangar and canteen, field and tent, there goes George, the modern minstrel. Everywhere he carries the language of commonsense, and when the band of victory plays, the star artist will be George!*

In June, having raised well over £10,000 for the trawlermen's dependents, George began work on his next ATP film, *Spare A Copper*, directed by John Paddy Carstairs and co-starring Dorothy Hyson (1914-96), the Chicago-born actress who had recently triumphed in the Old Vic's production of *A Midsummer Night's Dream*, alongside Vivien Leigh and Anthony Quayle.

Hyson was a rarity—a leading lady whom Beryl actually approved of, largely because while "researching" her she had learned about the married (to actor Robert Douglas) Hyson's clandestine involvement with Quayle, the great love of her life whom she would eventually marry. Hyson, however, found out during the first week of shooting that Beryl had "fixed things" with Michael Balcon so that she would fail her audition for *Let George Do It*, and her attitude towards Beryl was now openly frosty. Throughout the film, Hyson would refer too Beryl—and sometimes to her face, as "the diamond-studded bitch".

The screenplay and three of the film's four songs—not amongst George's most enduring, primarily because their composer is said to have purposely avoided the requisite double-entendres—were by Roger MacDougal, the Glaswegian chiefly remembered today from scripting two comedy classics of the next decade, *The Man In The White Suit* and *The Mouse That*

Roared. Even so, the numbers would prove popular enough with the fans for MacDougal to be commissioned to write for George again in the near future.

Spare A Copper was amongst George's better films, for though the editing and script are poor, and Dorothy Hyson is unconvincing as his leading lady, *he* is in sparkling form. The action takes place in Birkenhead on the eve of World War II. The battleship HMS *Hercules* is about to be launched—and also about to be sabotaged by enemy agents, an operation spearheaded by amusement park proprietor Edward Brewster (George Merritt), a plot which is ultimately foiled by bungling War Reserve, George Carter. George makes an uneasy entrance on a bicycle he has "borrowed" from Jane Gray (Hyson)—causing traffic mayhem. Henceforth the slapstick is continuous: numerous escapades when George inadvertently gets on the wrong side of the police *and* the crooks, culminating in a high-speed chase in a miniature racing-car which sees him zooming around a Wall of Death, after which he launches HMS *Hercules* himself just seconds before the bomb goes off.

The story, of course, *was* secondary to the slapstick, with George once more doing most of his own sometimes quite dangerous motorcycle stunts. Ignoring the clause in his contract which prevented him from even *riding* a machine, he heralded himself as "an angel with 200 horse-power wings" before charging around an obstacle course and ending up in an exploding first-aid hut. Jane works in a music-store, which just happens to have a large selection of ukuleles. He therefore sings "I'm The Ukulele Man" with an invading children's choir, after which he wrecks the place by rushing off to take his motorcycle test. "On The Beat" starts off quietly enough, but ends up as a rip-roaring free-for-all stomp complete with male trio, marching feet, and a raucous female obbligato…delivered by Beryl Reid in one of her earliest screen appearances!

Later, accompanied by a novachord, George croons "I'm Shy", and in the midst of a wild chase through a theatre he pauses long enough to participate in an amateur talent contest...where once more the uke is close at hand. The song was yet another that had been frowned upon by the BBC:

> *I went into a nightclub where a lady did a dance,*
> *She'd nothing on but pigeons,*
> *And she left the rest to chance!*
> *She didn't seem to feel the cold,*
> *The birds knew where to stay,*
> *I clapped my hands and shouted,*
> *But they didn't fly away!*
> *I wish she was down on our farm:*
> *She'd have nothing on whatever,*
> *'Cause our pigeons aren't so clever!*

The continuity errors in this one are few, but amusing nevertheless. In the scene where George sings "On The Beat", filmed in sections on different days and spliced together only after the director had decided to use Beryl Reid, the chain on his pocket-watch alternates in length and between the second and fourth buttons of his coat. Later, when he and the saboteurs are being pursued by the police and George ends up in a falling barrel, the frame pauses for a split-second, revealing the attached safety-wire. Towards the end of the film, during the car-chase when the crooks' car backs into a side-road, the fumes are actually sucked *back* into the exhaust because the cameraman, Ronald Neame, had filmed the car travelling forwards and reversed the shot!

Shortly after completing *Spare A Copper*, George was approached by Charles Forsythe, a Canadian comic-entrepreneur who was visiting Britain to put together a team of top-notch stars for a tour of North America, to raise money for the Spitfire Fund. Forsythe's project had been given full approval by the Ministry of Information, and he was confident that if he could talk George into participating, other artistes of a similar calibre would soon follow suit.

Forsythe, however, had not reckoned on the Formby's intense patriotism. Even if Canada was part of the Commonwealth, to their way of thinking in troubled times—when the emphasis was "looking after one's own"—it was just another foreign country which should have been able to take care of its own fund-raising. "If we want Spitfires, we'll pay for them ourselves without asking for help from foreigners," Beryl opined, while George cracked, "The only time *I'll* be leaving Britain is when they *blow* me out!"

The latter statement worried Basil Dean, who initially was led to believe that the Formbys would also refuse to do any more shows in France. George soon put him straight on this score. He told the press, "So far as I'm concerned, France and Britain are the same, especially those bits of France where are lads are. In the time it takes us just to get to Canada, Beryl and me can do a dozen shows across the Channel. Tell the Canadians to get Bing Crosby if they're so desperate to be entertained!"

The work for the Fleetwood trawlermen continued. Beryl placed announcements in the local papers that, for the time being, knitted articles sent to the Jump Fund would be donated to this cause, adding, "And if any of you hard-working ladies out there do have a few moments to spare, please knit me a few pairs of bootees for all those poor, fatherless babies." Within the week, more than a thousand pairs were sent to Singleton.

Beryl also began charging George's fans for his autograph—a few coppers, or whatever they could afford, which was dropped into a tin and counted up at the end of the week so that the money could be added to the fund.

In August, George and Beryl turned up at a RAF base near Newcastle to find an in-house concert-party in full swing and a young officer named Ted Coates impersonating George. Coates had written to him a few weeks previously, asking his permission to do this—wondering if George might see his way to loaning him an old ukulele which would be looked after and returned to him after the war. George had a far better idea: marching up to Coates, on the stage, he pushed a ukulele into his hand and told him, "That thing you're trying to play's out of tune. Here, have mine!"

George *should* have left for London in the middle of September to begin shooting his next film, but just as a game of marbles had delayed his journey to France, so too he was held back by a series of events which for him were of great significance. Firstly he stood in for an indisposed Bud Flanagan at Blackpool's Palace Theatre. After the show he was reunited with Fred Harrison, the manager of the Earlstown Hippodrome where he had made his first professional appearance nineteen years before. Harrison was celebrating his quarter-century at the theatre's helm, and suggested they get together and put on a concert. George said that he would be delighted to, but that it would have to be that weekend. For old times' sake he left his uke in the wings until the last two songs, and was accompanied at the piano by a Mrs Clements, who had played for him back in 1921. He raised over £100 for the Spitfire Fund.

The third event took place when illness forced Arthur Askey to drop of *The Show Of 1940* at Blackpool Opera House, and George insisted upon taking over for the last twelve performances—providing the producer agreed to hand over his salary and all the profits to the war-effort. This brought an angry reaction from ATP-Ealing's Michael Balcon, since George's new film was still waiting to begin shooting and the leading lady, Phyllis Calvert, was getting restless. George, and not Beryl, took the call, and he was not wearing this. At such critical times, he declared, helping others less fortunate than oneself was far more important than making films, and he put the phone down on the man who was ostensibly his boss.

Balcon is said to have become "wild with rage" upon reading a copy of George's current itinerary, which Beryl had had published in several national newspapers. This was the first in what would be a series of campaigns aimed at proving how much George was doing for his country, as opposed to some his "conscientious objector" colleagues who, over the next few years, would be constantly under the threat of being exposed by him:

> *I'm at Llandudno tomorrow night. I should have gone today. Instead I'll have to remain at home and prepare material for the Opera House. I'll go to Llandudno tomorrow and drive back in the middle of the night in time for rehearsals on Monday. On Tuesday I'll open a mile of pennies at Cleveleys. Wednesday's a dickens of a day. I'm appearing as Henry Hall's guest star at the Palace. In between I have a matinee at the Opera House, a couple of shows there at night, and a couple of Palace appearances in between. On Thursday I may go to Manchester for a consultation about the new film. On Friday I have two munitions concerts. On Saturday two more, and a lunchtime broadcast. And seeing as I'm in the Home Guard as well, I won't be forsaking them—I'll be out on patrol all Sunday. After that, who know? We all have to do our bit, Mr Balcon!*

At the beginning of November, George and Beryl were finally free to make what would be his final film for ATP: *Turned Out Nice Again,* once again directed by Marcel Varnel. Friends were concerned about him filming so close to London, the main target for the air-raids. George's journalist friend, Sylvia, even warned him that this might prove an "unlucky thirteenth" production—to which he responded that thirteen was his *lucky* number, for had he not wed "the girl on his dreams" on this date? Then he told everyone not to worry. *He* had given Michael Balcon an ultimatum: he and Beryl would spend just three weeks in London—which would include a full day at the recording studio—and the rest of the shooting schedule would take place in the North of England. This was not because he was afraid of working in the capital, but because he was still working flat-out for his Northern war charities *and* about to open in a pantomime at Blackpool Opera House. Balcon then informed him of ATP's latest dilemma: following the delays caused by George, the production would not be able to begin shooting because it no longer had a leading lady. "Miss Calvert has made such a success since her appearance with George Formby that it is feared she will be too busy," read the statement in the *Evening Standard*. This did not bother George, who just went off and did a few charity shows until Marcel Varnel summoned him back to the set.

George was next warned that the script had a jinx on it. It had started out as a hit West End play, *As You Are*, but its author, Hugh Mills, had yet to collect on his investment because he had been visiting Paris when the Germans had moved in and occupied the city. A homosexual, Mills had subsequently been interned and his London agent—fearing that he might be dead already—would not give ATP permission to transfer the play to the screen. The producer, Michael Balcon, got around this by signing a contract with Mills' mother, wherein it was agreed that the author's earnings from the film would be placed in a London bank account, and in the event of his demise be shared out amongst his relatives.

Like its predecessors, *Turned Out Nice Again* had more than its share of backstage problems. When told that his new leading lady, Peggy Bryan, was a former elocution teacher straight out of drama school, George steeled himself for "some pain-in-the-arse snob"...as he had once dismissed Polly Ward. Bryan (1916-96), however, was not posh at all. She hailed from Ireland, but had spent much of her life in Birmingham, hence an accent which was a combination of the two. Beryl, however, disliked her from the start. *This* actress was going to portray George's *wife*, the first time this had ever happened, and she anticipated that he would be expected to say and do all manner of things in front of the camera!

Before Beryl would get around to reading Bryan the riot act, part of the studio was hit by an incendiary bomb and almost totally gutted. Only George's ukuleles and Bryan's costumes were saved from the fire by quick-thinking but unnecessarily brave technicians. The fact that the actors and crew had vacated the area only hours before brought Beryl to her senses, and reminded her that there were better things to worry about than co-stars who were only "flighty" in her overworked imagination.

While he was in London, George joined a shelter-group organised by ENSA, for a series of underground shows in and around the capital. One of these, at the Aldwych tube station, was broadcast by the BBC on 27 November 1940 as part of its *Let The People Sing* series. George, one of several entertainers who participated in the event, cringed as he was introduced by Admiral Sir Edward Evans—who pronounced in his Etonesque accent, "You will hear George Formby, so typical of this country, and Geraldo and his orchestra. And you will hear London, below ground, making a night of it. George Formby. He needs no introduction. Good old George...not so old!"

When George realised that Evans had delivered his spiel from a script, and that he disliked Northern entertainers, he denounced him as a "snotty-nosed old bugger". The people, of course, were only interested in George, and roared their appreciation even when he quipped that many of them would be spending the night underground, when he had a comfortable flat to go back to—not that he would have minded roughing it for once. Pointing to a middle-aged woman, he chirped, "Shift up, missus, I'm coming in!" On a more serious note, he concluded, "I can tell you exactly what I feel about the English people today. We've got a King and Queen, and I think they're marvellous people for us lot to look up to. I think the way they're carrying on, they've got as much good in their little finger as Hitler and Gower-ring and all the damn lot put together. Don't forget, it's wonderful to be British!"

The four songs which George performed at Aldwych were recorded by the BBC, but during his lifetime never made it past the acetate stage. They included Fred Godfrey's "Bless 'Em All", written in 1917 and newly-revised by him especially for George...and Gifford and Cliffe's "Down The Old Coal Hole".

At the end of the month, shooting on *Turned Out Nice Again* transferred to Preston, where Horrockses-Crewdson & Co had placed their huge textile mill at ATP's disposal, giving the workers the week off and some of them a chance to become extras in the film. At their Singleton home, George ad Beryl once again invited their journalist friend Sylvia to tea, but instead of doing the interview there and then, George suggested that they meet the next morning on the set—at six on the dot! Sylvia tried to argue that this was way too early, until Beryl told her, "But you'll have to, dear. George has already told the director that you're going to be one of the extras!" George had already decided that "Sylvia" was not an appropriate name for a "film star", albeit that the journalist would only ever appear in a single scene, in just one film—two minutes into the scenario, she is the matronly factory girl with her hair in a bun—henceforth she would write under the pseudonym George had given her: Phyllis!

Turned Out Nice Again—named after the catchphrase which he uses umpteen times in his other films, but only once in this one—was, for most Formby fans, an inappropriate ATP swansong because it contained no slapstick. It did, however, a neat slap in the face for those detractors who had accused George of being unable to act. Indeed, *because* it brought his true thespian skills to the fore with its blend of pathos, humour and down to earth histrionics, in this respect it may justifiably be regarded as the best of all his films. Peggy Bryan—despite a sometimes "dodgy" Northern accent which reverts to her natural Irish-Brummie one when her temper flares—may likewise be deemed the most adept of his leading ladies.

George Pearson, the foreman at Dawson's underwear factory, suddenly finds himself promoted when Nelson, the overseer (Ronald Ward) is fired for fraud and goes to work for a rival firm. George is delighted, for this now means that he and his sweetheart, Lydia (Bryan) can wed. The Pearsons' home life, though, is anything but harmonious. George's Uncle Arnold (Edward Chapman) is paranoid because his prize pigeon will not lay an egg. Ruling the roost is George's mother, who interferes in every aspect of the couple's lives, including accompanying them on their honeymoon…feigning heart-attacks and persistently reminding him how long she spent "under the chloroform" bringing him into the world. The part had originally pencilled in for Thora Hird, an actress from Morecambe who was several years younger than George, though one cannot imagine a more immaculate portrayal than by Elliot Mason (1888-1949), who played stone-faced harridans on the screen but who in real life was nothing of the kind—almost a British Marie Dressler who, a few years later, would support Robert Donat and Deborah Kerr in *Perfect Strangers*.

The action jumps to the Pearsons' first wedding anniversary, when Lydia buys George a dinner-jacket—and is berated by her mother-in-law for living above her means. "Nothing's ice to look at till it's paid for," she chides. George, however, cannot make the party: he has to stand in for a colleague at an underwear exhibition in London. Here, he bumps into Nelson, showing off only the chicest lingerie whilst Dawsons parade it latest range of old fashioned corsets and bloomers. At the show, Nelson is sold the rights to a prototype yarn which, when he realises that the vendor may be a crook, he passes on to George. The next day he explains this to Lydia, in such a way that she initially thinks he has been with another woman: "It all started at the party last night...It was Mr Nelson who suggested it. I admit I rather liked the idea, but I didn't know what you'd think about it...So I went back and did it quickly. It cost three-hundred pounds...I gave an IOU for it."

When the penny drops, Lydia is enthusiastic. "Nothing ventured, nothing gained," she says. Then the Pearsons' marriage hits a rocky patch on account of the domineering old woman. The rows are vociferous and most un-Formby-like, and continue into the office when in a quick volte-face Lydia attacks George for failing to stand up for himself, and he resigns after the boss insults her. All turns out well in the end, however, when Lydia pretends to walk out on him. She has actually gone to London to model his samples, and when her picture appears in a newspaper, the bartering begins for George's yarn—just as the couple's furniture is about to be repossessed. George opts to go into partnership with Dawsons, even though the wily Nelson outbids them—so that he and Lydia can work at their London family, where they will be rid of his mother. And adding to the film's blissful ending, Uncle Arnold's pigeon finally lays an egg!

Turned Out Nice Again contained four excellent songs, amongst them Eddie Latta's pastiche—and another Formby "property" number—to the inventor of the potion, sold at every chemist for "one-and-a-kick" (1s 6d), which cures all ills:

> *Now if you get lumbago, rheumatics or gout,*
> *Or a pain in your Robert E Lee,*
> *Don't kick up a shindy,*
> *You'll never get windy,*
> *With Aunty Maggie's Remedy!*

Like Fred E Cliffe, Eddie Latta (Bruce Williams, 1902-72) was a gregarious Liverpudlian, born into a family of undertakers—a trade he reluctantly continued his whole life. Latta wrote just nine Formby sons, though doubtless there would have been more had he taken a leaf out of Gifford's and Cliffe's book and *demanded* his share of the royalties. He did not. Upon Beryl's insistence, George paid Latta a flat fee for each song, and added his name to the writing credits so he could pocket *all* the proceeds. When Latta realised that he had been duped he focused his talents elsewhere, which is a great pity. Songs such as "Auntie Maggie's Remedy" and "Guarding The Home Of The Home Guard" represent George at his most astute, and there should have been many more.

Meanwhile, the Formbys' first Blackpool pantomime, *Dick Whittington*—with George playing Idle Jack to Beryl's Polly Perkins—opened to fabulous reviews, despite there having only been enough time for one rehearsal. George donated his first week's salary--£1,000—to the Manchester Air-Raid Distress Fund, and despite Beryl's protestations actually registered for military service. The press turned up at the Labour Exchange and jokingly asked him how, as one of the highest-paid stars in British show business, he would be able to get by with such a colossal drop in salary, should he achieve his ambition and be accepted as an army dispatch rider. George cracked back, "I get less pocket money each week from the wife than they'd pay me, so I'd be laughing!" The examining board gave him a Grade Four classification and rejected him when he was discovered to have arthritic toes and a minor chest ailment.

For George, the pantomime run could not end soon enough. He was convinced that he had "bled the North dry" so far as his and Beryl's fund-raising was concerned, and was anxious to return to London and raise more money there, risking the dangers of the Blitz by joining the ranks of Flanagan and Allen, Elsie and Doris Waters, Max Miller and Al Bowlly—the much-loved crooner who, early in 1941, would become the Blitz's most celebrated casualty. "If London's good enough for her Majesty, then it'll do for Beryl and me," he declared, referring to the Queen's stolid determination not to leave Buckingham Palace even though persistently advised to do so.

George was a tremendous favourite with the royals, and at around this time there occurred his and Beryl's much-publicised visit to Windsor Castle, where they entertained the royal family and several hundred troops. A few weeks before the show, George was informed that he would be expected to sing all his big hits, including "When I'm Cleaning Windows", and fearful of offending "sensitive ears" he had contacted Fred E Cliffe and commissioned a set of "alternative" lyrics. When he and Beryl arrived at Windsor, however, they were told by a royal aide that the King and Queen were only interested in hearing the *uncensored* act with which George had delighted the troops—even though the young princesses Elizabeth and Margaret would be present. The show proved a triumph—afterwards, the King presented George with a set of gold cuff-links, and Beryl with a silver powder-compact, and three weeks later the Formbys appeared in a command performance for the Marlborough Troop, presided over by Queen Mary, the King's mother—a straight-laced woman who nevertheless requested George not to spare her blushes. *She* loved

"When I'm Cleaning Windows" so much that George was asked to sing it again, and the next morning news of this was relayed to the headquarters of the BBC, in the hope that the ban on the song would be lifted. It was not.

Before leaving London, George—or rather, Beryl—had informed Basil Dean and Michael Balcon that he would not be renewing his contract with ATP. *Turned Out Nice Again* had provided George with the opportunity to portray the kind of half-serious character he felt better suited to his acting abilities—one *not* suited to Ealing comedies—and no amount of persuasion or even a substantial increase in salary would get him to change his mind.

Being on the open market, so to speak, brought in a flood of offers, and when George finally signed a new contract, in March 1941, it was for Columbia Pictures. In a deal worth in excess of £500,000, he would head his own company, Hillcrest Productions—so named after his mother's house in Warrington, though he hardly ever saw Eliza—and over the next two years he would make a minimum of six films, with his own choice of theme, director and scriptwriter, though his leading ladies would be chosen by the studio.

The Columbia contract had been greatly influenced by the recent poll in *Motion Picture Herald*, which had placed George's films at the top of the British cinema box-office returns, just slightly ahead of Gracie Fields and Charles Laughton—and Number 5 in the International List, ahead of Errol Flynn, Bette Davis and even Bing Crosby. George himself stipulated just the one condition: though his films would be American-backed, they would have to be made in Britain.

George's defection to another company—one which was not British—caused ill-feeling in some circles. Anti-American detractors accused him of "selling out" on his country for the sake of lining his own pocket—and it was also suggested that he had only agreed to do charity concerts because his and Beryl's "expenses" included a percentage of the takings. This upset him so much that he began estimating how much each show would raise, and always made a point of making up any "deficit"—ridiculously unnecessary, of course.

The Formbys received poison-pen letters and menacing phone-calls, and on one occasion a brick was thrown through their car windscreen, narrowly missing Beryl's face. When interviewed by the police, George attempted to make light of the situation by suggesting the culprit had been a fan, too shy to ask for an autograph. He agreed to sign the brick, should its owner come forward, which of course never happened. The incident shook him badly, and for several days he tried to get out of the Columbia contract. This was not possible, though his attackers were placated for the time being by a statement issued by the studio, declaring that thus far in the conflict he had raised over £25,000 for the war-effort. Columbia were selling him short, for George had actually brought in twice this amount.

In May 1941, Beryl organised a lightning, 15-day "shilling" tour of those towns and cities worst affected by the Blitz. George told the press, "I know these people will get compensation after the war, but we don't know when that will be, and they want help now." The idea was that if just ten per cent of those who had so far not had properties damaged during air-raids subscribed one-shilling each, top-notch artistes such as George could easily raise as much as £10,000 a week. Advertising was essential, and the BBC had given over Sunday evenings for personal appeals from the stars, so that large sections of the public who would not normally have had a chance of seeing them in their neck of the woods would now know how to acquire tickets. Basil Dean and ENSA had agreed to handle artistes participating in the project and Oscar Deutsch, the managing director of Odeon Cinemas, had promised to supply the theatres free of charge.

Beryl at once hit a snag when she learned that the BBC, who clearly *did* believe that the Formbys had been dipping into war-effort funds, declined to offer George air-time to make his appeal—claiming that the station's Sunday evening appeal-slots were all fully booked until the end of the year.

For once, Beryl was justified in tearing a strip off the BBC director general, though her victory was decidedly Pyrrhic: George was allocated a mere two-minute slot in *Monday At Eight*, broadcast from North Wales, and he was not allowed to give out an address where contributions had to be sent. The BBC later admitted that because of this "oversight" just over a thousand contributions had been forwarded to their London headquarters, a mere fraction of Beryl's target.

Beryl was not the kind of entrepreneur to give up easily. The tour kicked off at Southampton on 10 June, and over the next two weeks took in Portsmouth, Plymouth, Bristol, Liverpool, Hull, Sheffield and Glasgow. Prior to each engagement, Beryl arranged to have slides projected on all the circuit cinema screens, informing fans exactly where George would be appearing, and where to send those all-important shillings. The tour brought in a staggering £23,000 in its first week, and even more in the second.

On 22 June, after Glasgow, George and Beryl played theatres in Stirling, Pitlochry and Fort William, before travelling to Inverness. Then—ignoring ENSA's warning that such a trip was too perilous to undertake—the couple flew to the Orkneys. Whilst here, they learned that a detachment of just twelve men were stationed in the Shetlands, and that their request to have George visit them had been turned down because their camp was out of bounds. The Formbys waited until after dark, then bribed the captain of a small boat to ferry them across. Other fans, over the last few weeks, had had to be content with thirty minutes of George's valuable time. These soldiers had him for four hours—

sipping mugs of coca laced with rum between songs, huddled around a camp-fire.

On 27 July 1941, George loaned his services to the London Tank Fund, taking part in the heavy infantry parade which "invaded" the West End. Driving a tank, he manned an unloaded tommy-gun to the delight of the 12,000 people who turned up to witness the event. Afterwards he appeared at the Tank Matinee at the Odeon Leicester Square—a snobbish occasion part-hosted by Ben Lyon and his wife, Bebe Daniels, who boasted to all and sundry of how much *they* had raised for the fund, whilst George quietly handed over a cheque for £3,000. He told one of the organisers, "Buy rivets, cock. That way I'll get more for my money!"

A few days later, the Formbys returned to Singleton for a well-earned rest. He told a reporter from the *Evening Standard*, "We're going to put our feet up, or maybe catch up on a bit of gardening. Well, hopefully. Ee, there's no rest for the wicked!" The couple ate one meal at home before dashing off to do a show in aid of the Fleetwood trawlermen, and the next morning George *did* get to tend his garden—digging up the potatoes he had planted in the front garden. "If you can't eat it, it's a weed," he told passers-by stopped off at the SPUDS FOR SALE sign, gasping at the exorbitant price he was charging for his produce...until they learned that the money would be going towards Beryl's Jump Fund.

At the end of August, following innumerable troops, factory and shelter concerts, George began shooting his debut film for Columbia. *South American George* saw him in a dual role—playing a gormless but loveable busker, and a Brazilian operatic tenor whose voice in the film was dubbed by Giovanni Martinelli. The latter, "disgusted" by the way in which Verdi's *Rigoletto* was sent up, subsequently demanded that his name be removed from the credits. Suffice to say, the music in this one is not always what one would expect in a Formby film!

The story begins in a provincial theatre, where the great Gilli Vannetti is giving the last performance of the opera season. When one of the non-singing extras fails to turn up, the producer sends out his scout who engages George Butters, whom he finds serenading an unappreciative barmaid at the nearby pub. Makes his stage debut dressed as a soldier: he drops his musket, and creates havoc with the soprano, in mid-aria. "Beg your pardon, missus," he says, then panics when he sees two relatives in the audience—one his father, who loathes the stage because his sister-in-law, Mabel, formerly a Gaiety Girl, is now a has-been residing at the Fernlands Artists' Retirement Home.

In the wings, George meets Vannetti's personal assistant, Carol Dean (Linden Travers), and overhears an argument between Ricardo, the theatre manager (Jacques Brown) and his lawyer. He learns that this last performance has been played to an entire house of concessionary ticket holders, for away from his own country no one wants to hear the arrogant Vannetti if they have to pay! Unfortunately, Ricardo has booked him for the next season, so to save his theatre from bankruptcy he must now find a way of getting the tenor to break his contract. In a fit of pique, Vannetti leaves for his next recital overseas, leaving Carol in the lurch—she has secured him for a charity engagement, to present a cheque to the residents of Fernlands.

George, meanwhile, leaves the theatre and on the way home—having told his parents, upon leaving the house that morning, that he is looking for a job, and having only received half-pay for his stage appearance—he accepts payment from a market-trader for demonstrating hair-curlers. This new hairstyle results in his becoming the spitting image of Vannetti, and when he visits Fernlands the next day to see Aunty Mable, he bumps into Carol, who transforms him—aided by a mascara brush and a false moustache—into a carbon copy of the tenor and saves herself from the embarrassment of having to tell everyone that Vannetti is not really a charitable man. When a picture of the presentation appears in the local newspaper, Carol persuades George to keep up the charade, and the rest of the film sees them trying to outwit the wily Ricardo—for George knows that if Vannetti does break his contract, *he* will never see Carol again, and he has fallen in love with her.

Because Vannetti's contract decrees that he must obey every instruction given to him by his manager, Ricardo forces his double to dance in the ballet corps. Then he makes him clean the stage, getting him to count every flake after he has switched on the snow-machine—before ordering him to climb the scaffolding outside the theatre to erect the neon lettering. Carol is impressed by his naïve determination. "I think you're the biggest little man I've ever met," she tells him, to which he replies in song that, no matter the challenge, so long as it is to please her he will do it with a smile.

Having failed to break George's spirit, Ricardo next attempts to catch him out with the contract's "undesirable publicity" clause. Hiring hammy actors, he sends a scantily clad woman up to George's apartment, trailed by a jealous "husband" who will find them in a compromising position. Before this can happen, we hear George being berated by Jiminy Cricket—the voice of his conscience which he chooses to ignore. "I love her," George says of Carol, to which the other half responds, "You *love* her! What could *you* give her? If turkeys were sixpence a pound you haven't enough to buy her a feather from a tom-tit's ear-hole!" Then Carol arrives on the scene, and the floosy is trussed up and shoved inside a blanket box until Ricardo and his cronies have left.

As a last resort, Ricardo hires the spivvish thug, Swifty (Shiner) to kidnap Vannetti and spirit him out of the country, but whilst Swifty is masterminding his plan the manager gets a call from the infamous entrepreneur, George White: his *Varieties of 1941* is about to open, but his star has gone missing. White offers Ricardo a huge fee to take Vannetti's contract off his hands, leaving George and Carol with a seemingly unsurmountable predicament—if the real Vannetti cannot be located and brought back to England in time for the opening night, George will have to sing opera! And now that Ricardo is about to rake in the money, he is all over the little man he has only treated like dirt.

The big performance takes place, with Aunty Mable and her pals opening the show—George's condition for helping out, now that Ricardo has been told his true identity—and with George having been forced to mime one to one of Vannetti's recordings. The real Vannetti has also turned up, and been knocked out by Ricardo's hitman. After George's successful opening aria, however, mayhem ensues when Swifty and his sidekick, assuming that their quarry has got away, chase him up and down the props, wrecking the scenery before *they* are knocked senseless by Carol. And finally, before blurting out that he loves her, after she has presented him with a show business contract—with her as his manager—George whips off his troubadour garb, under which he is wearing a matador's suit-of-lights. As "Don Tonsilitis" he entertains the crowd, having replaced his uke with a more appropriate instrument, with one of the finest of all the Formby film-songs, "My Spanish Guitar":

> *I've had lots of fights and I've had a few frights,*
> *There was one when the bull got me down.*
> *He jumped on my corns and stuck both his horns*
> *In my shanty in old shanty town!*
> *His eyes they were staring and glassy,*
> *I could feel his hot breath in my ear,*

So I stabbed him three times in the chassis,
And wished him a Happy New Year!
That bull got a shock, so he turned into Oxo,
You'll find him on sale in the bar!

South American George was completed in just six weeks, and its press-showing set for the end of November. Because many of George's fans had bemoaned the lack of slapstick in his last film, the distributors hit on a gimmick by taking out an insurance policy with Lloyds. At some cinemas, notices were posted to the playbills, declaring, "The aforementioned underwriter vows that for the receipt of a £1 premium, an agreement will be made wherein a sum of £500 will be paid in respect of each person who may die laughing whilst and as result of viewing this film." Lloyds did not have to fork out—not that the film was unfunny, quite simply that few of George's fans could afford the premium!

The Formbys, meanwhile, had ended up in another bust-up with Basil Dean. Since turning down Charles Forsythe's offer to tour Canada, George had been pestered by Dean to join ENSA's package to the country, scheduled to leave for Toronto in the New Year. Time and time again, George had told Dean that he was not interested, begging him to send him back into France, or even out to the Middle East. Dean, however, knew that it would prove difficult to put on any tour of North America without a headlining name to attract other artistes, and he piled on the pressure to such an extent that George almost gave in. Then on 13 October—a "lucky day"—George read a letter from an elderly fan, Frank Hannan, in Sylvia's column in the *Blackpool Gazette*:

> *Dear George. I feel very sorry for you, old boy, but you cannot please everybody. We all know that Canada would like you, that every country would like you, that even Hitler would like you. He would reckon it one of his*

> *biggest successes to get you. Anyway, take a tip from an old Lancashire lad and stop with us. You DO buck us up I these dark days and we shall not forget when this mess is over. I am talking to you as your father would. Stay put and carry on the good work!*

When George read in Hannan's postscript that he had once worked the music-halls—more than this, he had actually appeared on stage with Formby Sr—George called Basil Dean, who still would not take no for an answer. Beryl therefore paid for a piece to be placed in the national press in which her husband proclaimed:

> *George Formby is NOT going to Canada, Mr Dean. I appreciate your invitation, but I can't accept it. I've decided that I ought to remain with the lads in THIS country, singing to them whenever they want me. Sorry, but there it is!*

George even made light of the situation when his agent, Ben Henry, remarked that Basil Dean was extremely angry with him for so publicly forcing him to "eat humble pie". "If he doesn't like humble pie he can always join us for hot pot," George told Sylvia. The occasion was a hot pot supper at Fleetwood's Marine Hall, for 120 dependents of dead or missing trawlermen, after which he presented the mayor with a cheque for £1,200.

With Dean out of their hair for the time being, George and Beryl spent several days entertaining the troops on Salisbury Plain, and on 28 December they appeared at the Royal Albert Hall—in an ENSA concert in aid of the King's Fund For Sailors. Basil Dean was conspicuous by his absence.

The following afternoon, the Formbys paid their second visit to Windsor where they acted a sketch, "The Casting Office", and

and George sang seven songs with Geraldo's orchestra. The King requested "With My Little Stick Of Blackpool Rock", and Princess Elizabeth "Frank On His Tank"—after the show George and Beryl took tea with the royal family. The King and Queen presented them with a signed photograph, whilst Beryl dipped into her handbag and returned the compliment!

On 5 January, the Formbys embarked on a tour of Northern Ireland which should have begun four weeks previously, and for which George had foregone his annual pantomime. This offered detractors a little more ammunition to attack—concluding that if he had sacrificed £1,000 a week, he would be sure of getting his money elsewhere. This was untrue. Starting off with a "command" performance before the Ulster Prime Minister, he appeared in a minimum of three shows a day for six weeks, donating every penny he earned to Belfast air-raid victims. His travelling and hotel expenses came out of his own pocket. "Just keep me supplied with Guinness, and I'll do the rest," he cracked at an impromptu press-conference, before launching into "The Cook House Serenade":

> *My uniform is an apron,*
> *I'm learning to cook and bake.*
> *Now when I get out of the army,*
> *What a wonderful wife I'll make!*

It was during a troops contest in Belfast that George first publicly expressed his opinion—with no prompting from Beryl—about the "top brass" and their wives. Many of them did not even bother applauding between sketches and songs, though they invariably took up the first few rows of the concert halls—whilst the fighting men, his true fans, were relegated to the back of the auditorium. When one stuffy Irish matron was overheard saying how she hated these "tiresome little shows", but that at least they got her out of the house on an evening, George put his foot down. Marching on to the stage, he placed his ukulele at his feet and announced, "I'm come all this way to entertain the troops, the whole troops, and nothing *but* the troops!"

This brought gales of laughter from the boys at the back, though the military hierarchy were not amused, and George was cautioned never to say such a thing again. He promised the commanding officer that he would think about this—then adopted the saying as his wartime catchphrase, invariably causing pandemonium whenever he walked on to a stage. On one occasion he even called out for a telescope so that he could see his real fans, and on another he arrived early for a show—before the officers and their wives—and invited everyone to take their seats up front, declaring that he would personally "carry the can in the event of a bollocking". For this he was actually summoned to explain his actions to the War Office, though he did not attend the subsequent meeting, preferring to issue a simple statement that he was just an "ordinary citizen" doing his but for England—and for nothing.

The Irish did not always appreciate George's off-beat sense of humour. It was all very well for him to sing about "The Hindoo man", and slant his eyes before emulating Mr Wu, but another matter, some thought, to crack jokes—in the days before racial equality when it was not considered *wrong* to do so—about "Micks" and about Irish potatoes being better than English ones, "Because they make thicker chips!"

George's rank-and-file fans, in general, never found him in the least offensive because everything about his delivery was done only in fun, without the slightest touch of malice. One very straight-laced commanding officer's wife, however, complained so virulently about George's "vitriolic attack on this our beloved Emerald Isle" than within a few days the smear-campaign, mounted by the Limerick Ladies' Circle, brought an embargo on his films in that part of the country. Beryl was so annoyed that she contacted all the local newspapers and offered a £100 reward to be donated to a hospital of the editor's choosing, should he name this woman. ATP and Columbia Pictures offered similar incentives, and though George's detractor was never exposed, the embargo was lifted.

Early in 1942, George began shooting his second feature for Columbia, *Much Too Shy*, co-starring Eileen Bennett, Hilda Bayley and Kathleen Harrison. More fascinating than any of these, however, and making the production glow from start to finish, was Jimmy Clitheroe (1921-73)—the tiny, squeaky-voiced star who later appeared in British radio's longest-ever running comedy series, *The Clitheroe Kid*. Twenty when he made the film, he looked about eleven, the age he was in his radio series, and like George's friend Wee Georgie Wood was a perfectly formed (4 feet 3 inches) midget. Clitheroe never married, and lived his whole life in Blackpool with his mother—he committed suicide on the day of her funeral. There was also a fine cameo role from future *Carry On* star Charles Hawtrey, and others from Formby regulars Gus McNaughton and Wally Patch.

Much Too Shy was a gentle, part-sophisticated comedy, very much in the Ernst Lubitsch vein, set in the rural hamlet of Standstilton Green, where everyone knows everyone else's business. The story centres around three local women—Amelia Peabody (Harrison) who runs the village shop, the snooty Lady Driscol (Bayley) and farm girl Jackie Somers (Bennett), who is George's love-interest.

George Andy is the village handyman, and an amateur artist. The walls of his trailer, which she shares with little brother Jimmy (Clitheroe) are hung with head-and-shoulder portraits, and pride of place is awarded to Jackie's. Jimmy does not approve of George's infatuation with her—he never charges her for all of the odd jobs he does. "Show me a woman and I'll show you trouble," Jimmy persistently opines.

Sadly, Jackie is engaged to be married to the stuffy lawyer who serves George with a writ for non-payment of rent. His rent-money comes from what he earns designing posters for the local cinema, and the manager has dispensed with his services because he wants pretty female bodies, which George cannot draw. "I'd give a thousand pounds this minute to be a millionaire," he complains to Jimmy over his lack of cash. Then he sees an advertisement in his chip-paper for art-classes which boast an easy income after just the first lesson, and decides to give it a go.

At first the students, who are all into abstract art, poke fun at George, though he soon wins them over with a song…and when he draws three female heads on a canvas—copying a newspaper photograph of Peabody, Driscol and Jackie—the students add *naked* bodies. Outside the college, George leaves the painting with a pavement artist whilst making a telephone call, and the artist sells it, giving George half the proceeds. The picture ends up as part of a soap advertisement in newspapers and on hoardings, resulting in George being served with a writ by the outraged Lady Driscol. The painting, she declares, suggests that she has a 38-inch bust, whereas she claims she is a mere 36! "They've added two inches to my bust," she cries, bringing the response from George, "Well, isn't *that* making mountains out of molehills?"

The village women wreak their revenge on the hapless handyman. Marching on his trailer, they attempt to burn him out. The trailer breaks free and rolls down the hill into the village, flattening everything in sight and finally crashing into the shop. Then the court hearing takes place, with George defending himself, aided by Jimmy and Jackie. He proves that the offending portrait has *benefited* the three ladies—Miss Peabody's fame has enabled her to find a man, Jackie has seen sense and dumped her tiresome fiancé, and Lady Driscol has actually been complemented by being given a 38-inch bust...Jimmy has provided the court with a portrait of her, taken before she was married, when she was working as the showgirl, Connie Silver, and this is supplemented with evidence from a variety agent which states that in those days her bust measured thirty-*nine* inches! The case is dismissed, and George—still shy—rides away from the court-house in a hackney carriage with his sweetheart!

George described *Much Too Shy* as a "human interest story", though it was not well-received by the critics. The fans loved it, and it made a huge profit for Columbia. George had also added another string to his bow, that of associate producer—having been invited by Forces Sweetheart, Vera Lynn, to work on her first film, *We'll Meet Again*.

In *Spare A Copper* (1940)

With Eileen Bennett in *Much Too Shy* (1942)

Six:
I Did What I Could With My Gas Mask

"I'm just a clown without the make-up, the circus clown who magnifies the reactions of ordinary people to the things that happen around them." George Formby.

In the summer of 1942, George became embroiled in an argument with the then highly-influential Lord's Day Observance Society, an organisation which had already filed several suits against the BBC for playing non-secular music on Sundays. In an act of what may only be regarded as sheer spite, the LDOS now focused their attention on the theatrical profession, declaring that it was "unethical" for entertainers to work on the Sabbath, even if they *were* doing charity work. They even claimed support for their cause by dredging up the still-extant law of 1677 "forbidding any manner of thespian activity"—one which some sixty top-line artistes swallowed without question, announcing a sit-down strike!

George had been appearing in regular Sunday concerts since the beginning of the war, and saw no reason to heed what he dismissed as "the eternal damnation warblings of a bunch of meddling Bible-bashers". He was contacted by ENSA's Basil Dean and informed that whatever decision he made would affect the outcome of the strike on account of his high-standing. For five years running he had topped the *Motion Picture Herald*'s popularity poll—and though Gracie Fields, Leslie Howard and Robert Donat were not far behind him, Dean told George that *their* opinion did not count because they were not in England right now.

George opted to attack the LDOS head-on with what was for him an unusually hard-hitting statement, though there would be a good many of these over the next few years, usually penned by the ubiquitous Beryl. "I'll hang up my uke on Sundays only when our lads stop fighting and getting killed on Sundays," he announced. "As far as the Lord's Day Observation Society are concerned, they can mind their own bloody business. And in any case, what have *they* done for the war effort except get on everybody's nerves?" The next day, the strike was called off.

At the end of the year George began shooting *Get Cracking*, regarded by many contemporary critics as his finest film. It has an interesting assortment of peripheral characters—including a bungling gay recruit, very daring for the time—and a definitive villainous rival in the form of Ronald Shiner.

George's leading lady should have been Eileen Bennett, but Beryl quickly scuppered her chances off appearing opposite George for a second time, following the incident which had occurred at the trade showing of *Much Too Shy* when Bennett, wearing a low-cut gown, had swanned up to George and, in an act of genuine bravado, pecked him on the cheek! Beryl informed director Marcel Varnel that this time she would be sitting in on the auditions—"to ensure that he did not hire another tart".

Beryl's power, in fact, went further than this, as the successful "candidate", Dinah Sheridan—then employed as a secretary to Welwyn Council's Survey and Sanitary Inspector—divulged:

> *I walked into one of the large offices at Denham, and saw a very big desk with one lady behind it—no sign of anyone else at all. She told me she was Beryl Formby and that she wished to ask me some questions. First, was I married? I was able to say with blushes that I was [to Jimmy Hanley] and had been for four months. Presumably she considered that in any case I was hardly*

likely to look at anyone else but my delightful new husband, and no other questions were asked at all. She just said that I was what she had been looking for, and I left. Then, after the film I went back to my council office job, hoping the stories that all George Formby's leading ladies went on to better things was true.

Like Pat Kirkwood, Phyllis Calvert and only a handful of others, Dinah Sheridan (1920-2012) certainly did hit the big time, becoming one of Britain's most distinguished, best-loved stars. Her newlywed status, however, from Beryl's insanely jealous and blinkered perspective, did not necessarily mean that the young woman could be trusted. George, too, in a rare moment of allowing his guard to slip, confessed that life with Beryl may not always have been a bed of roses, as Dinah explained:

During the making of Get Cracking, I discovered that if I was on the nightly call-sheet, Beryl was also called. No "leading lady", no Beryl! When I was working, our lunch was taken in the dining room—most artists together—though not George. He was given his mean in his dressing room, cooked by Beryl. I remember very little about the actual making of the film, except one remark which has stayed with me. Some of the other male artists were talking to George, and I was there too. The subject of girlfriends came up and George was asked if he was a happily married man. I should have thought it was fairly obvious! His reply was, "Oh yes, it's all right—but when you have chicken every day you get tired of it by Friday!"

Unable to find fault with George's leading lady, Beryl vented her spleen on one of his co-stars, 42-year-old Irene Handl, renowned for her charlady and generally bedraggled roles. In this instance, a furore erupted on the set because the actress invited George to accompany her to the studio canteen. As she explained a few years before her death, in 1987:

> *I'd heard a lot about Beryl, but I never expected her to be so bad. She was such a nasty, spiteful piece of work to just about everyone, including George. I don't know whether she was thinking that I wanted to borrow money off him, or take him to bed. She was so twisted and conniving that it was impossible to work out what was going on inside that head of hers. I suppose I could have told her that all I wanted to do was share a pot of tea with him and have a little chat, but she was so blooming arrogant that I didn't even give her the satisfaction of letting her know that some of we actresses don't have sex on the brain every minute of the day!"*

Get Cracking was considerably more than a film. In the darkest days of the war it was an inspiration for the ones left behind—those who, unable to enlist on account of age or infirmity, formed Local Defence Volunteers groups all across Britain. It begins as a documentary, wherein we learn of the rivalry between the LDV divisions of the adjoining villages of Major and Minor Wallop. These hold regular military exercises, with the men of the former, as the name suggests, usually emerging as victors. George Singleton, the local hero who leads his contingency to muster—all lustily singing and whistling the film's title-song—is not, however, held in similar regard by his superiors. Throughout the scenario he is persistently losing and winning back his corporal's stripe.

When an unlabeled machine-gun turns up at the railway station shared by both villages, both lay claims on it. George—as his community's representative—is outwitted by Manley (Shiner), who has been tipped off by the barmaid at George's local. Not to be outdone, and confident that Minor Wallop *will* win the next exercise, George builds his own secret weapon—a tank, the *Mary Mk 1*—assisted by his sweetheart and an evacuee apprentice. In the closing moments of the film the tank makes an assault on the "enemy", also pursued by the army after Manley has reported that there is a German tank in the vicinity. George outwits everyone, as usual, and Minor Wallop wins the day...and as *Sergeant* Singleton leans against the tank with his girl, after bashing his rival, it drops to bits!

Get Cracking, amazingly, was completed in less than a month. It also brought complaints from some filmgoers when in one scene George calls someone "an old pillock", a term widely used today in Northern dramas like *Coronation Street*, but in those days about as "blue" as one could get. He actually told one reporter that he had not realised that the word was so offensive, but that in any case he had only repeated what had been written in the script. True, perhaps, but in years to come George would often refer to *Get Cracking* as "the pillock movie". It went on general release in May 1943, by which time George had completed a tour of the Orkneys and other remote British islands, *and* almost completed his next film, *Bell-Bottom George*.

George had also finally agreed to visit Canada, but the trip was again deferred when he was informed that Basil dean had added his name to the ENSA party which would be leaving for the Middle East as soon as the arrangements had been finalised. Marcel Varnel, the new film's director, was therefore told that he would be able to have George for a maximum of five weeks. Harry Parr-Davies, on leave from the army where he was with the Irish Guards Orchestra, was given just ten days to supply the music and songs.

Bell-Bottom George begins by combining fiction with fact—

thus the on-screen character, George Blake, *and* the man portraying him are both exempted from military service for having "flat feet and a groggy heart"—and again, as in real life, Blake is determined not to accept this rejection insisting on doing his bit for his country. The film is also unique in that the majority of the cast and almost every one of the male actors were unashamedly gay. Charles Farrell, Peter Murray Hill, Charles Hawtrey, Reginald Purdell and Manning were referred to by Beryl as "The Five Queens", and the scene in which George sings "It Serves You Right", surrounded by a bevvy of well-proportioned, posturing matelots, was a potent exercise in ultra-camp homoeroticism revered by George's surprisingly large, closeted gay following in wartime Britain—as indeed is the entire film.

The action takes place in Porthampton, a South Coast naval base where German agents led by the sneering Johnson (Elliot Makeham) are working in the cellar of his taxidermist's shop. They are transmitting wireless messages overseas and plotting to blow up a prototype warship, during its maiden voyage when all the Navy's top-notches and engineers will be aboard.

George Blake, the clumsy but far from stupid bar-steward at the Navy's Senior Service Club, develops a crush on the admiral's pretty blonde chauffeur, Pat (Anne Firth), after she knocks him off his bicycle whilst he shows off on his way to work. [This scene was filmed twice, firstly with 14-year-old extra Siv Joensen riding the cycle, over which the editor clumsily superimposed George's head, secondly with George himself in the saddle—in some prints, the first scene remains!] Anne gives him a piece of her mind—indeed, she rattles on for over minute without pausing for breath, and he is unable to get a word in edgeways. The admiral, meanwhile, takes pity on him and, as he too is on his way to the club, offers him a lift. Any admiration he may feel for George is short-lived when George wrecks the joint whilst putting up the blackouts. "You'd make a *rotten* sailor," says the admiral.

Fate intervenes in the form of Jim Bennett (Farrell), an old boxer pal assigned to sail on the HMS *Seaworthy*. When Jim's girlfriend invites him to a party, so that he will not be arrested by the "crushers"—the Navy's equivalent of the Military Police—he sneaks into George's room and borrows his only suit, leaving his sailor's uniform in its place. George of forced to evacuate the building wearing this when, after he has serenaded Egbert, his goldfish, there is an air-raid...Egbert goes down the drain, the crushers get George, and he is dispatched to Jim's ship, where the other men give him a hard time until he wins them over with a song and a nifty hornpipe.

George's unexpected popularity earns him a place in the Navy's band—Pat is their unheard vocalist—and he is engaged for a BBC broadcast. Meanwhile, he takes Pat to dinner, during which the taxidermist's dog steals her cap. George chases the animal through the restaurant—more mayhem—and eventually into the shop, where he hears the radio transmitting Morse code. Sufficiently gullible to believe Johnson's explanation that the cellar is infested with crickets, George later heard the same sound coming from a studio at the BBC, where they are recording an espionage play, and the penny drops.

Johnson's plan to blow up the ship is taking place. His chief agent, Shapley (Murray Hill),has a rendezvous on a train with a beautiful female spy, but when George and Pat end up on the same train it is George and not Shapley who ends up with the envelope containing the sabotage plans pushed inside his shirt, resulting in him being pursued by both. "Get away, you cheeky fast cat, you brazen hussy" he yells at her, whilst the beefy Shapley gropes George's chest and opines, "I'm feeling a bit queer myself!" Our hero, however, evades them both and eventually follows Shapley to the crooks' lair. This time, the dog steals *his* cap, and in chasing it a second time he is captured and stripped by Johnson's cronies, one of whom is a double-agent working for Naval Intelligence and helps him to get away.

Pursued by the crooks—and Jim Bennett, who has re-entered the scenario—George meets up with Pat and they set off with a life-or-death message for the admiral, who has set sail on the doomed warship...which by way of a producer's *faux pas* has considerably reduced in size! Their journey begins in the admiral's car, with Pat driving like a maniac, and concludes in no better fashion when George attempts to navigate a motor-boat after the steering comes off, crashing and flinging them both into the water. Then, whilst the spies are being rounded up, George tells his sweetheart to stop tickling him. The culprit, however, is Egbert, his missing goldfish, and the film ends with all three submerging beneath the briny after he has asked her, "Pat, will you be my missus—and Egbert's mum?" Brilliant stuff!

The songs from this production are exceptional, though special praise must go to two. "Swim Little Fish", George later said, always made him feel sad because it was a child's song, and he would always regret that he and Beryl had never had children of their own. And who could forget the beautiful pastiche which he croons to the woman he loves—and who, in this film, he has fallen for more quickly and more confidently than usual?

> *I'd never long for meals they'd ring a gong for,*
> *The shows they throng for, I would never view.*
> *I'd have pennies from heaven,*
> *I could live in a shoe,*
> *They could take my clothes coupons,*
> *If I had a girl like you!*

The locations for *Bell-Bottom George* were filmed in Fleetwood. During one scene George narrowly missed serious whilst piloting a speedboat, when the bottom of one leg of his flared trousers became caught in the open driving-shaft. George managed to drag himself free, leaving his mangled shoe and shredded trouser-leg trapped in the mechanism, but he required hospital treatment for a skinned foot. Again questions were raised as to whether she should still be allowed to perform most of his own stunts.

Having suffered Beryl's machinations on the film-set first-hand, Basil Dean was anxious that she would not be accompanying George on his ENSA tour, declaring, "Our boys out there have enough misery to contend with, without having to put up with her as well!" Dean had not reckoned with George's inability to cope on his own, and when he insisted that it would have to be *both* Formbys, or none at all, Dean gave in.

George was being very serious when he asked Basil Dean if he would be allowed to take his motorcycle with him on the tour. This way, he declared, he and Beryl would have no difficulty keeping up with the Eighth Army. The request was refused, so George bought a huge customised 1939 Ford Mercury from Sir Malcolm Campbell—17 feet by 6—which Campbell had commissioned to convey his team of technicians during speed-trial events, which had subsequently been cancelled on account of the war.

George had the car refitted so that its five rear seats folded down into beds, and he bought a special lean-to tent to provide sleeping accommodation for his valet and pianist. The vehicle took some getting used to: for several weeks before the tour the Formbys could be seen driving around Singleton. Basil Dean agreed that it would be ideal for desert conditions, though he complained when ENSA, who were responsible for their artistes' expenses, were sent a bill for the fuel. The car devoured petrol—the best George ever got out of it was fifteen miles to the gallon.

Little is known of the Formbys' tour. Unlike Gracie Fields, who later spent several months visiting the more remote—and menacing—areas in the Pacific and kept a detailed diary of her activities, Beryl does not appear to have put pen to paper in all this time, other than a log-book of sorts detailing the distances between shows and their content...and George, of course, was never allowed to become involved in any aspect of his career but entertaining. We must therefore rely on witness accounts, which are few and sketchy.

The couple flew to Lisbon at the beginning of August, then on to Tunis and Algiers, where George opened one show for the great French *chanteuse*, Damia, and shared top-billing in another with Joséphine Baker, secretly employed by the French Résistance. He strolled on to the stage whilst the soldiers were still applauding her famous "J'ai deux amours", pointed at the desert and chirped, "Ee, it's just like Blackpool sands!"

Some of George's comments after this show, however, to the Forces publication, *Union Jack*, cause a furore when made public back in England. Stars such as Damia, Baker, Gracie Fields and Arthur Askey had been risking their lives entertaining and helping others less fortunate than themselves since the beginning of the war, and these artistes loathed what Marlene Dietrich, like Baker an honorary lieutenant who had put herself in great danger, scathingly called "the lazy sunbathers"—those big names who could have done much good, had they been interested in helping anyone but themselves. When a young reporter from *Union Jack* asked George where all his contemporaries were, he could only reply honestly, "Most of them are in the West End, where we left them, though one or two *would* be willing to put on a show for the troops, I guess, providing the camps aren't too remote, and where there's no shortage of red carpets and cocktails."

The press were wrong in accusing George of attacking certain members of his profession, for his criticisms were well-justified.

Music-comedy star Florence Desmond had told him how she would love to sing to the troops, if only the dates did not clash with her new London season—and he knew of a young, very famous actor who had evaded call-up by the army because he had agreed to work for ENSA, then refused to do so outside London.

George refused to name names, even when threatened with action by the Variety Artists' Federation. Back in England, some fifty "available" entertainers of varying fame, not wishing to suffer prejudice from their peers, petitioned Basil Dean to publish the names of these "offenders" in the national press. These "lazy sunbathers" for their part threatened to go on strike unless Dean recalled the Formbys to face the music. Dean refused to submit to such pressure. Much as he disliked George and Beryl as individuals, he privately believed that George's comments had been justified, and was filled with admiration for the sterling job they were doing. In fifty-three days they would cover much of North Africa, Italy and Sicily, Malta, Libya, Gibraltar, Egypt, Lebanon and Palestine—thirteen countries, clocking up 25,000 miles and entertaining over 750,000 troops. George proved so popular that the Eighth Army made him their mascot, a worthy honour. The Formbys performed in burnt-out aircraft hangars, defunct opera houses, an ancient Roman amphitheatre—sitting on the backs of lawyers, and once perched on upturned dustbins. George would sometimes sing half a dozen songs if the going was tough, if not least twenty before being forced off the stage by heat. At most venues the troops drew lots for tickets, whilst letters for the soldiers' families were placed in a drum, and several pulled out at random by George, who countersigned them so that they could be posted upon his return to England.

There was nothing tactful about Beryl when she learned what the Variety Artists' Federation were up to, and of 9 September her response came in the form of a telegram to the *Blackpool Gazette*'s Sylvia:

THOSE ARTISTS THREATENING TO STRIKE OVER IN ENGLAND OUGHT TO BE SHOT OR SENT OUT HERE TO HAVE A BASINFUL OF WHAT THE LADS HAVE HAD

The following week Beryl's telegram, along with a letter from her, appeared in the national press—alongside a defence sent in from Algiers by Squadron Leader Frank Ellis and countersigned by eight of the officers who had been present at the Formby-Damia-Baker concerts, and at the *Union Jack* interview:

> *We had the pleasure of entertaining Mr and Mrs Formby in our humble desert mess, and on that occasion had the opportunity to share with them the absence of top-line artists in entertainments for the troops. They [and the others on the bill] were the first well-known stage personalities we had seen during the whole of the desert campaign, and we are glad someone had the courage and gumption to explode the myth, apparently current in some quarters, that the lights of the theatre world are shining on the battle fronts. Only by the personal efforts and honesty of people like Mr Formby can we hope "through trials to reach the stars".*

In the wake of the invasion of Italy, the Formbys were refused permission to enter the country—until Beryl learned that the Eighth Army had already been entertained by Damia, Marlene Dietrich, Alice Delysia and Joséphine Baker. Beryl kicked up a stink about this, and would not back down even when informed that each of these stars had opted to tour the Italian camp-circuit of their own volition, despised being advised not to do so by the authorities—and in any case, none of them were connected with ENSA. Gracie Fields was, and when Beryl was told this—George had performed in temperatures of 125 degrees F, in

Palermo, Sicily—she dashed off a letter to the *Daily Film Renter*, in London, which fortunately never made it into print. Two years previously, the publication's "Tatler"—his identity was never revealed—had signed his name to a piece which had actually been *written* by Beryl, attacking Gracie on account of her marriage to Monty Banks, at that time officially listed as an "enemy alien". In addition, she had blown all the facts out of proportion as far as George's benevolence towards his show business contemporaries was concerned:

> *Here's poor old George Formby literally working his fingers to the bone—traipsing all over the country—giving concerts everywhere unstintingly at his own expense—paying his fellow artists' hotel expenses, raising immense amounts of money and even better raising the morale of the people—and, blow me, George is slung into the background whilst an overwhelming amount of sob-stuff heralds the approach of the lil' lady who has been doing admirably similar work in Canada and America—but who, after all, has done it thousands of miles away and has been absent from this country for a year! Apart from which she took with her her mother, father, two sisters, sister-in-law, three nephews, one niece and an Italian-born husband...PLUS a considerable amount of dough!*

Beryl's letter to "Tatler", back then, had concluded that although she had nothing against Gracie, "This latest outburst of hysteria over her belated comeback rather makes me want to vomit." Why she should have been so unspeakably bitter towards this incredibly brave women—who laid herself open to more dangers during the war years than almost any other entertainer—cannot be readily determined. It may well be as Irene Bevan pointed out that, in essentially what was man's world, Beryl was jealous of any other female possessed of the same mettle as herself. The fact that Gracie, like herself, had spent her entire life pulling herself up by the bootstraps and, despite her intense naivety, had never allowed any man to push her around may have irked Beryl, too. Neither is it known what was written in Beryl's second letter to "Tatler" other than it must have been sufficiently unpleasant for the *Daily Film Renter* to refuse to publish it for fear of being sued!

Unable to bear the thought of Gracie Fields being in Italy when George had been told to stay away, Beryl bribed a Sicilian fisherman to ferry them across the Strait of Messina to the port of Reggio, where they gave an impromptu show to 5,000 troops on the beach within minutes of landing.

Two days later, just outside Naples, the Formbys' convoy caught up with the Eighth Army, and the couple were invited to dine—on bully beef, canned fruit and ersatz coffee—with General Montgomery. En route, according to a piece in a local newspaper, their escort jeep accidentally forced a group of Italian soldiers off the road, and two of these stepped on a landmine and were blown to bits. According to the story—made up, as will be seen—neither the jeep nor George's car stopped. After their meal, the trio posed for photographs which would be wired home, then George and Beryl drove back to Reggio. After several concerts they returned to Syracuse, in Sicily, where they stayed for a few days before heading for Gozo and Malta.

George and Beryl had always wanted to visit the Holy Land, and on 26 September 1943 they gave the first of two shows at a base near Tel Aviv, one of which was attended by J H Dunn, a 23-year-old RASC driver. Dunn's letters home to his sister, Margaret, in Kent, have been preserved by the Imperial War Museum and make for fascinating reading. Of this first Formby concert, the young man very quaintly observed:

I went to an ENSA show with George Formby heading the bill. I was one of the lucky ones to draw a ticket, and he sang a song about Mr Woo being an air-raid warden, and if you have a chink in your window you will have a chink at your door, get it, and others just as laughable. In fact he was great, and the funniest thing of all was, when he came on the stage in his shorts about ten sizes too big, and during his act with his wife, he was looking through his shorts and laughing and saying, "Ee, I've never seen those through here before!"—and after playing about the stage and us laughing and thinking of course the obvious, he finished up with saying he could see his feet! He played three guitars [sic] and, singing about ten songs he spoke to us, saying he would meet us coming into Berlin, and that he had been in ten countries on thirty-one days—some travelling, nearly as fast as the 8th Army, and they are still going strong and George will have to get a move on if he is going to keep his appointment.

From Palestine, the Formby convoy drove further north to Syria, where the weather posed a bigger threat than the enemy. At Damascus and Zebdani temperatures were well in the hundreds, whereas at a fighter station high in the Lebanon Mountains it was below freezing. In Aleppo, a locust flew into George's mouth whilst he was singing "It Serves You Right", to gales of laughter from the 10,000 soldiers. Then the next day he and Beryl went down with malaria, and their subsequent shows in Syria and Turkey had to be cancelled. They were back in shape—more or less—one week later for their tour of Egypt, though when Beryl appeared on stage in Cairo for their very last tour in the Middle East, despite the scorching heat she was wearing thick stockings to conceal the dozens of bug-bites on her legs.

The Formbys arrived home during the first week of October 1943, thoroughly exhausted and each of them a stone lighter than when they had left. Yet within hours of reaching their London flat a representative from the Variety Artists' Federation was hammering on their door, demanding that George offer an explanation for his outburst in *Union Jack*, and that he disclose all the names in his supposed blacklist. Beryl's response was to tell the man, "Bugger off!", before slamming the door in his face—the consequences of which would later prove dire, and come close to irreparably damaging George's reputation and career. In the meantime, the couple did consent to attending a press-conference a few days later at the Waldorf Hotel, to which they were accompanied by their manager, Ben Henry, and representatives from ATV and Columbia.

George thought of taking his uke with him, hoping this might bring a little light relief to the proceedings, but Henry advised him not to. It *was* a solemn affair, with Beryl bursting into tears whilst recalling the truth about what had really happened when the two young soldiers had been killed in Italy. These had been escorting George's convoy across a minefield, and he and Beryl had watched them being blown to bits in front of their eyes.

To extricate himself from the predicament which he had only put himself in by being honest, George explained that he had been chatting with several soldiers in Algiers, unaware that one of them had been on *Union Jack*'s payroll. This was untrue, though the interrogating committee did not press: they wanted George to be more specific, and name names. A nod or shake of the head would suffice, he was told, after each name was read out from their "list of suspects"—in other words, entertainers who had something to feel guilty about to have assumed they had been blacklisted at all. George would have nothing to do with this. "It's a classic case of 'If the cap fits, wear it'," he told the gathering, before leaving.

A few weeks later, On 23 January 1944, having in the meantime received countless poison-pen letters and obscene telephone calls, George once more left his ukulele at home and gave a broadcast for the BBC, immediately after the nine o'clock news, describing his recent experiences in Europe and the Middle East. The broadcast would be his last in Britain for another three years. "With all respect to the many learned, expert and scientific broadcasts there have been about Middle East affairs, there has not been one which got home to the hearts of the listeners more than this," observed the London *Evening Standard*.

George told listeners that the most important aspects of the tour had been his chats with the soldiers after each show, adding:

> *They wanted to talk to somebody from home. We used to sit around, always with mugs of tea, like a lot of old women gaffing...what was the beer like, was it getting stronger, how often does it rain, how are the food and cigarettes...are the people being looked after? They were worrying quite a lot about you folks at home, but we soon put them right about that. We told them that after four and a half years, Britain was still the best country to live in...We never met a grumble or a grouse. All you mothers and wives and sweethearts at home—don't worry about your boys. When they write home and tell you they're fit and well and happy, please believe them. They're telling the truth!*

A few days later, George started shooting his next film for Columbia, *Asking For Trouble*, a title which the Formbys considered inappropriate after their run-in with the Variety Agents' Federation. It was changed to the even less apt, as shall be seen, *He Snoops To Conquer*. His co-stars were Elizabeth Allen and Robertson Hare.

Snoops, as it is affectionately known by the few Formby fans who had seen it until the more recent DVD release—like George's other films it was not re-released for the cinema, and to date has never been seen on British television—is a hugely entertaining tale of the fight between the "little man" and bureaucratic corruption. Tanglewood is depicted as a small town representative of many in wartime Britain, where the civic powers cream off the fat of the land and live in the lap of luxury, whilst the ordinary citizens who are the lifeblood of industry are forced to eke out a miserable existence in poverty and sometimes appalling housing conditions. When reporters from a London newspaper visit the town to investigate this, the crooked council officials, headed by the odious Oxbold (Claude Bailey) plan to pull the wool over their eyes but do not reckon on the visitors encountering George Gribble, the town-hall factotum who innocuously shows them around. Thus the public are outraged to observe photographs of the massive Oxbold mansion, which houses just four people, next to the Gribbles' tiny terraced house on the pretentiously-named Paradise Row, which houses fourteen.

There is further skullduggery when a government scheme grants £200 to the council so that it may carry out a Public Opinion Investigation into housing conditions. The officials need £150 for a new road-sweeper, so they decide to appoint their own officer to conduct the survey, and pay him the remaining £50. "Any idiot can do that, even Gribble," one says, and when George is asked to name his own fee they get an even better bargain: all he wants is £27 10s to repay a loan-shark from whom he had borrowed money to help out a friend.

George visits every house in Tanglewood save one—that of millionaire philanthropist, benefactor and inventor, Sir Timothy Strawbridge (Hare), whom hardly anyone in the town has ever seen—and who is so caught up in his self-centred world that he is completely oblivious to the suffering around him. Oxbold is hoping that if Sir Timothy can be persuaded to stand for councillor, he and his fellow conspirators will be able to rake in more money from the government and line their own pockets. Oxbold also had another hold over them: as the local bank manager, he will continue giving them loans so long as they do as he says.

George fills in hundreds of survey forms, of which only those on behalf of householders who are content with the council's running of the town—in other words the councillors themselves and the wealthy—are dispatched to Whitehall. The rest are given to George to be placed in the salvage bin. Whilst doing this, George accidentally meets Sir Timothy, just as the newly-acquired road-sweeper passes by. When this breaks down, the pair lend a helping hand, resulting in the machine running amock through the town, drenching passers-by, billowing out clouds of dust…and regurgitating the survey forms.

Forced to hide in Sir Timothy's house, George familiarises himself with a multitude of gadgets—and meets the inventor's daughter, Jane (Allen). George also has to cope with his own financial problems, when Oxbold fires him for speaking to the press: a bailiff moves into his room and vows to stay there until his debt to the loan-shark has been paid. He then suffers the wrath of the townspeople who, having seen their forms scattered through the streets, believe that it is *he* who has conned them. When he leaves the house they chase him back into it, and he ends up frozen stiff in Sir Timothy's newfangled refrigerator.

After this episode Jane suggests that *George*, as one of the "little people" who has been wronged, should stand against Oxbold at the next council elections. He is further persuaded by Sir Timothy, who opines of him, "Don't need brains. Look at the Commons, the House of Lords. He knows one fool from another, he can drive a road-sweeper backwards and sideways, and he can dive through a window and didn't freeze solid at zero temperature. If he can stand all that, he can stand politics!"

The film ends with the big showdown between the corrupt officials and the public during his first election rally. The bailiff has seized George's goods, including the vase where he has hidden the survey forms which were dispatched to the salvage bin, and this has ended up in the canal. Sir Timothy, however, has recorded these on his latest patent—uncannily, a precursor to the modern microfiche—and after Oxbold has been exposed as a swindler and the inevitable brawl has taken place between the honest, hardworking folk of Tanglewood and the crooks, George emerges at the local hero...and he of course gets the girl.

George later said that working on *Snoops* was a nightmare, but never added *why*, or why he always considered his worst film, when it was anything but...leaving everyone to assume that any dissention must have been linked to onset problems. This was not true. Both he and Beryl got on well with Elizabeth Allen, and Robertson Hare was just as dotty and as much fun to be with away from the camera as he was in front of it. The real reason for his unhappiness was much more sinister.

One morning, George and Beryl were on the set—he had just completed his first scene with Elizabeth Allen—when they received a visit from Mr Madden, the Dance Music Supervisor with the DMPC (Dance Music Policy Committee). This was the body responsible for vetting songs, music and comedy routines, and for investigating artistes' possible political and collaborationist leanings during wartime. The Formbys were told that though they themselves were not and never had been suspected of having Nazi sympathies, their names had been included on a list compiled by the DMPC because the committee had declared three of George's songs "enemy-friendly". All had been written by Harry Parr-Davies, for *Bell-Bottom George*: "If I

Had A Girl Like You", "Swim Little Fish", and the film's title-track.

The Formbys were horrified. Madden showed them a document drawn up by the BBC. French stars Mistinguett, Maurice Chevalier, Sacha Guitry, Lucienne Boyer, Charles Trenet and the pianist Alfred Cortot had all been denounced as collaborators, and the English performers Stella Ramon, Geraldo and George Elrick had their names included in a clause headed "PASSED BUT WATCH". Madden concluded that a huge question mark would hang over the Formby's trips into France until their "fate" had been decided at the DMPC's next monthly meeting.

That same afternoon there was an emergency meeting with George and beryl, their manager Ben Henry, a representative from ENSA, and as many Columbia executives as could be mustered as such short notice. Incredibly, the press were excluded and never found out that the name of Britain's foremost entertainer had been published in a DMPC document—in full, whereas his "accusers" were represented only by their initials; AC, ADM, GD, PO, DV and DM. Only Madden's name appeared in full.

George had recorded the three songs in question, but the records were yet to be released, so he was instructed to perform them in front of the DMPC committee within the BBC's Criterion Music Room—by no means an easy task under such harrowing conditions—and his versions were checked against the sheet-music supplied by the Victoria Music Publishing Company. George was then told that the committee would come to a decision within several days. If this was not in his favour, the "offending" songs would have to be removed from his repertoire, Columbia would have to withdraw the film from cinemas, and the Formbys would be prohibited from ever entertaining the troops again.

It must have been an agonising wait, and a totally unnecessary one. There was absolutely nothing seditious about the songs, and the only likely explanation for George's name appearing on the DMPC list seems that it had been put forward by someone from the Variety Artists' Federation-an act of revenge by one of those entertainers he had branded a "lazy sunbather". Lucienne Boyer had also complained about her name being included on the list, as had Mistinguett—both were actively engaged by the French Résistance, the former organising British parachutist drops in Normandy, while Mistinguett was raising funds for French Food Aid. Nevertheless, George's sheet-music was re-examined at the next DMPC meeting on 1 February 1944, and the following morning George was informed by Mr Madden that the "offending" songs had been re-categorised in a special document headed "PASSED WITH PROVISOS". The minutes of the meeting observed, "Mr Formby may be permitted to perform these works, but no additional chorus may be added to them without reference to the Dance Music Supervisor." The most ridiculous situation of George's career had been resolved, though it would leave an aftertaste of bitterness.

Throughout this latest ordeal, the Formbys had stayed in touch with General Montgomery's office—which had also been made aware of the DMPC list—and now that they had been "cleared", Beryl told Marcel Varnel, the director of *Snoops*, that should the invasion of France begin before the film's completion, this would be abandoned until their return from France. "Our boys over there are much more important than a few feet of celluloid," she told him.

Only days after finishing the film, Beryl received a telephone call from Montgomery himself. George's services were required in France, the great man told her, though in view of the danger she was advised to stay at home. Beryl told him sharply that *she* would be the judge of that. A few years later, in an impromptu radio interview in Melbourne, George's "shadow"—as Beryl announced herself—spoke of her run-in with Monty:

> *We were having a meal with Monty in his tent one evening after we'd done a show for his boys, and he said, "George, there are some boys who made the initial landing on D-Day, the paratroops over the other side of the Orme—and they haven't been relieved yet. It really would do them a world of good if they could see your face for a few minutes." So George said, "All right, I'll go up and have a look at them." Then Monty said, "Of course, Beryl won't be able to go." So I told him, "In that case George doesn't go either!" So he said to me, "All right, Beryl, if you want to risk your silly neck, go ahead and do it!"*

George's first show in Normandy, straight after a dreadful four-hour Channel crossing, was not given aboard HMS *Ambitious*, as has been frequently stated. Prior to this, he sang to fifty soldiers in a Bayeux farmyard! Over the next four weeks, he and Beryl appeared in seventy hastily-arranged shows, some lasting only minutes on account of the fighting, others running on for hours. At Caen they bumped into Gracie Fields. A few weeks earlier she had crossed the Channel incognito to join up with the 53rd Welsh Division, who had just taken Carpiquet airport, two miles from one of the main German artillery lines. As far as is known, however, these two great British institutions did not get around to performing in the same show.

At some "venues", George handed out sticks of Blackpool rock after singing that particular song—at others, mere years from the enemy line, he was not allowed to sing at all and had to make do with crawling into the trenches, and sharing a few jokes with the lads. In Amiens, when told that the Formbys were Catholic, a priest invited them to evening service, insisting that George bring his uke along. When he arrived he realised why: part of the church, including the organ, had been damaged by a shell and he was asked to accompany the congregation whilst they sang hymns! *Only* George could have got away with singing the Hargreaves-Dammerell number, with its unmistakable echoes of the Anglo-Belgian singer Harry Fragson, which had appeared on the flipside of "The Ghost", back in 1937:

> *I'm a Frenchie dirty-doggie…*
> *I'm a mais-song, a tres-bong!*
> *Perhaps I can-can, I'm not sure!*
> *The shirt that I'm now wearing*
> *Is pomme-de-terre-ing,*
> *I'm a Froggie, I'm a Lancashire main-sewer!*

Before leaving for France, George had agree upon his next film for Columbia—very reluctantly, for he was the first to admit that these "tiresome pictures" were starting to interfere with his war work. For this reason, just days after returning home he renewed his ENSA permit, then informed Marcel Varnel that he had just eight weeks to complete the project.

I Didn't Do It, a tragi-comedy in the finest Grand Guignol tradition, within which the high-camp action is in the major whilst the songs are relegated to the minor key, concerned the weirdest but most fascinating assortment of characters ever assembled for a Formby film. There are hammy actors, an Irish conman, a bungling magician, a psychopathic ex-circus performer, Siamese twins, and an alcoholic landlord. The setting is Ma Tubbs' theatrical boarding house, to which Manchester millworker George Trotter arrives, aspiring to become an actor. Some years before he had met Terry O'Rourke (Jack Daly) who, after giving him his autograph told him to look him up if ever he was in London. O'Rourke has completely forgotten him, bit knows a soft touch when he sees one—therefore when George misleads him into thinking he is rich, the actor coerces him into funding a West End cabaret revue wherein this gaggle of has-been thespians will make their comeback—something the house's resident agent, Vance (Carl Jaffe), has thus far failed to effect.

An improbable but effective drams begins when one Tom Driscoll (Dennis Wyndham) arrives on the scene—a wealthy, arrogant Australian trapezist who boasts that the troupe he is about to assemble will take the country by storm. Driscoll and Vance were once two-thirds of the famous Flying White Devils, a partnership which ended twenty years ago when Driscoll had an affair with the act's third member, Vance's wife. During their last performance in Sidney, Driscoll deliberately allowed Vance to fall, leaving him crippled and disfigured in hospital, and running off with his wife. Because these injuries and the passage of time have greatly changed his appearance, Driscoll has not recognised him.

George's and Vance's rooms are next to each other, their exterior windows connected by a narrow ledge. Vance uses this to his advantage when he abseils down the side of the building into Driscoll's room, kills him, then swings along the ledge using his hands to plant the incriminating evidence in George's room: George's plimsolls which he has worn on his hands, his handkerchief and blood-stained gloves, the scouting knife with which he stabbed his victim, and a wad of Australian banknotes which Vance hopes the police will assume to be George's motive for the crime.

The police arrest George, but soon release him when they realise that the killer has left *too* much evidence—they assume that now he is free, the real criminal will slip up.

For no apparent reason, a famous impresario turns up at Ma Tubbs' with a £2,000 cheque for George to finance his project, but is waylaid by O'Rourke, who announces that he is George's agent. George, meanwhile, is in grave danger. Vance tells him that Driscoll also owned two valuable diamond rings, items not found by the police because *he* has hidden them in the eyes of the stuffed owl which George keeps in his room! When George finds these, Vance forces him at gunpoint to sign a confession that he murdered Driscoll, then orders him to swallow poison. He does, using a trick glass he has borrowed from a magician, and pretends to be dead. The film ends with a denouement straight out of Edgar Wallace. O'Rourke gets to put on his show, involving all the acts from the boarding house, but with a mysterious "Mr X" topping the bill. Surrounded by mirrors so that the audience cannot differentiate between himself and his reflection, George sings "The Daring Young Man", a number centered around the Driscoll-Vance saga, and the killer—exposed by him as "Mr X"—is apprehended by the police.

As usual, Beryl made her presence known on the set of *I Didn't Do It*, particularly when she heard a rumour that George's leading lady, Marjorie Browne, intended making a play for him. Browne had little to do in the film. She was neither pretty nor convincing in her part, and when Beryl saw her without make-up—in her words, "with a face like the back of a bus"—she did not feel it necessary to read her the riot-act. The Boswell Twins, on the other hand, were the personification of glamour and had a bad but undeserved reputation. Born in Loughborough in 1920, Honor and Beryl Boswell had toured England as a song and dance act until the outbreak of the war, whereupon they had created their infamous "Tassel Dance" and played some of the less reputable cabarets and halls. Though he claimed it was impossible to tell the sisters apart, George did engage in a brief affair with Beryl Boswell.

As had happened during the shooting of *I See Ice*, Beryl Formby found a suitable excuse for turning a blind eye, as Irene Bevan explained:

> *The Boswell Sisters were little more than strippers—"naughty revue-dancers" they used to call them in those days. Gracie [Fields] knew them well, and she also knew Jack Daly, the young Irish comedian who had begun his career as a warm-up in one of her shows. During the thirties, Daly had had a brief but passionate affair with Gracie, since which time he had slept with more women than most of us have had hot dinners. It was as if he knew that he was going to die young, as if he was packing them in, so to speak, whilst there was still time. Beryl Formby was just another notch in his bedpost, something she must have known considering his dreadful reputation. I'm sure that, had this one got out—as opposed to her earlier fling with Gavin Gordon—despite George's own indiscretions it would have signalled the end of the Formby marriage. Not that George would have divorced Beryl, though I am certain that he would have left her.*

Meanwhile, still incensed by the media's attitude towards George following the *Union Jack* fiasco, Beryl pleaded with Columbia not to invite any critics to the premiere of *Snoops*, which took place on 8 January 1945 at the Strand's Tivoli Cinema. Initially, the studio objected to this—until she supplied them with real proof of George's popularity...a list of the names of the 20,000-plus members of his fan club.

Ten days later, the Formbys were amongst the first contingent of ninety ENSA artistes who flew to Karachi, in Pakistan, where they remained for four days before crossing the border into India.

There were few concerts here, but on a "day off" George and Beryl chartered a private plane to Imphal, the capital on the Manipur state, close to the Burmese border, which had been besieged the previous year when Japan had invaded Assam. No shows at all had been scheduled for this region—indeed, ENSA forbade the Formbys from making the trip, to which Beryl responded, "It's our money we're spending and our neck's we're risking. Mind you own business!"

Several weeks later, the Formbys' "mysterious trip into the middle of nowhere" was explained, not to anyone at ENSA or anyone else of official status, but their friend Sylvia back in Blackpool. During their tour of Scotland in aid of the Shilling Fund, Beryl had shared a pot of tea with a Glasgow housewife. And here she had made a heartfelt promise, one which she had every intention she had of keeping, no matter what it entailed:

> *She asked us to find the grave of her brother, who was killed fifteen miles from Imphal, and take a photograph of it. I never thought for one moment that I would be able to carry out her request. So I got in touch with the Graves Commission officer, helped him look through the files, and found what we wanted. The boy had been brought in from where he was buried, and re-buried in the Military Cemetery at Imphal. We found the grave, and George took the picture.*

From India, the Formbys travelled to Ceylon and Burma. In Columbo, in a football field and in temperatures of 130 degrees F, that George had 15,000 soldiers in hysterics with the most recent episode in the saga of Mr Wu, whose talents were by now extended to putting out small fires—without using sand—for, having dispensed with the laundry *and* the window cleaning business, the honourable gentleman was helping the war-effort:

> *His cousin, Wun-Way-Hin, was one day helping him*
> *To move a time-bomb from the shop, I know,*
> *But it went off Bang! And there's no doubt,*
> *Wun-Way-Hin flew one way out,*
> *And Mr Wu's an air-raid warden now!*

During this tour, George refused to speak to the press and risk being drawn into any arguments such as the one sparked off by his comments to *Union Jack*. No sooner had the Formbys arrived home, however, at the end of March, than they and a number of other artists found themselves in the firing line following remarks broadcast by Basil Dean on All Air India. Though her name had not been mentioned, Dean had been referring to Beryl when, after praising his "team" for their bravery and loyalty, he had confessed his disappointment that, "Certain parties had demanded privileges way and beyond the norm, including first-class hotel rooms, maids and batmen and the unnecessary chartering of special aircraft...and an expectation that the order of battle should be altered to suit their convenience."

In the Formbys' case, much of this seems unlikely to have been true: one cannot imagine them risking their lives on what was, to be perfectly honest, a well-meaning but costly and some would think futile expedition to photograph a soldier's grave, then suddenly beginning to lay the law down about hotel conditions and luxury flight arrangements. Even if they had, they would not have been the only ones. After all, the ENSA chiefs and military hierarchy were never expected to rough it, and unlike George and Beryl were getting paid considerably more than just £10 a week. Beryl was therefore justified in seeing red, and such was her anger that she was even prepared to mount a "mini insurrection" with the comic Wee Georgie Wood, who was also chairman of the hated Variety Artists' Federation by penning a letter—signed by Wood and George—which was, equally bizarrely, published in the 3 April edition of *The Times*...the newspaper which George had once dismissed as, "Only fit for wrapping fish and chips in."

> *There is much criticism directed at the stars, that they prefer to work comfortably in the large base areas instead of going forward. The fact is, of course, that we have to go where ENSA sends us. The George Formby party played to over 250,000 troops, the Georgie Wood party played nineteen more shows than ENSA had scheduled for their tour. General Leese made it possible for Mr Formby to get to Burma. Air Marshall Joubert arranged for Mr Wood to go there. It is nonsense to suggest that they would pander to artists by making it possible for them to have special aircraft unless they saw good reasons for giving the actors such valuable transport...The suggestion that the stars expected the order of battle to be changed to suit their convenience is childish. We certainly have not suggested that our services were not wanted because we could not be accepted in the front line at a particular moment. We did suggest that our services were wanted in the forward areas and ENSA seemingly did not realise this.*

The second section of the Formby/Wood does not make sense. Basil Dean had not commented on this point in his broadcast, only the inordinate demands of some of his artistes—and Beryl *had* put her foot down about the Burma trip, declaring that unless she and George could be guaranteed their safety, in so far as this was possible, then they would not set foot in the country. But if the Formbys were expecting an apology from Dean, they were to be disappointed. Their letter was ignored.

In July 1945, *I Didn't Do It* went on general release, though if it proved *almost* as popular with George's fans as his previous films, it did little to endear him to those critics who in the past had raved over his every gesture—cheerful, loveable old Formby, he of the toothy grin and bungling disposition simply was not convincing in the role of a murder suspect. The reviews upset George a great deal. His contract with Columbia Pictures was drawing to a close, with just one more production in the pipeline, and he announced that he was not in any hurry to renew it or solicit another. It would be far better, he declared, to go out riding the crest of a wave than to fade into celluloid obscurity...in which direction, according to Basil Dean, he was clearly heading, as the producer explained in a television interview of 1966:

> *George wasn't an easy person to find the right vehicle for. His range was limited, though fortunately he had a very shrewd idea of his own capabilities, and was always determined never to step outside them. It was never a case of a comedian wanting to play Hamlet. Of course, the real secret of his success was personality. That wide grin of his seemed to spread right across the screen. George never acted gormless like some successful comedians. He was gormless as far as the audiences were concerned, and they took him to their hearts accordingly.*

Irene Handl, on the other hand, strongly disagreed with Dean, believing that much of George's genius had been left untapped:

> *He was a sort of elemental that would have needed a very, very clever director, quite out of the class of the kind of film he did. And of course, those directors didn't*

> *direct his kind of film. But I think if you'd have got him with an ace director, they'd have got something really special out of him. He didn't know what he held in him. It was like a very frail glass with something very precious in it. And that thing would never come out because what people liked about him wasn't that!*

After almost two decades at the top of his profession—six years of which he had been Britain's Number One draw—and still unable to work out *why* he was so popular, George had suddenly become convinced that he was losing his appeal. He had recently even been ousted from the top of the *Motion Picture Herald* poll by James Mason and David Niven. This was a relatively unimportant factor, for his records were still selling in vast quantities, even the older songs, which had been re-issued by Regal Zonophone. If the critics generally regarded his Columbia films as inferior to his ATP/Ealing comedies, the fans were just as ecstatic about them.

To ensure his and Beryl's financial security—though he had around £150,000 in the bank—George sold their Singleton home in the summer of 1945 and bought Sullom End, a farmhouse a few miles away at Barnacre, near Garstang. Beryl's elderly parents moved in with them. The main building comprised six bedrooms, three reception rooms, and servants' quarters. Annexed to it were two smaller houses and a pair of labourers' cottages. "I intend to become a gentleman farmer and breed cows," he announced. "That way Beryl and me need never starve!" He posed for photographs with four Ayrshire calves he had bought at the Penrith cattle-market, the first of the proposed "Beryldene" herd—Beryldene Beryl, Beryldene George, Beryldene John Willie and Beryldene Funny! His most important acquisition was the new motorcycle he said would be used for his and Beryl's shopping trips into Garstang and Fleetwood.

A few weeks after moving into Sullom End, George began shooting *George In Civvy Street* for Columbia. This enabled his film career to end on a high note. There were none of the overworked routine gags and lines, the slapstick was sophisticated, the songs first-class. When one hears the big production number—"We've Been A Long Time Gone"—at the *start* of the film and witness the spectacle of George doing the Argentinian Tango with Ronald Shiner, one instinctively knows that one is in for a treat. And *what* a treat!

Like *Bell-Bottom George*, this is a rip-roaring, hand-on-hips high-camp extravaganza. Indeed, the director Marcel Varnel brought in all the "lavender extras" from the earlier film, utilised many gay in-house jokes which must have sailed above the heads of George's heterosexual fans. Even one of the characters was called Lavender!

The war is over, and the boys are coming home to their wives and sweethearts. Amongst them are George Harper and his pickpocket pal, Fingers (Shiner). During his absence, George's father has died, bequeathing him the Unicorn, a run-down riverside pub which for months has had only one regular customer—Shadrack (Ian Fleming), an artist who donates his works to the establishment in exchange for board and lodgings. Across the river is the Lion, an up-market hostelry which used to be run by George's sweetheart Mary Colton (Rosalyn Boulter) and her father. Since the old man's death, however, it has been managed by the unscrupulous Jed Brindle (Frank Drew) and his domineering mother, who treat Mary like dirt.

Not long after George's return home, he is visited by a pair of crooks who try to con him into selling the property for less than its actual value. The ploy fails, so they join forces with Brindle and plot to have him relieved on his license. First they tamper with the clock in the bar so that he can be charged with serving after hours, then they spike the beer with paraffin. None of these schemes work, but George does temporarily fall out with Mary, and to cheer him up Fingers sends for some of their old army chums. George then goes off to dream *Alice Through The Looking Glass*—he is the Mad March Hare to Mary's Alice and Fingers' Mad Hatter, and the dream takes on a symbolic theme when the Unicorn fights the Lion in the boxing-ring, emerging as victor and inspiring George to tackle his rivals head-on.

The Unicorn is closed for refurbishment: his pals all "muck in" to get the place ready for its re-opening as a pantheon for the opulent river-trade. The big day arrives, and George hires the real-life bandleader, Johnny Claes—the only black actor to appear in a Formby film. His rivals, however, bring in their "secret weapon"—a showgirl named Mitzi Montrose (Daphne Elphinstone), who tells George that she is a singer. She is actually a stripper—earning this film an "A" certificate—and when she gets down to her undies, an all-out brawl erupts, whereupon the crooks get their come-uppance. Then into this confusion an art expert arrives from London. Mary, now reunited with George, has sent one of Shadrack's paintings (of George) to the Royal Academy, and is has caused a sensation. The rest of Shadrack's canvases, in effect George's property, are then bought for a small fortune…and as per usual the hero gets to live happily ever after with the girl—in this instance literally—girl of his dreams.

A scene from *Get Cracking* (1943) with Dinah Sheridan. (Dinah Sheridan)

With Ronald Shiner in *George In Civvy Street* (1946), George's final film. (ATP)

Preparing for a show during World War II (courtesy of Imperial War Museum)

George and Beryl "somewhere in North Africa", visiting the troops during World War II. (courtesy Imperial War Museum)

Seven:
Sitting Pretty With My Fingers Crossed

"George Formby's more obscure songs are so hilarious, the language so flat and Lancastrian, always focused on domestic things. Not academically funny, not witty, just morosely humorous. That really appeals to me." Morrissey, singer.

George's career, certainly in Britain, did suffer a temporary slump in the first few years after the war. In March 1946 he was guest of honour at the very first *Daily Mail* Film Festival, held at the Leicester Square Theatre. This paid tribute to some of the British screen stars who had risen to prominence during the conflict. One was James Mason, whose handsome, brooding looks and seductive voice had set hearts a-flutter—and not just female ones—as the calculating aristocrat in the 1943 film, *The Man In Grey*. Mason had rocketed to the top of the *Motion Picture Herald*'s popularity poll, and along with contemporaries such as Stewart Granger, David Niven and Laurence Olivier was largely responsible for the declining screen careers of not just George, but those of Tommy Trinder, Will Hay and even Gracie Fields. To all intents and purposes, not that the bad times were no longer just around the corner, mirth was no longer the only order of the day. The public had begun clamouring for intrigue and suspense, but above all romance.

George suffered celluloid rejection very badly, and after the *Daily Mail* Film Festival, he became so chronically depressed that his doctor and Beryl genuinely believed that he was losing his mind. But whereas George's doctors prescribed complete rest,

Beryl had him admitted—under the name Ingham, her maiden name—to a psychiatric hospital in York, where he remained for five weeks. His only visitors were Beryl—and his mother and sister Louisa, anxious to get their hands on his money, should he be sectioned. Since becoming famous, George had hardly seen his family, and these two turned up with a long list of demands. Eliza began her tirade by accusing Beryl of neglecting her son, declaring that she was here to take him home. She and Louisa then read out a list of demands—for money, which she said George was morally obliged to acknowledge. His brother, Frank, had been sent to prison for theft and his wife could not afford to feed their children. His sister Ethel was in debt had had been threatened by the bailiffs. His sister Mary needed money to pay for specialised hospital treatment and if George could not help, was in danger of losing her sight. Beryl sent these odious women packing, though her own behaviour left much to be desired. The press and worried fans who turned up at Sullom End were told that he was in bed, suffering from the flu. A hospital spokesman, who cannot be named for legal reasons, told me:

> *He suffered a complete nervous breakdown. For years, Formby had been one of the country's top box-office draws, and his insensitive wife had more or less convinced him that he was a has-been. According to our records he wasn't put into a strait-jacket or anything like that. He was given medication, and afforded a little peace and quiet. Certain aspects of the case are, however, very disturbing. Mrs Formby insisted that her husband remain here until he was fully recovered, and that in the event of failure in this respect he should be committed to a suitable institution. He stayed here for over a month—then one day, after Mrs Formby had signed an overseas contract, she came to collect him and*

> SHE told the doctor that in her opinion he was well enough to go home. As the doctor refused to discharge him, Mrs Formby signed the discharge papers herself.

The overseas contract was for a tour of Scandinavia, astonishing everyone because this was one part of the world where George was virtually unknown. It came about as a result of his being "spotted" by a Swedish variety agent. Not only this, the tour proved that even the usually impeccably organised Beryl, the undisputed queen of wheeling and dealing, could be taken for a ride.

The couple flew to Stockholm on 13 May, and Beryl's first tantrum took place in the lounge at the Bromma Flyfalt airport when one of the small contingency or reporters—seeing George in his dark glasses—rushed to his aid, thinking that he was blind! "No, he isn't," Beryl snarled. "And neither is he as daft as you, thank God. Get out of our way!"

Beryl lost her cool with the Swedish promoter—whose name has never been revealed—when he informed her that George's first show would not be taking place in one of the smaller, more intimate venues she had specifically requested so that he might feel more at ease, but at the huge, 12,000-seater theatre within Stockholm's Nojesfaltet Amusement Park. She soon calmed down when told that *all* the tickets for the event had sold out in record time, such had been the hype of the past week when a national radio station had played his records, non-stop, for several hours.

The show did not get off to a good start, however. Several artistes preceded George in the programme—he was in fact the *vedette-américaine*, which on the Continent is the artiste secondary to the top of the bill, who closes the first half of the show. So contrary to what has been said, the audience were not there solely to see him but one of Sweden's top female singers—

Ulla Billquist (1907-46), one of the most neurotic performers to ever appear on a stage. Three times married, Billquist had spent her entire career in the shadow of the country's number one entertainer, Zarah Leander, who she emulated. Two months after working with George, Billquist was found dead in her kitchen, having gassed herself. The Master of Ceremonies was his Swedish near-equivalent, the actor-comedian Thor Modéen (1898-1950), who was also Billquist's closest friend and often appeared on the same bill. Beryl did not mind this, though she had objected to the clause in George's contract dictating *how* and *what* he should perform. He had wanted to appear on the stage alone, with just his ukuleles, but the in-house bandleader, a tetchy individual named Thor Jedderbys, had objected—claiming that his musicians would have to be paid for sitting around for more than an hour with nothing to do until the headline act came on. Beryl was left with no option but to supply Jedderbys with a selection of George's records borrowed from the radio station—there was no time for rehearsals—hoping that by listening to these, his musicians might have some idea how to accompany an artiste they were wholly unfamiliar with.

The orchestra proved hopeless. George opened with "When The Boys Of The Village Get Cracking", but was forced to abandon it halfway through. During his next number, "I'm The Ukulele Man", he had to struggle whilst Jedderby's musicians played the wrong tune! Matter were then made worse by a very tipsy Thor Modéen, who strode on to the stage between songs to explain to the audience what each one was about, but spent more time clowning around than doing this. George pressed on and completed his set—at one stage he even executed a little jig with Modéen—but there were no encores, just a polite thank you before he walked off. In their dressing room Beryl was already on the phone to the airport, trying to book seats on the next plane back to England.

The next morning, 15 May, in the breakfast room of Stockholm's Grand Hotel, the Formbys where shown a photograph of George on the front page of a national newspaper, and a fellow guest translated the accompanying feature. There were no references to the bungled orchestration, or Modéen and Billquist, and George was described as, "The greatest British phenomenon of all time...a consummate professional who last evening overcame every adversity to entertain us."

Beryl contacted the tour promoter at once, and within two hours he had found George a new set of musicians who *were* familiar with his work...which was just as well, for his next show was that very evening, again supporting Ulla Billquist, at Malmo's vast Folkets Park in front of a crowd of 20,000. This time there were no problems, and two evenings later George himself topped the bill at the Bernsbee, Sweden's most prestigious music-hall. Because there was no continuity-robbing MC, some of his quick-fire numbers had to be slowed down and have many of their Northern colloquialisms removed. Even so he scored a big success singing about his plus-fours, his horoscope and snapshot album, and about the ubiquitous Fanny and Mr Wu, and he had them rolling in the aisles with "Believe It Or Not", another "ghost" song which he had recorded back in 1934:

> *I whispered, "My dear, don't give way to fright,*
> *But, in the room you sleep a ghost appears every night."*
> *"No silly ghost," said she, "Could ever frighten me!"*
> *Just as the light she turned out,*
> *"Who's that in my room?" she cried,*
> *And started to shout.*
> *I whispered, Shut up! I'm the ghost I told you about!"*

From Stockholm, the Formbys flew to Copenhagen, where they spent two days sightseeing, before knuckling down to the serious business of work. George was photographed with the Little Mermaid and could not resist pointing to the statue's breasts and cracking, "Ee, I bet you don't get many of them to the pound!" He then went on to earn £1,200 for three appearances at the city's Tivoli Gardens—a record fee which would not be exceeded until Marlene Dietrich's season there some years later—before ending the tour with concerts in Odense and Aarhus.

Back in England, barring a handful of charity concerts to aid relatives of deceased servicemen, George spent much of his time at Sullom End, "tending the herd" and tinkering with his motorcycles. It did not take him long to realise that the life of a gentleman farmer was not for him. The expense by far swamped any income, so the farmstead was put on the market, along with the still four-strong Beryldene herd. It would eventually be sold to the Thompson family, then the proprietors of Blackpool Pleasure Beach, by which time the Formbys would have acquired a new property. The Spinney was set in two acres of landscaped gardens, near Knutsford in the Cheshire countryside. Again, Beryl's parents moved in with them, though sadly, not long afterwards, her father died.

On 24 June—he and Beryl were appearing at Blackpool Opera House in the revue, *Starry Way*—George was awarded the OBE in the King's Birthday Honours List, for all that he had done for his country during the war. Receiving similar accolades were fellow entertainers Elsie and Doris Waters, Doris Hare, and Wee Georgie Wood. Though obviously delighted by the award, George was unable to conceal his disappointment—and anger—that Beryl had been completely ignored. He told Sylvia, "It should have been something the wife and I should have shared—not that we ever expected anything for entertaining the lads overseas. Now, *that* was an honour!"

George's comments to his friend were very much of an understatement. Two skippers from Fleetwood had been awarded the MBE, and two local women the BEM: the latter pair had worked side by side with Beryl, raising money for her Jump Fund, and Beryl of course had been the brains behind every one of George's charity drives. He firmly believed that she had not only been snubbed by "the establishment", but deliberately insulted, and there seems to be no reason to believe that he was wrong. For her unselfish and tireless dedication, no one deserved to be recognised for her wartime efforts than Beryl Formby.

In October 1946, the Formbys flew to South Africa for what would prove the most problematic tour of George's career—one which would be curtailed on account of Beryl's (and later George's) political views, and her strangely alternating fits of greed and intense compassion in a country torn apart by poverty and racial oppression.

Beryl had cabled ahead, as with every major series of engagements, to ensure that she and George be afforded maximum publicity, only to be told that if they were expecting this, they would have to foot the bill. They were, on the other hand, promised that a high-ranking delegation would meet their plane at Johannesburg's Palmietfintein airport, along with a limousine which would convey them to the railway station, where George's first show was scheduled to take place...on the actual platform. Both the delegation and the car failed to turn up, but George's fans did not let him down. Five-hundred of these, some plucking ukuleles, mobbed the couple the instant they set foot on the tarmac, and *these* escorted them to the station. Many of these people had greeted Gracie Fields when she had first visited South Africa in 1935. Indeed, to capitalise on the publicity, the distributors of Gracie's films were showing them back-to-back with George's...and just in case anyone did *not* know who he was, he was billed in some cinemas as "The Male Gracie Fields With The Banjo"!

Such measures were wholly unnecessary. At each stop along

the journey to Cape Town, George was obliged to get off the train for an impromptu performance on the platform—once on top of the train itself—and between the railway station in Cape Town and his hotel there, over 20,000 people lined the streets, chanting his name. The intense heat and this noisy welcome—though appreciated—did George no good at all. His health was just starting to fail, though for a few years more he would often give a variety of excuses as to why he was feeling unwell, and whilst he and Beryl were being manhandled from their car into the foyer he tottered and very nearly collapsed.

George was back on form for his performance that evening at the Alhambra Theatre, and after singing twenty of his best-loved songs he rewarded the enthusiastic audience with his own arrangement of "Sara Maraise", which he sang phonetically in Afrikaans...halfway through he giggled, and announced, "Ee, it's ever so funny when you don't know what you're singing about!"

The Formbys moved on to Pretoria, and a massive controversy when Beryl learned that the civic luncheon. Arranged in their honour, was to be presided over by Daniel Francois Malan—the head of the National Party who, two years hence, would introduce apartheid. George was not in the least interested in politics, but even he disapproved of the man known as "The Boers Black-Veldt Moses"—a man who had already cautioned Beryl that she and her husband would not be permitted to perform to black audiences, even on station platforms.

Much has to be said in praise of Beryl's audacity and courage in ripping up Malan's message and telling the courier, "If that man turns up at the do, George and I will be on the first plane back to England." Astonishingly, Malan was "replaced" by D P Van Heerden, the Mayor of Pretoria, who informed Beryl—as he had Gracie Fields, ten years previously—that, on account of the country's abject poverty it had always been customary for visiting entertainers to pay for their own civic receptions. She hit the roof, telling a press-conference, "Imagine the cheek of the man. He invites over two hundred people to a slap-up lunch—people *we* don't know from Adam—then expects us to pay the bill. Well, he knows *exactly* what he can do!"

Beryl's outburst was certainly justified, though not so some of her mercenary demands. When George had been interviewed in the lobby of their four-star hotel—and photographed tipping a porter with English money!—he had commented that his room was "champion", and that he and Beryl planned travelling around the city the same as everyone else, by taxi, or "Shank's pony". Beryl, however, complained to their tour organiser that their accommodation was not up to her expectations. Mayor Van Heerden therefore arranged for the couple to stay at the most expensive hotel in Pretoria, and supplied them with a limousine, a liveried chauffeur *and* a manservant. The cost came out of the City Council's already severely depleted funds.

Today it would be argued that words such as "darkie", "nigger" and "Chink" are politically incorrect, and rightly so, though in George's day such terms were largely acceptable, even by those to whom the terms were applied. George's Chinese fans were never offended by Mr Wu, just as *he* remained unaffected by suggestions from some quarters that all Lancastrians wore flat caps and clogs, raced pigeons, kept ferrets and thrived on hot-pot. The harsh prejudices of South Africa, however, affected him badly—until Beryl suggested, to her eternal credit, that they should defy Malan's instructions and put on a series of shows for blacks-only audiences, a move which resulted in the Formbys being virtually *ordered* to leave the country.

Most of these blacks-only venues were flea-pit cinemas in the city's most run-down districts, where anything could happen. Beryl was advised to dress down whilst they were being driven to them…not in a civic limousine, but in an armoured police truck flanked by a fleet of motorcycles. George and Beryl bore the cost of this, the people were allowed in free of charge, and George did not accept one cent in salary for each of the twenty shows.

It was during one of these performances that Beryl sparked off a massive row. George had just sung "When I'm Cleaning Windows", and had called Beryl on to the stage to join him for a curtain-call when a three-year-old girl toddled on to present Beryl with a box of chocolates. She instinctively picked the child up, gave her a big kiss, then passed her to George—a perfectly natural reaction, though something of a historic one for this part of the world.

Outside the theatre, a hundred or so of the most hardened thugs the couple had ever seen cheered them and pelted them with flowers, and for almost an hour the Formbys chatted to these people and signed autographs. The next morning, at their hotel, a delegation arrived sent by Malan, warning Beryl that she must never pull such a "despicable stunt" again. She reacted by slamming the door in their faces, and that same evening she overstepped the mark again—by handing out sweets, and more hugs, to a crowd of children who had gathered around the stage-door. This time she received a call from Malan personally and Beryl, almost always the lady even when laying into someone, quietly told him before putting the phone down, "Why don't you piss off, you horrible little man?"

Within the hour, Malan exacted his revenge. Throughout the tour there had been speculation that the Formbys might purchase a property in Pretoria or Cape Town where they could spend the winter months. George's doctor had told Beryl that there was every chance of his developing his father's chest complaint, and had advocated a warm climate. Now, they were told by Malan's office that, not only were they no longer welcome in South Africa—the tour still had a week to go, and the organisers had arranged for an extension—they would have to leave the country at once. This time there was no civic vehicle to convey them to the airport, and shortly before boarding their place another message was delivered from Daniel Francois Malan—"Never come here again!"

The Formbys returned to England and began rehearsals for their annual pantomime. *Dick Whittington*, at the Leeds grand, was a resounding success and sold out every evening for two months, a pleasing antidote to the dreadful reviews for *George In Civvy Street*, still playing to capacity audiences five months after its release. There would be no more Formby films, he vowed, even when approached with a possible Hollywood contract. Gregory Ratoff, the former actor who had recently directed Gracie Fields in *Madame Pimpernel*, saw no reason why George could not be as big as Gracie, Stateside. George told Ratoff that he would mull over his offer—then promptly forgot about it when, in the February, Beryl suddenly fell ill.

The couple had rented a boat for the weekend on the Norfolk Broads, and were just outside Great Yarmouth when Beryl collapsed and was rushed to a private clinic. At first the doctors suspected that she might have been anaemic, but tests revealed a small growth on her cervix. This proved benign, but it was worrying all the same and after surgery she was hospitalised for nineteen days. George only left her side once—Beryl's doctors had advised him that she would need plenty of fresh air, so he went out and, on impulse, bought a 48-foot boat, the *Maudau*, which over the coming weeks would be converted into a handsome, two-berth cruiser which George would relaunch as the *Lady Beryl*.

Following Beryl's brief recuperation, George played two weeks at the London Palladium, where he was supported by Billy Russell, the Birmingham comic—renowned for his mother-in-law jokes, he was a precursor of Les Dawson. Again, the season was a sell-out…again, George was hammered by the

London critics. "Formby is in such bad taste, and so mechanical," observed *The Times*' Paul Dehn, a man who despised any artiste hailing from "North of Watford Gap", and who received dozens of poison-pen letters and even death-threats for his barbed comments.

In July, George and Beryl travelled to Birmingham, where they appeared on the hugely popular radio show, *Workers' Playtime*. This particular edition was broadcast live from Norton's Motorcycle Factory, and though the event was to raise more money for charity, George was more than compensated when the managing director presented him with a prototype 490cc International, the first machine to roll off the company's production line since the end of the war. The couple posed for photographs, with Beryl perched precariously on the pillion. George would hardly ever ride the bike, declaring that it was too powerful even for him, and a few months later he sold it to a drinking pal for £250 and donated the money to a children's charity. While they were here they received the tragic news that their favourite director, Marcel Varnel, had died in a car accident in West Sussex on 13 July. George later said that he had been given another reason never to face a movie camera again—for who would ever replace Varnel?

In September 1947, the Formbys embarked on a six-week tour of Australia—flying there in what he termed "arse-about-face fashion", stopping off in New York, and then Hollywood. George, with his easy-going mien, took an instant dislike to the rowdy, hectic pace of the film capital. He and Beryl were invited to several glitzy parties, one of which was attended by Marlene Dietrich, who told me:

> *He spent most of the evening looking very much like a fish out of water, and his wife never left his side for a minute. He was a friendly man—I would meet him a few*

> *years later, when he was doing a musical in London—but he seemed really scared of this woman, who scowled at him every time a pretty actress stopped by to chat. I remember him in Hollywood, not playing his [ukulele], but singing "Remember Me". But I don't think appearing in American films would have done his career any good. George Formby was too special to appear in anything that was not entirely English.*

From Hollywood, the Formbys flew to Sydney, where within hours of their arrival George was invited to address a film convention. The actual tour kicked off in Melbourne, where on the morning of his first show he was asked by the organisers if he and Beryl would be doing comedy sketches, or just singing. When George replied that they would be doing both, he was told that in order to perform non-musical routines he would have to join Australian Equity—providing his application would be processed within the eight hours before curtain-up, otherwise he might not be allowed to perform at all!

George's initial reaction was to ask Beryl to book seats on the next plane back to London. Then he changed his mind, and with his penchant for saving pennies asked if there would be a discount if he joined the actors' union for just a few weeks, as opposed to the full year. This was not possible, and again he submitted to defeat—until Beryl stepped in, defiant as ever, telling a press-conference, "We won't be submitting to petty bureaucracy, if that's what they're expecting. We don't make this much fuss when your people come to England, so Australian Equity can like us or lump us. We're off to New Zealand in the morning, so that'll give them a couple of days to decide whether they want us or not. We don't care either way!"

The couple arrived in Auckland during the afternoon of 24 September, and there was another row when Beryl was informed that George would not be permitted to sing "When I'm Cleaning Windows" because the New Zealand authorities considered it too vulgar. She told reporters outside the IZB Radio studios, "If he can't do that one, then he won't be doing any of the others. Bugger the lot of them!"

More sparks flew within the studio when Beryl was shown the stations "Not To Be Played" list, for this contained no fewer than twenty Formby songs, many of these his best known. And when she saw the woman assigned to George's interview—a flirtation, pretty blonde named Alice—she declared that he would not be doing the broadcast. After a great deal of unpleasant wrangling, during which the object of everyone's attention sat smoking in a corner, a compromise was reached. "Mr Formby is very tired after his long journey here," Alice told her listeners. "But, Mrs Formby has kindly consented to address the nation this evening, when hopefully we'll be able to play some of Mr Formby's recordings after the ten o'clock watershed!"

Again, Beryl hit the roof, snarling at Alice that she and George always went to bed before ten when overseas. The situation was saved by a technician and his assistant. George was escorted to an adjacent studio, where he taped ten songs which could be edited and aired at the producer's discretion. Beryl likewise recorded her interview—but if she sounds pleasant and friendly towards Alice, according to the studio records she never stopped glaring at her during their conversation which, for the better part only touched on the Formby's quest for food parcels, centering mostly around their fondness for the British royal family, and Beryl's tastes in fashion:

> *Several American women asked me about my clothes and said, "My, what a lovely little suit you have on. We can see that you come from England by the cut of it." I thought that was rather complimentary...I think our hats*

> *too are definitely smarter than anywhere in America. Our hats are mostly trimmed with feathers, now. We have lovely birds of paradise, ospreys, and of course the ostrich feathers which the Queen made so popular. And they do look very smart and becoming...*

The biggest glare of all, witnessed by a reporter covering the visit for one of the Australian dailies, came from Beryl when George walked into the studio—his performance having been recorded without hitch, perhaps because Beryl had not been there—and pronounced, "As usual, once two women start talking, you can't stop 'em!" Beryl was also disapproving as they were leaving the building. Two-hundred fans had gathered in the forecourt to see them off, and when they began chanting his name, George grabbed an empty litter-bin, turned it upside-down to sit on, and reprised the ten songs he had just taped.

Later that evening, George's recital was broadcast on the national network and IZB's switchboard received so many calls that it was repeated the following evening, along with some of Beryl's comments—not just on IZB but on most of the independent stations. At the end of Beryl's conversation with Alice, George had said that he would only be staying in Auckland for two weeks—meaning to say two *days*. This was just as well, for within hours of the broadcast so many offers came flooding in that the Formbys did indeed end up staying in New Zealand for over a fortnight, and as a result of this the Australian tour had to be extended.

Their success however had little effect on their problems with Australian Equity—they were hounded by the union throughout the tour, though the adverse publicity worked in their favour when theatres which had originally turned George down now clamoured for him—enabling the wily Beryl to demand a hefty increase in his fees, which in any case were handed straight back to charity. George refused to perform at any Equity functions after its members picketed a Melbourne cinema where they were showing a short season of his films. The union hit back at him by putting out a statement that, when invited to participate in benefits concerts to raise money for the Food For Britain Fund—rationing was still taking place here—he had denounced his compatriots with a sharp, "Don't talk to me about British workers. They're not even worth the effort!" This was ridiculous propaganda. George had never said such a thing, and a few weeks later the charity thanked the Formbys in the press for the staggering £35,000 they had raised, enabling 75,000 food parcels to be dispatched from Sydney.

In Sydney, in the middle of November, there was also an altercation between George and one of Australia's leading jockeys, Derby Munro. The two should have competed against each other in a one-mile race, with the proceeds going to the Food For Britain Fund, but when George arrived at the course he was informed that the race had been cancelled because of an "insurance matter". He assumed that his tour-promoter had stepped in to prevent the stunt from taking place, as had happened with Basil Dean when George had arranged to climb Blackpool Tower. Munro then swaggered up to him in the bar and bellowed, for all to hear, "Sorry, sport, but I didn't want a little fella like you to get hurt!" George rounded on him and yelled back, "I was good enough to ride in races in England, *sport*, and I'll give you a run for your money any day!" Despite his protestations, however, the course committee refused to reschedule the race, and when the Formbys flew out of Australia a few days later, in view of all the problems they had accounted here must have been asking themselves why they had bothered going there in the first place.

Back in England, George was besieged with more film offers,

all of which he turned down. "When I look back on some of the films I've done in the past, it makes me want to cringe," he said. "I'm afraid the days of the clown are gone. From now on I'm only going to be doing variety."

It was at around this time that the media began speculating about George's health. The reports in the British press about his South African and Australian tours had been second-hand. Now they could observe for themselves that he was looking more than a little peaky, though he laughed this off as fatigue, which was at least partly true. His doctors were treating him for a suspected gastric ulcer, and he had started to have breathing problems on account of his heavy smoking. He had certainly not begun hitting the bottle, as one of the tabloids suggested, though Beryl did nag him into booking himself into the same York psychiatric hospital where she had incarcerated him earlier. This time he stayed for just two weeks, and left when the *doctors* discharged him.

In December, George opened in *Cinderella*, playing his first Buttons to Beryl's Dandini at the Liverpool Empire. The production hit a snag when, two weeks into the run, the chorus went on strike because of Beryl's boasts to the press that the management had acquired George for a "snip"—his usual £1,000 a week plus a share of the profits—whilst most of them were struggling on £20 a week, if they were lucky. George, in a rare outburst which he later claimed had only been a joke, called them "a bunch of communists" and threatened to fire his personal assistant, Harry Scott, for publicly declaring that they were probably justified in taking action. Scott saved him the trouble by storming out of the dressing room, yelling that he was going home to Blackpool. This upset the Formbys more than the potential strike. With mere hours to go before curtain-up, Beryl told the chorus that they could have to pay-rise they so badly needed—without even checking with the management to see if this would be all right!—then she and George climbed into their

Rolls Royce and sped off to Blackpool, where they found Scott drowning his sorrows in the bar at the Opera House. Two hours later, the trio were back in Liverpool, still the best of friends.

Although they hung on to their Cheshire home for the time being, the Formbys were far from happy living out in the sticks, and in June 1949 George bought Linden Lea, a few miles outside Blackpool. The house, close to Fairhaven Lake and overlooking Grannie's bay, set them back £10,000. On 24 September, the couple celebrated their silver wedding anniversary during a long-awaited, much delayed tour of Canada. Indeed, they should have left England at the end of August, but George, with his flair for stepping into the breach, had replaced a laryngitic Donald Peers in *Buttons And Bows*, at Blackpool's Grand Theatre—in one of the revue's tableaux he sang a cod-opera duet with the Manchester-born tenor, Frederick Ferrari.

By now, the Formbys had become reduced to little more than a marriage in name only—not entirely loveless, but more a mutually respectful business partnership. Some of course were willing to swear that it had never been anything else, and that the pair had become institutionalised to each other's ways—Beryl, the bullying *patronne*, and George the underling provider…and that neither would have been capable of surviving without the other. "Darby and Joan precursors to George and Mildred," was how Irene Bevan described them, alluding to the characters from the Seventies' television sit-com.

Cynics too have often wondered why, if George had been dealt so hapless a hand in the marriage stakes, he did not just take advantage of his established reputation and walk out on her. This is not a difficult question to answer. In George's day, especially in Northern England, the adage still held strong that, as one makes one's bed, so one must be prepared to lie on it…one which the Formbys would harness themselves to, forcibly or otherwise, until the end. In 1949 the general public knew nothing of what transpired within the portals of the latest Beryldene. Whenever the Formbys put in an appearance, with Beryl linking George's arm with seemingly genuine affection, gently chiding him whenever they were in proximity of an attractive younger woman, they gave a convincing display of marital harmony...as happened in Ontario whilst cutting their cake, with George still joking that it was not too late to hear the patter of tiny feet!

The couple had flown into the country five days previously. Beryl caused an immediate furore by demanding a four-star hotel instead of the modest guest-house provided by the tour promoter—not an unreasonable request—and George told reporters, with a deadpan expression, that he had been unable to offer the airport porter a tip because he had only £4 17s 6d in English money on him, and he would need this for cigarettes when he arrived home! Beryl had also insisted that he be paid after each engagement in hard cash--$1,000 for each of his twenty shows, and $500 for radio appearances, which she could convert into pounds at a time when the exchange rate was the highest it had been for years.

The entire tour was a sell-out, with most of the tickets snapped up within hours of the box-office opening. Not all of the venues were legitimate theatres, enabling Beryl a better opportunity of bartering with the management. In Saskatoon, George performed at the Kinsmen Club. A rowdy dance-hall frequented by a largely gay clientele who must have wondered what lay in store for them when he strolled on to the stage and opened his set with "Dare Devil Dick". The applause for the song, needless to say, was deafening. In Brandon, he discovered that he had been booked to appear at the local ice-rink—on the same evening the establishment were holding a cattle auction in the car-park. George could not resist opening with "I Wish I Was Back On The Farm", which he sang in an almost incomprehensible Devonshire brogue!

In Toronto, George strolled on to the stage at the Royal Alexandra Theatre, and before launching into his opening number pointed to a middle-aged man sitting in the front row and shouted, "Ee, Walter, is that really you?" The fan was Walter Nicholson, a Blackpool man who had emigrated to Canada some years before with his wife. After the show the couple dined with the Formbys at their hotel, and George explained that this was his first decent meal in two days. He had been so worked up about his first appearance in a Canadian theatre that he had been virtually unable to keep anything down.

Another fan was not so lucky. Dennis Poulter, the son of the Middleham shoemaker who had befriended George thirty years previously, was now living in Canada. He told me:

> *I wrote to George, relating the association of himself and my father, but all I got was a very curt letter from Beryl which more or less suggested that if I wanted to see her husband, tickets were available at the box-office. Needless to say, I didn't bother...*

The show business reporter with the *Toronto Star* readily appreciated the Formby genius:

> *George Formby is one of those fortunate theatrical personalities who can stand in the middle of a bare stage and carry a show on his own—like Jolson, or Cantor, or Gracie Fields. His infectious personality ricochets across the footlights and makes everybody feel at home. Here he was, thousands of miles from his Blackpool in a strange country among strange people who say "street car" instead of "tram", "elevator" instead of "lift", and talk of dimes instead of sixpences. He wasn't even sure they'd know who he was, or if they'd enjoy his songs. Yet*

after that first split second of jitters, it was roses, rose all the way!

George and Beryl arrived back in Liverpool on 25 November. Both looked unwell, having spent much of the crossing in their cabin on the *Empress of France*, suffering from flu. Three weeks later they opened in *Cinderella* at Leeds' Grand Theatre. As had happened earlier in Liverpool, the chorus and bit-parts complained about George's massive salary, and Beryl's demands that he should not be stared at whilst working his way through the wings towards the footlights…an exercise described by his former co-star, Garry Marsh, as "the parting of the Red Sea". George only added fuel to the flames by telling a reporter from *Yorkshire Post*, "I always say the managers should pay everybody what they think they're worth, so don't go blaming everything on me!" Again, a strike was narrowly averted, and for four weeks the show played to packed houses. Then, a few days before Christmas, during the interval, George collapsed in his dressing room. The theatre manager, terrified that he was having a heart attack exacerbated by all the in-house problems, called for an ambulance—but before this arrived, George had been examined by an off-duty doctor who had been sitting in the audience. He diagnosed a simple dose of food-poisoning, and George was driven back to his hotel. The next afternoon he was back on stage for the matinee performance, looking a little green but still bubbling over with the inimitable Formby magic. What the audience did not know was that only minutes before curtain-up his own doctor, summoned from Blackpool, had administered a shot of morphine…to which he would soon, but thankfully only temporarily, become addicted.

On 21 January 1950, unsteady on his feet and his face bloated on account of the drugs he was taking, George entered the Decca studios in London and in single takes re-recorded three of his old hits—"When I'm Cleaning Windows", "Auntie Maggie's Remedy" and "Leaning On A Lamp Post"—along with a new song, Max Miller's "Come Hither With Your Zither". The comic known as "The Cheeky Chappie" stayed with him throughout the session, which would be George's last for almost two years.

Though still only forty-five, in these recordings George sounds much older, though this mellow timbre befits him inordinately well and gives one cause to rue that his health and his heavy schedule did not permit him to spend more time in the studio. On 7 March, he was taken ill again at his home, and this time his doctor *thought* he was suffering from dysentery, a condition which had plagued him off and on since his return from North Africa. In absolute agony, he was rushed to Blackpool's Victoria Hospital, where surgeons performed an emergency appendectomy. Because of his doctor's misdiagnosis he very nearly died, and his daily dose of morphine was increased, affecting his features to such an extent that when he left the hospital, the photographers waiting outside respected Beryl's wishes not to take any pictures—a far cry from what would have happened today. For a month he recuperated aboard the *Lady Beryl*, cruising the Norfolk Broads and spotting a cottage which was for sale at Wroxham—a tiny, quaint residence with a thatched roof and no amenities. The price was just £2,000. George bought it on impulse, then arranged for it to be renovated. Over the next six months he forked out another £2,000 and turned it into a riverside showpiece, but he spent little time there, preferring to recover his investment by renting the place out to friends. By April, he was suitably recovered to top the bill in a Lifeguards Variety Show at Windsor Castle, before virtually the entire royal family. Princess Margaret met him beforehand and asked him to do "Leaning On A Lamp Post". He obliged, dedicating it to her.

One week later, the Formbys embarked on their second tour of

Scandinavia. There were two shows at the Tivoli Gardens in aid of the wartime resistance movement, another at the Bernsbee, and part of George's 90-minute return-visit concert at Nejesfaltet was televised. While in Stockholm he and Beryl were courted by the film director, Alf Sjoberg (1903-80), whose screen version of August Strindberg's novel, *Froken Julie*, had recently been released to huge critical acclaim—the following year it would be awarded the Grand Prix at the Cannes Film Festival.

Sjoberg's intention was to make a film in Sweden with each scene shot twice—in English, then Swedish—teaming George with Anita Bjork, the voluptuous blonde star of *Froken Julie*. The Formbys were invited to sit through a private screening of the un-subtitled film, which must have been grim. Bjork (1923-2012) was more appealing to the eye than *any* of George's previous leading ladies, but the stark reality of this film frightened the life out of him—it ends with Miss Julie grabbing her lover's razor and slashing her throat! Beryl was extremely apprehensive about leaving her husband alone with an actress who also, inexplicably, had taken a shine to him. The Formbys, Sjoberg and Bjork spent several days discussing the project, which would follow a similar theme to Marcel Carné's *Les Enfants du Paradis*, made in 1945 and generally regarded as the greatest French film of all time.

Sjoberg had observed the immense similarities between the type of character George had played in most of his films, and Carné's tragic mime Baptiste, immortalised by Jean-Louis Barrault. George's role in the new film was therefore to be a largely silent one, though his singing voice would be used over the opening-closing credits. George called Eddie Latta from Stockholm and commissioned him to write two songs, one which would see him duetting with Bjork, and even made a screen-test. This however was quickly consigned to a vault after Beryl put a very firm damper on the proceedings…having discovered that the secret of Sjoberg's success in producing atmospheric dramas and sparkling comedies was that outsiders were never allowed on to the set, no matter who they were. The next morning, the Formbys returned to London.

In May 1950, Beryl received a cable from a Canadian entrepreneur, inviting George to participate in a gala performance at Toronto's Maple Leaf Gardens, in aid of the Winnipeg Flood Relief Fund. The other artistes had all agreed to pay their own expenses, and Beryl saw no problem with this, though she was initially far from happy with George travelling such a long way for a one-off engagement, particularly as he had been so unwell of late. "Better that I send you a cheque to cover what George might have earned," she cabled back. The sponsors, however, would not take No for an answer for they, like George's transatlantic record companies, stood to make a lot of money out of his appearance. Beryl swallowed the bait when told that the entire three-hour show would be broadcast to 40 million listeners on 730 radio stations right across the North American continent—ironically, on 26 May, George's forty-sixth birthday—and that, in view of this, Decca Canada and Canadian Columbia were anticipating a sudden rush for George's records.

George performed just six songs, before a hypercritical audience of 20,000, and caused a sensation. He walked on to the stage to chants of "Happy Birthday", and afterwards he and Beryl were presented with a huge horse-shoe of one-thousand red roses...which they sold for a dollar each to fans, the money augmenting the £30,000 already raised by the event.

The next day, George was inundated with offers to tour the United States, including $10,000 for an eight-day stint in Chicago, and $5,000 for a single performance at the pantheon of American entertainment, New York's Carnegie Hall. Beryl was all for accepting, but this time George put his foot down. The "Yanks", he declared, would never understand him—they would laugh *at* him, not with him. He did agree to a compromise: a full-length tour of Canada at the end of the year.

The summer of 1950 was spent quietly at home. Between recurring bouts of dysentery and chronic depression George worked but little—a handful of variety engagements, and the switching on of Morecambe's illuminations. There were two more trips to the hospital in York and several discreet visits to Dublin where the Formbys hoped to find a property. "I'm sick to death of the tax-man robbing me of ninety per cent of earnings," George complained to a reporter who trailed them to an estate agent's office. For this reason, he furthered, he and Beryl would not be appearing in pantomime this year.

There was a little light relief, not to mention what George called "handbags at fifty paces", on 4 August when he participated in the second "Petit Prix"—the Blackpool theatrical set's annual one-mile charity horse race between Squires Gate and St Annes. Over 5,000 holidaymakers jostled along the promenade to watch the event, whose "jockeys" included the handlebar-moustached comic Jimmy Edwards, Terry-Thomas, and that other infamous exponent of the ukulele, Tessie O'Shea.

The trouble began when Terry-Thomas complained that George should not be allowed in the race because he had once been a professional jockey, and as such would have an advantage over everyone else. At this, "Two-Ton" Tessie, a great admirer of George, yelled that she was hoping that Terry-Thomas' mount would throw him so that *he* would be barred from the race for having a broken neck! There then followed a fierce argument between Jimmy Edwards and the actor-stooge, Jerry Desmonde, a pal of Terry-Thomas, and who had won the race the previous year. Edwards' horse, Desmonde declared, was too good for him—he should be riding an ass! Upon this, the comic dismounted and strode off in a huff, leaving his horse in the middle of the prom. A few minutes later the race took place, with

George emerging victor by eight lengths—Desmonde coming last. Then the squabbling resumed...until Beryl silenced everyone by bellowing, "Grow up, for heaven's sake. The whole damn lot of you are worse than a load of bloody schoolkids!"

At the end of August, George and Beryl boarded the *Empress of France* for Montreal, and the first leg of their Canadian tour—seven weeks which would be extended to ten, mostly one-off shows in different towns and cities—for which George was paid up to $4,000 a time, often with a heavy percentage of the profits. Asked *why* he had elected to do one-night stands at selected venues, he cracked, "Because most of the time I can only stand one night in the flipping place!"

At one show, the couple were presented with traditional, multi-striped Hudson Bay coats, and George was given a ten-gallon Stetson to match the one he had at home. After another show, on Vancouver Island, a Kwakiutl Indian chief handed Beryl a miniature totem-pole fertility symbol!

George was inundated with offers to do radio shows, but accepted only one—a short spot on Norm Pringle's *Midnight Merry-go-Round* in Alberta, where he sand the number most requested by Canadian fans, "It's No Use Looking At Me". George had introduced this back in 1934, and one can well imagine him having a crack at the Bard and sending up Hamlet:

> *I got rather muddled when I dressed for the part,*
> *The audience were full of grins.*
> *I shouted out, "Odds-boddikins!"...*
> *I was feeling a draught around my anatomy,*
> *I must have looked the sight of sights!*
> *I shouted, "Ee, turn out the lights!"*
> *'Cause I'd only got one leg in me tights...*

In all, the tour earned George around $200,000, of which $68,000 was paid back in Canadian taxes, and some 90 per cent of the balance collected by the British Inland Revenue. As he had been working almost exclusively for charity, George was well justified in telling reporters, upon his return to England, "That's it. So long as this government keeps bleeding me dry, I shan't be in much of a hurry to work again!"

For almost six months, barring a charity show in Dublin in February 1951, George was as good as his word, and many fans truly believed they had seen the last of him. Much of this time was spent on the Norfolk Broads, where the *Lady Beryl* was moored at Potter Heigham, between Great Yarmouth and Hoveton. Here, his eccentricities—and some might say roguish fondness for making a fast buck out of absolutely any situation—reached a new level. After he had guided a fellow yachtsman through a tricky bridge, the had asked for his autograph and joked that if George ever gave up the stage, then at least he would be able to get a job as a lock-keeper. The next day, George put on a cap and dark glasses so that no one would recognise him, and began charging for his services! It has to be said, however, that he gave every penny of his "salary" to a local children's hospital.

Then, just as he was beginning to enjoy his "dotage"—at the age of forty-seven—he received an offer to appear in his very first West End musical, a wholly unexpected volte-face which would see him catapulted back into the limelight after almost five years in the virtual wilderness.

October 1946: a smiling George and Beryl arrive in South Africa. The smiles would not last long.

The picture, said by the Formbys to have been their favourite, sent to friends at Christmas 1950

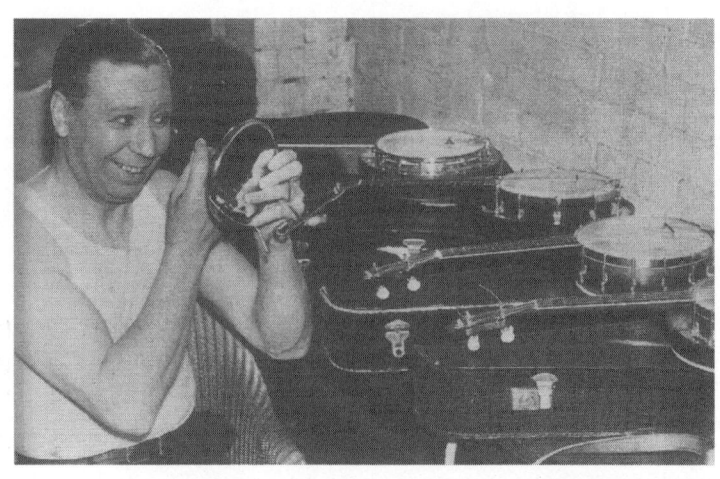

Two shots of George c.1950, preparing for a show in his Spartan dressing-room (GFS)

Eight:
Like The Big Pots Do!

"It wasn't the songs, so much as how George Formby sang them. He could have an audience in the palm of his hand more quickly than any other entertainer I've ever seen." Harry Scott, personal assistant.

Brewster's Millions had a chequered history. Based on the novel by George Barr-McCutcheon, it had been adapted for the stage by the author and Winchell Smith, and first produced in 1907. Jack Buchanan had starred in the 1935 British film version, and ten years later there had been a Hollywood remake with Dennis O'Keefe. More recently the rights had been acquired by Emile Littler—famed for his recent London production of *Annie Get Your Gun*—who had commissioned a libretto from Eric Maschwitz, renowned for his screenplays for *Balalaika* and *Goodbye Mr Chips*.

Both Littler and Maschwitz later said that the musical version of the story of Percy Piggott, the man who had to dispense with one fortune in order to inherit an even bigger legacy, had not been created with any specific actor in mind—though it had not taken them long to figure out that the role could have been tailor-made for George Formby. Beryl, on the other hand, began telling everyone that she had been wanting George to appear in the *film* version of *Brewster's Millions* for twenty years. Having been disappointed with the play and the Buchanan film, she told the press, she was certain that George would have turned it into his biggest hit ever, if only one of the better directors she had approached had listened. Wishful thinking, most certainly, it did not take her long to negotiate a pre-contract with Littler—*before* telling George, who fortunately would be just as excited about the project as she was.

It was only after the actual contract had been argued over and signed—and the title changed to *Zip Goes A Million*—that both George and Beryl began having serious misgivings about what they were letting themselves in for. The West End of London, with the exception of the Palladium, had never been really Formby-friendly, and George had done himself few favours by once denouncing its producers and clientele as, "A bunch of snobs who know nowt about seal life." Emile Littler reminded himself of this comment before rehearsals got under way, adding that he was taking an enormous risk by staging a musical at the imposing Palace Theatre with a Northern comedian playing the lead...and that as such, George should not anticipate the £1,000 a week he had been paid in the past for his pantomimes. For once, Beryl was justified in jumping down the producer's throat. Littler was told that the so-called "common" North had just as much talent as anywhere else in England, if not more, and that if he could not pay George what she and every other producer in the country obviously thought he was worth, the he would be quite happy to stick with pantomimes. Littler knew that she was right, and George's salary was set at an unprecedented £1,500 a week plus a share of the box-office.

Eric Maschwitz's libretto, scored by George Posford—who had also worked with him on *Balalaika*—differed from the original play in that it was set in the United States. Percy Piggot, a Newton-le-Willows window cleaner—a last minute change of occupation, Maschwitz later confessed—inherits £1 million from his uncle in Piggotsville, Texas. There is a coda attached to the old man's will: Percy must spend every last cent of this within four months in order to inherit another $7 million—moreover, he must not divulge to anyone why he is doing this, especially his sweetheart Sally, who was played by Australian musical-comedy star, Sara Gregory. The other leads were Wallace Eaton, Ward Donovan and Barbara Perry—the latter two American, because Maschwitz said he wanted to give the play an "authentic feel". George therefore invests his windfall in a musical comedy, *The Garter Girl*, assuming this will be a failure. Furthermore he invests money in the stock market, and bests vast amounts of money on horses—only succeeding with each enterprise, despite the events of a crooked banker to swindle him. In the end, as had happened in his films, he comes out on top and ends up with the girl. The piece contained several fine songs, four of which constituted George's penultimate visit to the recording studio on 5 November 1951, while that same evening he performed them on the BBC Light Programme's *Henry Hall's Guest Night* before dashing off to the theatre. Three were new, but Gifford and Cliffe's "The Pleasure Cruise" had been in his repertoire since 1935.

As George was extremely apprehensive about opening in London with such a vast change of direction, *Zip Goes A Million* premiered at the Coventry Hippodrome on 4 September…where there were just as many backstage squabbles as there had been on the sets of his films.

Emile Littler, himself gay, objected virulently to the middle-aged Wallace Eaton's pursuit of the rough-trade male prostitutes who often hung around the stage-door, and who were sometimes sneaked into the actor's dressing room. When Eaton became amorously interested in the handsome, 35-year-old Ward Donovan, the show's adagio dancer, Little threatened to fire him unless he behaved himself. Beryl also fell for Donovan, who despite his two marriages—the latter to comedienne Phyllis Diller, who wrote about his "antics" in her autobiography, *Like A Lampshade In A Whorehouse*—was only ever interested in men. Thus while Donovan snubbed both Beryl's and Eaton's advances, both compromised by getting their lovers to meet them in a local pub—though by the time the production hit the West End of London, Littler actually began *accompanying* Eaton and Donovan to well-known pick-up spots around Piccadilly and Waterloo, frequented by the so-called "Dilly Boys".

The production's most threatening dilemma was at the time said to have been instigated by the second female lead, Barbara Perry, a voluptuous but volatile 28-year-old blonde already known to British audiences. Having played bit-parts and walk-ons in several Hollywood films, she had appeared on the London stage—perhaps most noticeably in *Starlight Roof* with Pat Kirkwood. It is now known, however, that most of the backstage problems were instigated by Emile Littler, by Perry's mother who chaperoned her everywhere—and by Beryl.

Littler had originally wanted Perry to play the part of sally, for which he had agreed a salary of £100 a week. However, when he realised before rehearsals got under way that Sara Gregory was by far the better singer, she was promoted on the proviso that she retain her salary of around £50 a week, whilst Perry was expected to take a pay-cut! Not unexpectedly, her mother objected to this, but rather than tell her the truth, Littler informed Mrs Perry that her daughter had been moved down the cast because she was not a member of Equity. This had not hindered her in the past, for Barbara was a fully paid-up member of the Variety Artists' Federation and been warned by Littler that *if* she joined Equity, she would be fired from the production!

Simon Blumenfeld—writing for *The Stage*, and one of the most respected journalists in show business who rarely had a bad word to say about anyone—told me:

> *Emile Littler was an absolute martinet, a thoroughly nasty piece of work who would stop at nothing to get his own way. He would do this sort of thing often—hire someone for a certain fee, then try to get rid of them once*

> he'd found someone else who could do the job for less money. Hardly anybody in show business liked him, yet working for him was such a bonus because his productions were always so phenomenally successful.

Barbara Perry's mother had done her homework as far as the Formbys were concerned. When Beryl quietly pointed out that it was the "done thing" for visiting thespians to temporarily join the actors' union, Mrs Perry pointed accusingly at George and levelled, "*He* didn't, when he went to Australia!" Henceforth, he and Beryl would publicly declare that the dispute between Perry and Equity had nothing to do with them—then in true Machiavellian style, whilst being nice to her face they worked behind the scenes to ensure that the rest of the cast snubbed her, and even persuaded Equity to instruct its members to disrupt or boycott rehearsals. "It seemed a bit daft, sending somebody to Coventry when they were there already, but it had to be done," George later said.

Barbara Perry submitted to the pressure. Only hours before the dress-rehearsal she handed Eric Maschwitz a receipt which proved she had joined Equity. This was shown to the press, though Perry herself refused to speak to reporters. Half a century later, she broke her silence to Peter Holland and Dennis Taylor of the George Formby Society. And, *still* unaware of the Formbys' machinations, she recalled them with great reverence:

> *I've got to tell you the nice things about Beryl because you'll hear plenty of the other. I was the oldest virgin in captivity, so she trusted me, though the fact that she took me under her wing was the worst thing that could have happened so far as the rest of the cast were concerned. She told me, "You know, people don't like me. They're inclined to say that North Country women are dumb, and*

> *I made up my mind years ago to show them that North Country women are smarter than any men in the business." When she told me that, tears came to my eyes. As for George, he had magnetism, a charm which never stopped. I only saw one of his films, No Limit. I never saw his vaudeville act, so I can only judge him on that one show. But to me he was a lovely actor.*

Perry had, however, nurtured one big regret:

> *I'd had rave reviews, everybody loved my dancing. I got second reviews to George even though I couldn't sing a song with him. That was terrible. There could at least have been a reprise of "Ordinary People" somewhere in the show...*

Barbara Perry would find herself persistently rubbed up the wrong way throughout the run of the play. Though undoubtedly a talented all-rounder, this *was* George's triumph. Audiences were interested *only* in him, so much so that sometimes when he was not on the stage they chatted noisily and ignored whatever else was happening. Declaring the plot secondary to the songs and that infectious Formby grin, the *Coventry Evening Telegraph* dubbed him, "The one-man pantomime that never palls." Indeed, every time George produced his ukulele—as in his films, at the silliest or most inopportune moment—the audience became hysterical, so much so that he contributed an additional line to the script which he repeated every evening—"Ee, you're not supposed to do *that*. You're holding up the play!" And, milking the situation for all it was worth—it is no understatement that George Formby was having a similar effect on his admittedly smaller fan base as the Beatles would have on their, in the next decade—Emile Littler made room for more Formby songs by cutting some of the other parts, including Barbara Perry's.

By the time *Zip Goes A Million* reached the Manchester Palace at the end of the month—the next stop before London—Perry's part had been so reduced, on top of hardly any of the cast speaking to her, that she was close to throwing in the towel. Matters were made far worse when the BBC announced that they were to broadcast excerpts from the first night—Beryl "persuaded" the producer to record only George's numbers, and was not surprised when he informed her that this had been his intention in any case. After the show, Perry marched into Emile Littler's office and demanded that he release her from her contract. This was not possible, and on 20 October the played opened in London.

Because this was ostensibly a showcase for George's spellbinding on-stage antics, hit-songs and lousy jokes, critics who were non-fans and had never fully understood his appeal did not know what to make of a middle-aged man—now portly, and looking older than he actually was—whose every gesture brought him screams of approval and endless standing ovations. *The Times* did not like him at all, declaring that he lacked any vestige of finesse, and Kenneth Tynan positively loathed the way that, in his opinion, a tedious plot had been woven around George's lack-lustre personality:

> *It is only when the music stops that I start raising provisos like a palisade around my liking for him. I cannot laugh as he fidgets, gapes and fusses flat-footed across the stage...and I am unable to accept the theory that banality or catchphrase acquires wit or philosophy when delivered in a North Country accent. Simplicity and unaffectedness can be carried to extremes. Mr Formby works with what Henry James called "great economy of means and—oh—effect".*

George pretended not to be offended by Tynan's snooty, scathing attack on his roots, but he was deeply hurt. Even Cecil Wilson's otherwise enthusiastic euphemism in the *Daily Mail*, that he was "Lancashire hot-pot served on a silver platter" did not detract from the fact that, from these people's point of view, he would never be anything but common. "I wish I'd have stayed in bloody Manchester," he told Gracie Fields over the phone. "At least up there folk know what I'm all about!"

Neither was George impressed when he read in the press that Oscar Hammerstein had called him "Britain's most characteristic comedian"...Hammerstein later confessed that he had never heard of him until earlier in the week, and that he had only attended one of the performances because Emile Littler had persuaded him to do so—hoping that the great man might "see his way" into writing something for George which would tempt him into crossing the Atlantic. "If that's his game, he's just wasting his time," was George's response.

Beryl also left herself wide open to sarcastic criticism when she compiled the notes for the second edition of the *Zip Goes A Million* programme. Writing in the third person, she spoke of how she and George had met in Castleford, how devoted they were towards each other, how happy their marriage had always been. Critics already aware of Beryl's well-intentioned machinations must have cringed when reading such ace quotes as, "The general question of all concerned is that his wife is conscientiously carrying out a good job," and, "As an established actress in her own right, Beryl Formby possesses her own vivid personality, on stage and off." She was most criticised for stating that *she* had written some of George's songs, and for including what she said was the play's best review: "The zippiest, snappiest and happiest musical comedy that's happened in a long while!"...for this had come not from a show business column, but from the *Weekly Sporting Review*!

What most of the critics thought or said was of course immaterial. Not one performance of *Zip Goes A Million* played to a less than capacity house, though after the first few weeks George's own enthusiasm for the production started to wane. Emile Littler had told him to expect a very long run, and this he did not want. He had proved the cynics and the "anti-North brigade" wrong by triumphing in the West End, and he now wanted his life to resume normality, at least as far as his failing health would allow.

The biggest threat of all, hanging over George's head like the Sword of Damocles, *was* his state of health, one aspect which Emile Littler had apparently chosen to ignore whilst attempting to insure George for the show. Prior to rehearsals, George had undergone a medical examination and been pronounced unfit to perform in a production which, having set Littler back a cool £40,000 before the first curtain-up, would *have* to have a long run in order for him to recover his investment. George had shrugged at this, genuinely believing that the show would prove a flop and that in next to no time he would be heading home, or back to the *Lady Beryl,* on the Norfolk Broads. Littler too had chosen to break the law by completely ignoring the insurance report and hoping for the best.

The best was not to be. Early in April 1952, on the Thursday before *Zip Goes A Million* broke off for the Easter weekend, the Formbys set off for Potter Heigham. George was driving. That morning he had made up his mind to tell Emile Littler that, come Whitsuntide, he would be dropping out of the production—this would give the producer ample time to find a replacement. The couple were twenty miles outside London when George felt a sudden bolt of pain shoot through his chest. Nevertheless he still managed to bring the car to a halt at the side of the road before passing out. Beryl flagged down a motorist, and between them they moved George into the passenger seat. However, instead of calling for an ambulance, Beryl drove back to London, put George to bed in their flat, and summoned a doctor. Why on earth *he* did not admit George to a hospital is not known: all he did was inform Beryl that George was displaying the symptoms of a duodenal ulcer, and advise her to get him to drink plenty of milk.

The show, of course, had to go on. Absolutely no statement was given as to why George would not be returning to the Palace Theatre. All the seats for the next two weeks' performances had been sold, and Emile Littler announced that there would be no refunds. George's understudy, Geoffrey Piddock, made a valiant attempt to bridge the gap. He proved hopeless in the role of Percy Piggott, though in retrospect it is extremely difficult to imagine *anyone* stepping into George's shoes, and he was eventually replaced by Reg Dixon, the Coventry-born comedian who ate least restored a little life and dignity to the part.

Dixon would carry the show to the end of its London run. It closed in February 1953 after 544 performances, toured for two years, and finally ground to a halt with Charlie Chester in the coveted but by then over-worked role of Percy Piggott.

Meanwhile, an interview which George had given to a reporter from the *Sunday People* halfway through the Palace run—ostensibly to complain about all the begging letters he was being pestered with, many of these from his own family—now surfaced, giving many people who knew nothing about his health problems cause to believe that he had abandoned *Zip Goes A Million* because of an argument over his salary. If this particular interview was anything to go by, George was not just interested in making money, he was obsessed by it. The interviewee, of course, had been Beryl:

> *The gossips forget our old friend the income-tax man. He stung me for nearly £800,000 during the war years, even*

though I spent most of that time entertaining the troops all over the world for £10 a week, singing in shelters and war factories. Nowadays, with surtax higher than Mount Everest, I have to earn a pound before I can afford two packets of potato crisps, and seven more for a packet of fags! Even when I earned $100,000 for Britain during my Canada tours, all I had left after tax and expenses was $800...I think I can claim to have made a lot of people happy, and in return they made me both happy and rich. Their appreciation totted up to around £84,000 a year...I have made two pictures a year—that's £50,000. My percentage of the takings added another £10,000. I earned more than £500 a week in pantomime—the BBC and commercial radio forked up another £8,000. If you add on my income from gramophone records and "George Formby" ukuleles it makes a grand—and I do mean grand—total of £84,000. On top of all the rest, I earned about £20,000 a year for charity...unfortunately, today I am taxed at 19s 6d for every pound I give to charity, which makes it difficult. I hope the begging-letter merchants will take note of that. Last week they asked me for a cool £4,000.

It took George's doctor an incredible *five days* to realise that something was seriously wrong, and that he had in fact suffered a coronary. On 4 May 1952 he was admitted to the London Clinic where he was tended by the King's former physician, Sir Horace Evans (George VI had died in the February), who told him that he was lucky to be alive. Here, George was finally weaned off his morphine addiction, and when Beryl issued a public statement explaining to George's fans *why* he had been forced to drop out of *Zip Goes A Million*, over the next few days he received thousands of get-well messages and cards, including several from the royal family. Beryl kept unwelcome visitors—members of George's family, reporters, and press-photographers—at bay. George once again announced his retirement...not that anyone believed him. On 4 June, having spent almost nine weeks in hospital, George returned to his Fairhaven home. Suffering from acute depression, his features bloated once more, he insisted upon inviting old pal Sylvia for tea. This interview was a grim one, for by and large he was only interested in speaking about his death, which he believed to be imminent, and his tax problems:

> *The doctor will only let me walk to the garden gate and back once a day. It'll be nine or twelve months before—if—I'm right. Still, I've had a grand life and I'm sorry it's had to end like this. I've topped the bill for nearly thirty years and I hate to have to give up now. But what can you do? We're not wealthy, but we're all right. We've enough to live on. We're also thinking about selling this house. We've never spent much time here, and now there doesn't seem to be any point in keeping it on.*

Two evenings later, George and Beryl turned up at Max Wall's Blackpool Palace Theatre revue, but so as not to create too much of a fuss watched the show from the wings. The manager, however, asked George if he would not mind stepping on to the stage, just to surprise the audience and prove to everyone that he was back in circulation. George obliged—halfway through Wall's patter—and as he made his entrance, leaning heavily on Beryl's arm, the orchestra struck up "Chinese Laundry Blues". He looked so ill that at first many people failed to recognise him—but when he approached the microphone and muttered, "Ee, this *is* a grand tonic!" the audience went mad.

During George's illness, the Formbys' other house in Cheshire had been put on the market, and Ben Henry had bought another on their behalf—one of several they had viewed several months previously. The move, George declared, would get him away from the taxman, besides which he now wanted to breed horses. Aldon was a 24-roomed mansion near Foxrock, just outside Dublin, originally been built as a club but for refused a liquor licence. George paid £20,000 for it, and like the others it was rebaptised Beryldene.

The Formbys would spend little time in Ireland. Away from his beloved Lancashire, George was like the proverbial fish out of water. By January 1953 *this* house would have been put up for sale, along with the one in Fairhaven, enabling George to buy a six-roomed residence but a stone's throw from the latter. It was an astute move. The house, Cintra, belonged to the popular tenor, Joseph Locke, a massive star in Britain at this time, but who was experiencing severe financial difficulties and needed the money fast. Soon afterwards he would flee England for tax evasion. Beryl therefore did not have to bargain too strongly to get Locke to drop the price to just £15,000—though only on condition that if George ever sold the place, he would be able to buy it back at the same price—*if* he had any money! The papers would be signed on 22 February. This particular Beryldene would remain George's favourite, the one within whose walls he would achieve eventual peace of mind.

In the middle of September 1952 there was another drama when George choked on a fish-bone which pierced and became lodged in his oesophagus. He was taken to Blackpool's Victoria Hospital in considerable pain, but the surgeons were terrified of operating on him because of his heart condition. After forty-eight hours and with the threat of serious infection, they were left with no choice. It took him several hours to come out of the anaesthetic, and his first visitors were Beryl and Sylvia. His first words, Silvia said, were, "Ee, everything seems to happen to me.

And they *still* can't keep a good man down!" He was right. The doctors told him he would have to stay in hospital for at least a week, but he discharged himself after just four days because, he said, he had a "pressing engagement"—judging a beauty contest at the Middleton Towers holiday camp, in Morecambe!

In March 1953, the Formbys were spotted by the Michael Walsh of the *Daily Express*, at what was for them an unusual location—a West End nightclub where they were offering moral support to an obscure comic named Arthur Riscoe, making his cabaret debut. Walsh observed how George had put on weight, but that he looked sun-tanned and healthy. He told the journalist, "I'm going to plunge in and work again. I think I can make it in another musical. The winter in Dublin did it—eating Irish steak and drinking Scotch. My doctor's orders were a daily ration of six doubles and a single. Relaxes the arteries, they say!"

In April, looking far from well but claiming that his doctor had okayed him to travel, George and Beryl flew to Bulawayo in Southern Rhodesia, for a series of seventeen shows which formed part of the Rhodes Centenary Exhibition. Each evening he opened the show with "In The Congo" or "Wunga Bunga Boo", which in today's politically correct climate he would never have got away with. In what may only be regarded as an act of devilment—if not sheer folly, bearing in mind how their last visit to South Africa had concluded—they took a few days off to fly to Johannesburg, then on to Palmietfontaine, where George gave an impromptu concert on the tarmac before taking a 15-minute "pleasure trip" in the country's very first jet. Then it was back to Bulawayo, where the Formbys stayed at the home of the Prime Minister, Sir Godfrey Huggins.

At the end of August, George opened at Southport's Garrick Theatre, billed as "A Formby Come-Back Special". A few weeks later, he switched on the Blackpool Illuminations—kissing Beryl on the cheek after crooning "Leaning On A Lamp Post" to her, he told the crowd, "It's the old woman's birthday today. Twenty-one summers, but I won't tell you how many winters!" Beryl looked far from pleased.

In October, after a great deal of wrestling with his "inner demons", as he called them—and after consulting Sir Horace Evans—George returned to the West End. There had been talk of his replacing Reg Dixon in *Zip Goes A Million*, still raking in the money but now only playing to 75 per cent audiences...but in George's eyes, a jinxed piece all the same. He had therefore opted for his only "lucky" London theatre, the Palladium, and opened in Val Parnell's revue, *Fun And The Fair*. With him were Terry-Thomas, the Deep River Boys, Audrey Jeans, and Billy Cotton and his Band. Parnell, who had never been a Formby fan—George did not like him at all—had initially insisted as one of the terms of the contract that George to come up with a set of brand new songs. George, however, was less interested in learning new material than he was in giving fans what they really wanted—the standards he had made his own—and Parnell gave in. Having Formby in any revue was enough to guarantee standing-room only—besides which, Beryl had confided in him that these performances might well be her husband's last.

Strictly speaking, *Fun And The Fair* had not started out as a Formby vehicle. It had originally been put together by producer Charles Henry to showcase the then limited talents of Terry-Thomas. Though their names appeared side by side and in same-sized letters on the playbills, Terry-Thomas was being paid £1,400 a week—£400 more than George—and he was closing the show. Beryl had complained about this to the producer during rehearsals, for George's sketches—one a spoof on the television series, *What's My Line?*—were weak, and she did not believe that the seven numbers he had chosen for his solo spot would be sufficient to placate his fans. In fact, it was only when the curtain fell on what the audience took to be the close of the first half that the real magic began. The first time this happened, an announcement over the tannoy urged the audience, "Ladies and gentlemen, you are requested to keep your seats, please!" Then curtain then rose on a pitch-black stage, and a few seconds later a spotlight picked out a small couch upon which were three ukuleles, and the orchestra struck up "Chinese Laundry Blues" as George materialised, stage-left. This was Beryl's *coup de grace*…not seven, as arranged, but fifteen songs, beginning with "I Wonder Who's Under Her Balcony Now?", each one greeted with hysterical cheers and the stomping of feet. "He's back!" screamed the headline in the *Sunday Express*, whilst the feature added, "George Formby is back, in good health and spirit. Last night at the premiere we were one big happy family rejoicing at the return of the prodigal!"

Terry-Thomas, who like Audrey Jeans had risen to prominence in *Piccadilly Hayride*, the 1946 Sid Field extravaganza, was not amused:

> *I closed the show with my impression of a sergeant-major impersonating Noel Coward. The trouble was, George Formby put the audience in a certain mood which made them non-receptive to whatever followed…Even though the closing act was the star spot, I felt on this occasion that being there was an anti-climax. I told Charles Henry, "George Formby is really the star of the show. He should go on last. Put him where he belongs and make it easier for me." But Charles liked my work and wasn't keen on Formby's. "What?" he said, "Put him on last with all those fucking awful parrot stories?"*

In fact, Terry-Thomas had asked for George to be *removed* from

George from the show because he was stealing all his thunder, and when Henry refused, the comic threatened to take up the matter with Equity—not that they could have done anything. This brought a sharp response from Beryl, who cornered Terry-Thomas in his dressing room and told him, "It's no use complaining to the union. The fans have clearly decided who *they* prefer. So why not just pack your bags and go to America? They're used to your brand of rubbish over there!"

The Palladium run should have lasted six weeks, but on account of George's popularity was extended to nine. It was also a tremendous triumph of mind over matter for him. For the first time since his debut in 1921 he had started to suffer from stage fright, and between performances often endured lengthy bouts of depression, aggravated by recurrent stomach problems, themselves brought on by worrying about his heart condition.

Towards the end of 1953, on the strength of his *What's My Line?* Skit, George made two appearances on the programme—first as the week's mystery guest, then replacing the indisposed Gilbert Harding in the Christmas edition. The latter reunited him with Pat Kirkwood, his co-star from *Come On George* who later sympathised with him for having to tolerate Beryl's interference—mouthing the responses to his questions—in the Shepherd's Bush television studio in full view of the contestants and audience. To be honest, he should never have been asked to do the show. Gilbert Harding was noted for his acerbic, sometimes cruel sense of humour, and George was far too naïve to realise that the other team members were taking him for a ride, certainly whilst the programme was on air. He did have a run-in off the set with regular panelist Lady Isabel Barnet, whom he accused of looking down her nose at him, and who he learned had been the one demanding that he not be allowed to crack any gags because she had always found them, and him, "decidedly crude".

For six months George did virtually nothing. His annual pantomime—*Dick Whittington* yet again, this time in Manchester—had been cancelled after his doctor had warned him that the strain might prove fatal, and his place had been taken by the *PC 49* actor, Brian Reece. In February, George's car was involved in an accident on the Great North Road, just outside Peterborough. Overtaking a lorry on a bend, he crashed into the side of an oncoming saloon. No one was injured, but the other car was a write-off. The police were summoned but the driver, Owen Watling, did not press charges when George agreed to buy him a new car. Had the matter gone to court, George would almost certainly have had his licence take from him, for he clearly should not have been driving in his fragile state of health. "He's been so ill, I'd feel awful adding to the poor man's problems," Aveling told reporters, whilst George quipped, "Oh, well. I suppose it was just one of those sings, as they say I the song!"

The accident affected George badly. Within the week, without even bothering to have it repaired, he had sold his car and even talked about *burning* his driving licence—until Beryl persuaded him otherwise and, at the end of May, he bought another Rolls Royce. The first time he took it out, he parked it opposite Blackpool Tower and was walking away when another vehicle backed into it—not only this, the driver stuck his head out of the window, yelled an obscenity and drove off. George took the man's number, and he was later arrested and fined.

During the first half of 1954 there were a few shows here and there, the rejection of another film script, and a cancelled recording session with His Master's Voice. He also turned down another season in the West End, choosing instead a summer show in Blackpool where he shared top-billing with Joseph Locke—though Beryl insisted that the title of the revue should be named after George's catchphrase and not after one of the tenor's songs, as Locke had wanted.

Turned Out Nice Again, produced by Jack Taylor and premiered at the recently refurbished Hippodrome on 25 June, should have run for thirteen weeks. It closed after just six when George again fell ill with dysentery and depression. This time, his doctors *ordered* him to take things easy. George was pushing himself so hard that he was slowly but surely killing himself.

Again, George announced his retirement, and a few days after pulling out of the show he and Beryl drove down to Wroxham, where over the next few months they moved between their cottage and long, relaxing outings on the *Lady Beryl*. It was at Heronby, on the August Bank Holiday Monday, that the Formbys organised a tea-party for the Fred and Kathleen Howson, friends who were holidaying on the Norfolk Broads. Fred was general manager of a motor firm in Penwortham, near Preston, where Formbys had been taking their cars to be serviced for the past twenty years. George had become particularly fond of the Howsons' daughter, Pat, always calling her his "sweetheart" and occasionally taking her little gifts. Now, the little girl had blossomed into a pretty, vivacious brunette, still unattached at twenty-nine, and working as a schoolteacher. And that afternoon in Wroxham—right under Beryl's nose—George promptly fell in love with her, though it would take him a little longer to actually *do* anything about his feelings.

Meanwhile, incapable of just sitting around twiddling his thumbs—"I've got to pick up my knitting again," he told Sylvia, using the expression he had borrowed from Gracie Fields. "Otherwise, what else have I got to do with my time?"—George made his "comeback" on New Year's Eve, performing a medley of his hits on *Ask Pickles*. This was followed, on 9 January 1955, by a longer television slot headlining the BBC's *Top Of The Town*. He performed two sketches, sang "The Pleasure Cruise" from *Zip Goes A Million*, and duetted—very much against his will—with terry-Thomas on "Leaning On A Lamp Post".

The broadcast was so popular that George was booked for the programme's 20 February edition, along with singing star Eve Boswell. This had to be cancelled on account of the severe winter, when six-foot snowdrifts prevented the Formbys from leaving their home.

At the beginning of March, George and Beryl made their second (official, though technically it was their third) trip to South Africa for a series of engagements which would raise £15,000 for the National Cancer Fund. Daniel Francois Malan, the country's prime minister since 1948 and Beryl's sworn enemy, had recently resigned, so she was hoping that this extended visit would prove trouble-free.

Once again, the Formbys were instructed not to perform in the townships at exclusively black venues, though this time Beryl got around the problem a little more diplomatically—telling the private secretary of Malan's equally austere, whites-only pulpiteering successor, Johannes Strijdom, "The deal is this. George sings to whom he hikes, *where* he likes, and we hand over all the money to a charity of your choosing."

Strijdom reluctantly agreed, but his charity—whatever this was, would never receive a penny. George had agreed to raise funds for the NCF, and this is where the money went. From their base in Johannesburg, the couple toured the whole Witwatersrand region, culminating with a show at Witwatersrand University—the very first appearance there of a European entertainer—which George was advised to cancel at the last minute because of Beryl's quite vociferous anti-apartheid comments at an earlier press-conference. She had stupefied journalists by exclaiming, with a few mild expletives, "All this racial stuff is just rubbish. We're all the same colour inside, so why pick on people just because they're a different colour on the outside? Black, white, or sky-blue pink with yellow dots on, they're just as good as you!"

The concert went ahead, despite the death-threat received by Beryl one hour before curtain-up, and which necessitated in the pair being guarded, by armed police standing in the wings, and at the end of the performance the organisers presented George with the establishment's most prestigious accolade, a Kruger half-sovereign medallion. Then, after wiping the tears from his eyes, George rewarded the 5,000-strong audience with "Sara Maraise", which he recorded a few days later in Cape Town, but which would not be commercially released until after his death. British admirers heard this for the first time on 16 April 1955 when he sang it on the BBC Light Programme's *In Town Tonight*.

Prior to this, on 13 April, George appeared in the Royal Variety Performance at Blackpool Opera House—only the second time this famous event had taken place outside London, the other being at Knowsley Hall in 1913 when George's father had topped the bill. George replaced Gracie Fields, who a few weeks previously had undergone an emergency operation for gallstones. The other big names on the bill were Joan Regan, Arthur Askey, and American singer Eddie Fisher. George brought the house down with "Sitting At The Top Of Blackpool Tower". Copyrighted under this title in 1943, until now George had always performed it as "*Spotting* On The Top Of Blackpool Tower"—the spotting not alluding to seagull droppings, as he often joked, but to wartime "fire-spotting".

The impromptu command performance did wonders for George's flagging career, which in the past had always been successfully resuscitated by Beryl's persuasive nagging and unfailing faith in his abilities. Now, however, indolence had been tragically superseded by rapidly failing health. For George, time was running out and, well aware of this, he embarked on a reckless, near-suicidal binge of events which he knew could quite possibly end up killing him. In May, he embarked on a gruelling ten-day tour of Canada, raising $50,000 for the Variety Club of Canada, for which he was presented with a Gold Life-Time Membership card. Zigzagging back and forth across the country, he only found time to relax during the homeward journey aboard the Empress of Scotland...and was laid low with an attack of bronchial pneumonia. Yet no sooner had he recovered from this than he was back in the spotlight, starring in his first straight, virtually non-musical play.

Too Young To Marry had been written by Martin Flavin and first produced at the Liverpool Playhouse in 1935, with Michael Redgrave playing the central character, a hen-pecked Scotsman who stands up to his carping wife—but only when drunk. Cynics might have agreed that such a scenario was a little *too* apt as far as the Formbys were concerned, save that for once George was the one doing all the nagging, because Beryl had started hitting the bottle. And with good cause.

For months, Beryl had complained of feeling tired and ill, always blaming her condition on overwork, and the stress of having recently lost both her parents. In August 1955, she was admitted to a Norfolk hospital for tests—the same one that had cared for her in 1947—and this time the results were devastating. She was found to have incurable cancer of the cervix, and the doctors told that at best she would have just two more years to live.

With Ward Donovan, in *Zip Goes A Million* (1951)

With Barbara Perry in *Zip Goes A Million* (1951)

George with Beryl, in 1953. By this time both were seriously ill.

Nine:
Goodnight, Little Fellow, Goodnight...

"I thought to myself, 'What a charming man,' and I hoped that he would eventually find a nice girl. But I never dreamt it would be me." Pat Howson, fiancée.

The press, in the days when "women's problems" were never discussed by the media, were told that Beryl was suffering from leukemia. Irene Bevan recalled,

> *There was this silly story going around that if the truth came out, people would think she'd developed cancer there because she'd been promiscuous, which was absolute rot. Beryl had had a scare back in 1947, but this time it was the real thing and nothing to do with the few flings she'd had while playing George at his own game.*

George coped with the devastating news the only way he knew how—by working. His own doctors had warned him that by stretching himself to the limit he was well on target for another heart-attack, one which might prove fatal. With this in mind, he began taking stock of his life. His wife was dying, and hastening the end with a daily bottle of whisky. For as long as he cared to remember, his marriage had been sexless, something which had never perturbed him because in this respect there had never been any shortage of offers. Cynics made persistent fun of George's looks. He himself had mused about the potent pulling powers of unattractive men in fictitious songs such as "Why Don't Women Like Me?" Yet to be truthful, *he* did not fit into this category. In his youth he had been extremely athletic and even now, in his early fifties, many much younger women still found him appealing. George was a man with a warm, outgoing streak which had been forcibly cooled by an overlong union with a woman who, in spite of being his anchor and saving grace, had always treated him like an errant schoolboy and never offered him the normality of a conjugal bed.

Now, George Formby was standing at the crossroads. Behind him, a glorious career—constructed and nurtured by the very same beautiful tyrant who, in turning him into an international icon, had for not intentionally selfish reasons robbed him of so many of life's pleasures, not least the opportunity to become a father. And for what? So that she could predecease him and leave him alone in a world within which he had depended upon her for so long? For all that he had given to this world, George deserved at least some happiness before he left it.

"If only God could procure some tiny miracle," he told Sylvia over the phone. "Wouldn't that be nice?"

The miracle occurred in July 1955, when George bumped into Pat Howson again—for this time he told the pretty schoolma'am just how miserable his life had become, and for the first time in years, Beryl was not breathing down his neck.

George and Pat Howson became soul-mates during the summer of 1955, of this there is no doubt. Just how far their relationship progressed beyond the platonic is not known, though on the face of it this would seem unlikely. George was a very sick man who had already taken far too many risks with his health to jeopardise it any further by extraneous sexual activity. He was also, despite his occasional meanderings from the sanctity of his marriage vows, a moral man who, though he may have begun to hate his wife and thus long for a release from the invisible prison she had built around him, would not have wished to hurt her feelings and create a public and ecumenical scandal by letting the world know that he had found a "replacement" whilst she was still alive. For this reason, even his friendship with Pat had to remain a closely-guarded secret—by no means an easy task, for over the coming years, whilst Beryl's life slowly ebbed away, necessitating sometimes lengthy periods when she could not be with her husband, George's movements would be carefully monitored by the eagle-eyed, Beryl-worshipping factotum, Harry Scott.

Too Young To Marry was completely revamped by Emile Littler, to bring the main character into line with George's homely, cheerful mien. One song was added: "If You Don't Like The Goods, Don't Maul 'Em", which he had recorded with Jack Hylton back in 1932. The play toured spasmodically between September 1955 and November 1956, though for once not always to packed audiences and to generally poor reviews. Several performances were recorded and ended up on bootleg tapes, notably the one in Glasgow where George was booed on account of his dreadful Scottish accent, and that at the Golders Green Hippodrome on 4 September 1956. Between venues, there were concert appearances—some forcibly shorter than they had been during George's heyday—and during the winter, the annual pantomime, *Babes In The Wood* at the Liverpool Empire.

For the very first time, George appeared on stage without Beryl. She told the press, "I have quite enough to do, looking after George backstage. I'm up like the proverbial lark every morning, getting all the correspondence out of the way before he gets up. I think I'm entitled to a rest, don't you?" It was of course her progressively worsening condition which was tiring her—and the fact that in order to cope with the pain, Beryl was drinking heavily. This, in addition to the cortisone she was taking, had bloated her features considerably and she, like her husband, had piled on the pounds.

George's first West End pantomime—that perennial favourite,

Dick Whittington, yet again—opened at the Palace Theatre in December 1956. The premiere was attended by the Queen and Princess Margaret, Prince Charles and Princess Anne, and the royal party shared "a pot of tea" with George and Beryl during the interval. Later in the season, part of the show was televised by the BBC. Again, the London critics were nothing less than severe, and unduly so. "If George Formby were long absent from the stage, he would not be missed," *The Times* opined...two days before George was compelled to drop out of the production with a throat and lung infection, to be replaced by Gracie's brother, Tommy Fields.

The year 1957 saw George doing virtually nothing. He and Beryl attended the premiere of the re-released *Keep Fit* in London, following this with a visit to the TT races on the Isle of Man. In June, he hosted his own television spectacular with guests David Niven, Petula Clark, and opera star Tito Gobbi. At the end of the year he appeared on ABC Television's *Top Of The Bill*, where at the last minute he replaced "When I'm Cleaning Windows" with the rarely performed "Trailing Around In A Trailer" as a tribute to Fred E Cliffe, who had recently died. On the strength of this performance he was offered a tour with Leslie Sands' musical-comedy, *Beside The Seaside*.

Subtitled *A Holiday Romp*, and already well-played on the repertory circuit before George took over, the play opened in Hull on 10 March 1958. After a short season in Blackpool it moved to Birmingham's Alexandra Theatre. Its audiences began dwindling until the promoter, Derek Salberg, pulled the plug in the May, whilst it was playing at half-capacity at the Brighton Hippodrome. The critics—and the public—in this part of the country were simply not interested in witnessing the exploits of "a boring family of Northerners" whose only pleasure in life appeared to be spending a rowdy week in Blackpool, engaged in a full-scale battle with a battleaxe guest-house landlady.

Blackpool theatregoers, on the other hand, had loved the play and every house had been a sell-out. "It may not be true, but it's funny," declared the *Gazette*'s Brian Hargreaves, though he was not so sure that it would do the guest-house trade much good:

> *One imagines that the only thing likely to stop its success would be a picket of landladies around the theatre. The place in which it is set is a shocker and the landlady, Mrs Austin, a horrible termagant, a cruel but comic caricature. She meets her match, though, in Wilf Pearson, a cheerful, naturally easy-going chap. The clashes between the landlady with the face as long as a fiddle, and the boarder with the face as round and beaming as a ukulele are formidable and funny. Stock characters certainly, but they have been written with acute and good-humoured insight...George has a part which fits him as well as his suit (surely too smart a piece of tailoring for a Wakes week visitor?). He gathers the guffaws in easy, accomplished fashion, and can be most touching at times, too. It really has turned out nice again!*

George did not even care that the people of Brighton had rejected him as a dismal failure. Blackpool was his *home*, his second heart, and all that really mattered were the opinions of *its* public. He therefore told the producer, Maxwell Wray, that the production would more than recuperate if he allowed him to add a few more songs and return with it to the Blackpool Grand, or the Opera House. Wray would not hear of this, and George lost his temper, vowing that he would never appear in another stage musical. This time, he would keep his word.

1958 was the leanest year of George's career. Friends stated at this time that he was closer to Beryl than ever—perhaps as much through unnecessary guilt that he would soon lose her, as through genuine affection—and that he wanted to spend as much time with her as he could, whilst he could. He certainly experienced severe difficulties staying at the helm when, on bad days, Beryl was unable to leave their Fairhaven home—not just turning down a film appearance, by now a regular occurrence, but also cancelling several radio broadcasts and a recording session with His Master's Voice, who reciprocated by informing him that he would never be offered another. There were three television dates: an appearance on *The Frankie Vaughan Show*, another on ABC's *Second Birthday Show*, and his rock and roll debut with the Deep River Boys, performing "Rock Around The Clock" and a medley of his hits.

In October, convinced that this would be their last holiday together, George arranged to take Beryl on a Mediterranean cruise. Stubborn almost to the end, *she* cancelled this and booked them a cabin on the *Empress of Britain*, about to embark on a twelve week cruise to the United States and Canada...having negotiated a crafty means of getting back most of the £3,000 she had forked out for the trip. The entrepreneur Hughie Green was shooting a television spectacular, *Atlantic Showboat*, aboard the vessel. David Whitfield, Shirley Bassey and Duke Ellington had already been signed up, and George now completed the line-up.

The couple spent much of the time they were at sea below deck, emerging only to do the show. George performed four songs, only two of which were left in Green's film—"The Pleasure Cruise" and "Hello Canada!"—which was screened by ABC on 13 December.

It has been stated that George was suffering from stress at this time, on account of having to hide the fact from Beryl that she was terminally ill. This is not true. Not only had she been told the truth by her doctors, she in turn had confided the grim news to her friend, Sylvia, now on her early seventies and herself ailing:

> *I first became ill two years ago, after a fall in a Liverpool theatre. I broke two ribs and a thumb, but evidently the worst result of it all was the shock to my nervous system. I got to such a pitch that I could scarcely walk downstairs as I had no sense of balance. The crisis seemed to come when I had to be helped up the gangplank for this last visit to Canada. On board, the ship's doctor looked at me and he said to George, "Your wife is a very sick woman, you know." He told me that I had pernicious anaemia [sic], and straight away started me on a course of injections. After five days, even though it was a very rough crossing, I was able to walk back and forth across our cabin with perfect ease. I feel a different person, now. We're even planning another cruise to Africa, or to one of the sunshine countries.*

The doctor had administered cortisone, and *this* had contributed to Beryl's lulled feeling of well-being, along with her gradual addiction to alcohol. In this respect, George was much more of a companion than a moderator, matching her glass for glass and quietly getting smashed within the privacy of their cabin. Only once did Beryl's secret almost become public knowledge—this was when the *Empress of Britain* stopped off in Montreal, and she was too drunk to go ashore and George had to announce that she was suffering from the flu.

In public, Beryl handled herself well, grimacing every now and then when a fresh wave of pain shot through her body, and steadily getting plumper on account of her medication. Like some latter-day Christian martyr, she refused to go into hospital and in April 1959 when she accompanied George to the BBC studios, in London, for the filming of *Steppin' Out With Formby*, she could hardly walk. George had to keep sitting down because of dizzy spells, though his performance was as bouncy as always. He sang seven songs, including two new ones which should have been recorded during the aborted session with His Master's Voice: "Piccolo Pete" and "It Ain't No Sin To Take Off Your Skin".

Two months later, George opened in summer season at Great Yarmouth's Windmill Theatre, by which time Beryl's condition had deteriorated to such an extent that even on better days she was unable to appear on stage with him. She was replaced, as his stooge, by Bettina Richman—with her husband, John Jackson, a minor but popular comedy duo at the time—though this did not prevent her from ruling over the proceedings, from a wheelchair within the wings.

One afternoon, Beryl was well enough to accompany George to the Windboats boatyard for the launching of his new yacht, *Lady Beryl II*. The old vessel had been traded in for a superior model, though George had taken his wife's advice *not* to pay the £500 difference, as James Spencer, a former Windboats employee—seventeen at the time, and bought his first pint of beer, albeit illegally, by his idol—explained:

> *Beryl had told us that a public appearance by the Formbys would be worth much more that £500—you know, a good advertisement for business. She also complained about the champagne, declaring how she hoped SHE was not paying for an expensive vintage to be smashed against the side of a boat. And she absolutely hit the roof when George disobeyed her instructions not to go to the men-only bar and left her standing outside! I remember my boss telling me that it was probably the first time George Formby had dipped his hand into his pocket to buy a round of drinks. Then [my boss] concluded, "If that was MY wife, showing me up in public like that, I'd throw her into the water!" She really was a pain in the arse...*

Great Yarmouth was George's penultimate triumph. Every night was a sell-out, and o two shows were ever the same. "Lamp Post" and "Windows" had to be there, of course, but as the season progressed the sketches became shorter as George made way for more songs—the pauses between which were longer, taking advantage of the hysterical applause to get his breath back. Sometimes, and it would appear purposely, he forgot the words so that the audience would prompt him. No matter how obscure the song, they seemed to know the lyrics, turning each evening into a wondrous singalong experience. He told Sylvia over the phone, "I only wish it would go on for ever. But all good things have to come to an end, don't they?"

This particular "thing" almost ended prematurely at the beginning of August when, on their way back to Great Yarmouth following a lightning visit to Fairhaven, George's Jaguar was involved in a collision with another car near Norfolk. Neither vehicle was badly damaged, and the other driver only suffered cuts and bruises. Beryl, in the back of their car, slept through the whole thing. George however went into a cataleptic shock, and the doctor who tended him at the scene of the crash was co convinced that he was about to have a coronary that he drove him, and the still-groggy Beryl, to the hospital at King's Lynn rather than risk waiting until the ambulance arrived. Tommy Trinder, holidaying in the region, heard what had happened on the mid-day news. He had bought tickets for George's show that evening—now he kindly stood in for him.

When the doctors in King's Lynn examined George, they declared it a miracle that he had survived this long. His blood-pressure was sky-high, his lungs irreparably damaged through smoking upwards of forty cigarettes a day since the age of twelve—the so-called "coffin-nail" brands such as Woodbines and Capstan Full-Strength—he was three stones overweight, and his heart in such a pitiful state that they did not expect him to last the night. Yet all he could tell a reporter who suggested that he at least ought to try and stop smoking was, "Ee, lad. What good would that do me now?"

After three days in intensive care, followed by a week in a private ward, George discharged himself from the hospital and returned to the Windmill Theatre, picking up where he had left off as if nothing had happened. When the season ended early in October, he learned that he had broken the all-time attendance record. "Proof, if ever proof were needed, that George Formby is *still* Britain's greatest entertainer," observed a local newspaper.

During this second run in Great Yarmouth the offers poured in: a tour of provincial theatres spearheaded by Harold Fielding, a record contract with Pye International, yet another film, a summer season in Blackpool, and a twenty-week tour of Australia.

George's spirit was willing enough, but he was terrified of straying too far from Blackpool in case anything happened to him. "I'd never forgive myself if I died abroad," he told Sylvia, half-joking, whilst Beryl told the Australian promoter, quite seriously, "Our real problem isn't George's health, this time, but that of our dog, Willie Waterbucket. He'll be fifteen this October, and we'd hate anything to happen to him whilst we were away. So I'm afraid George and I won't be coming to Australia just yet."

The Blackpool season accepted George accepted without hesitation, along with the two-session record deal at the beginning of May. The executives at Pye were hoping that even in this limited time George would tape enough of his old material to cover at least two album sides, though he soon made it clear that he had no intention of reviving any of his former hits.

This in itself presented George with a major problem. Fred E Cliffe was dead, whilst Harry Gifford had died whilst George had been negotiating the Pye contract. Such was his reputation for insisting his name be added to the credits so that he could rake in the lion's share of the royalties, that no established composers wanted anything to do with him. Neither did he do himself any favours by lashing out at the mediocrity of modern "pop-song" writers, telling *Melody Maker*, when asked to explain why he had been as popular in his heyday as Tommy Steele and Cliff Richard were now, "I don't know. I suppose I used to be what Cliff Richard is now—not very good, but what the public wanted."

The two songs chosen by George for his studio comeback, but which ended up being his last, were, in comparison with his *grandes oeuvres*, no better than the pop ditties he had condemned. Indeed, their importance in the immensely rich and varied Formby catalogue may be determined by the *manner* in which they were recorded—in just ten minutes, with George not even bothering to remove his hat and coat, and leaving the studio without waiting to hear if the takes were of an acceptable standard. Of the two, "Banjo Boy" is perhaps the more passable, with a jaunty ambience reminiscent of the unsurpassable Formby style. "Happy Go Lucky Me", on the other hand, is a contradiction of terms if ever there was one, for George sounds anything but. Every chuckle in the voice, an integral and natural element prevalent in his work for over three decades, is not simply contrived, but embarrassing—a pathetic, uninspired swansong to a mighty recorded legacy. "I would rather never work again and let people remember me the way I was, than disappoint them now," he told the press after the record had been released, and many of his fans believe that he should have applied this maxim *before* cutting this final disc.

On 4 June 1960, George opened in *The Time Of Your Life* at Blackpool's Queen's Theatre. He should have shared top-billing with Jimmy Clitheroe, but Beryl complained about this to the producer, Ross Taylor. The pipe-voiced little comic therefore had his part in the revue cropped to make way for George's infamous but horrendous parrot jokes, and the Italian tenor Tony Dalli was brought in at the last minute. Glamour came in the shapely form of Yana—a busty, sultry-voiced Essex-born *chanteuse* renowned for her fish-tail dresses, and whose hits in England included "I Need You" and "Mr Wonderful", both of which were woven into the flimsy plot.

George fell for Yana (Pamella Guard, 1932-89) in a big way. She performed her showpiece number, "Climb Up The Garden Wall", sitting on a swing surrounded by an ocean of artificial flowers. Blatantly lesbian despite being thrice married, and with a huge gay following, she was living with an American actress at the time, though George did not know this. Neither did he realise, until it was almost too late, that Yana was deliberately leading him on—interested not in the tired, prematurely-aged man making a last desperate attempt to recapture his lost youth, but in his very healthy bank-balance.

Despite the hefty £1,500 a week fee, George insisted that he would only sing for twenty minutes, immediately before the interval. After some arguing with Ross Taylor, he then agreed that he would appear in some sketches with the other artistes, and that his spot could be moved to the end of the show. The latter change came after an objection from Yana, who claimed that if George claimed the first half, the audience would begin vacating the theatre. George then threatened to pull out of the show altogether when told that, in keeping with BBC tradition, the audience would be admitted free for the performance of 14 July, which was to be televised. "It's not that I object to people getting summat for nowt," he told the *Blackpool Gazette*'s Brian Hargreaves. "But I am against all those civic dignitaries and scroungers who wouldn't normally give me light of day if they had to pay to get in." He then upset the rest of the cast by refusing to turn up for rehearsals, declaring that these would only overtire him, which of course was true—and that in any case, he had been singing most of the songs in his programme for so long, that there was no need. "Just stick a lamp post and I'll do the rest when the time comes," he told the producer.

Several people *did* storm out of the theatre during George's second show when, between "Lamp Post" and "Happy Go Lucky Me", he pointed to a young woman sitting in the front row and announced that he would like to dedicate a limerick to her:

> *There was a young man called Vickers,*
> *Who took his girlfriend to the flickers,*
> *He saw some white wool and he started to pull,*
> *And that's how the girl lost her—hankie!*

The Time Of Your Life broke all box-office records at the theatre, and instead of closing in September was extended for two months. Jimmy Brennan, the impresario who had booked George for this show, had no trouble signing him for a the summer of 1961…Beryl was not around to complicate matters. He also consented to an in-depth interview with Brian Hargreaves—the first *ever* when Beryl would not be present to vet his answers or reply on his behalf. At the last minute, Hargreaves fell ill, but George was just as candid with his stand-in, Michael Berry:

> BERRY: *No other British comedian has topped the bill for as long as you have. Why have you managed to remain an established star for such a long time?*
>
> GEORGE: *Because I've never overworked myself and let the public see too much of me. It's foolish how some of these newer comics are on television so often. No matter how good you are, the public don't want to see your face every time they switch on the television.*

BERRY: *Would you call yourself an artist of international appeal?*

GEORGE: *I've performed in every country but Russia and China and haven't had any eggs thrown at me yet!*

BERRY: *You have a reputation for being an extremely rich man...*

GEORGE: *I usually say "I'm comfortably off" to that question, but I'll tell you this. During my career I've earned over £1 million...and I've paid out £300,000 in income tax.*

BERRY: *How would you describe your type of comedy?*

GEORGE: *Natural. I never have to be anything but myself when I go on stage...*

BERRY: *And what type of comedian applies to YOU the most?*

GEORGE: *Straightforward, uncomplicated stuff. Jimmy James. Morecambe and Wise...*

BERRY: *And no blue jokes. Why is this?*

GEORGE: *Because it's not necessary. If you can't make people laugh without being vulgar, then it's about time you packed it in.*

BERRY: *Which is your favourite medium—films, television, or the stage?*

GEORGE: *The stage every time. You can get another chance the next night if you make a mistake—you only get one chance on television. And when I see myself in my old films, I always think I'd like to have another go at them and do them better.*

BERRY: *George, do you smoke or drink?*

GEORGE: *[cigarette in one hand, tumbler of whisky in the other] Both, but not a great deal, ha-ha!*

BERRY: *Throughout your career, your wife Beryl has accompanied you everywhere and managed your affairs. Has this been one of the contributory factors to your success?*

GEORGE: *Beryl and I have always been a team. As far as my career is concerned, I would not be where I am today if it had not been for her help.*

This latter observation, of course, cannot be reiterated often enough, though by now George and Beryl were no longer the team they had once been. She missed more of the Blackpool performances than she attended—initially through illness, but later on account of her unacceptable behaviour, which saw her actually banned from entering the theatre. Beryl fell into drunken, violent rages more often than not sparked off by the latest reports on George's amorous activities from resident "spy", Harry Scott. "For almost thirty years, George's lackey—and that's *all* he was, never a friend—had been waiting to jump into bed with Beryl," Irene Bevan said. "The mere thought of George doing the same thing when *he* never achieved his own goal drove the pathetic little man half out of his head with jealousy."

George's relationship with Yana cannot be denied. They were seen checking into hotels not just in Blackpool, on his doorstep, but in Manchester and later in Bristol. There is some doubt as to how long they had been an item. Though Scott does not refer to Yana by name in his heavily-ghosted memoirs—she was still alive at the time—he leaves us with no doubts about her identity, and states that the affair had been going strong for two *years*:

> *When Beryl wasn't around she used to go to his dressing-room and cheer him up, but she never went near George when Beryl was there. While they were playing together at one particular theatre during the time that Beryl's health started to fail, after the evening's show George used to take this lady back to the flat she had rented. Beryl knew that he had struck up this friendship with this girl, whose talent and youthful beauty had captured his imagination. George told her so himself. Yet all Beryl had said was, "Let him play, he's only like a big boy, really!" And she forgave him. Mrs Formby was, I think, tempering her fierce love and jealousy with unexpected tolerance. Her ill health was making "Our Beryl" an even sweeter and more understanding person than before.*

If the latter part of Scott's diatribe was true—not an easy conclusion to reach when one considers his almost manic affection for Beryl—then George had exacted the ultimate revenge on his wife, flaunting in her face his affair with a much younger, much prettier woman, and doing so whilst the person to whom he owed absolutely everything was virtually on her deathbed. Taking into consideration George's track-record for being British show business's archetypal "easy-going chap", one cannot begin to imagine that he could have acted with such calculating cruelty...or indeed that, if he had confessed all to Beryl, she would have forgiven him, given her own jaundiced temperament. On the other hand, one must also consider the fact that for thirty-six years this indomitable woman had ruled the Formby household like a Spartan tyrant—granting George neither his freedom to enjoy the fruits of his labours, nor the requisites of a normal and happy marriage. It may well be that he had had no alternative but to seize upon this final moment of weakness to burst free of his chains. Perhaps one can come to this conclusion: Beryl had been pushing George towards exacting his revenge for years, and despite the bad timing she should have counted her blessings that this had not happened, on such a scale, much sooner.

Michael Berry is thought to have asked George about his "friendship" with Yana, but to have been requested not to print the reply. Another subject touched upon in his interview for the *Gazette* was that a film was about to be made about George's rise to fame—with Tommy Steele, already a big star at twenty-three, in the title role. "And why not?" George had posed. "He can be made to look like me. He's got the same mouth—though whether he can master a Northern accent's another matter, if course." The venture is believed to have been scuppered by a statement from Beryl, "If George *does* make the film, it will be properly handled because *I'll* be on the set at all times to make sure the project runs smoothly." Ill or not, Beryl's name was still a by-word for terror in show business circles.

George saw a lot of Pat Howson during these anxious months when he had absolutely no one else to turn to. In September, Beryl was rushed to the La Sagesse Convent Hospital, where she lay at death's door for a week. By the end of the month, however, she had discharged herself. The doctors had told her she would be lucky to live beyond the end of the year, and her greatest wish was that she should die, "religion free", in her own bed at home.

In November 1960, George sang in public for the last time, at the grand Order of Water Rats Ball, at London's Dorchester Hotel. Afterwards he spoke to reporters about his enthusiasm for the future. The film-project with Tommy Steele had been cancelled, but he had received another offer and he was also looking forward to his pantomime season in Bristol. Having failed to secure him for the tour circuit, Harold Fielding had persuaded George to star in *Aladdin*, playing Mr Wu, at the Hippodrome. At the ABC studios in Manchester, George had also filmed three short introductions to *I See Ice*, *Spare A Copper* and *Turned Out Nice Again*. These would be used during the *Formby Festival*, a retrospective of his films to be screened by the BBC during the winter.

On 16 December, what is generally regarded as George's greatest performance—it was certainly his most sincere and moving—was broadcast on BBC Television's acclaimed *Friday Show*...effectively, a virtual tete-a-tete containing the laughter, and the tears, of the finest singing clown Britain had ever produced, one whose like we shall never see again. Like a sad, tired old man reliving his life whilst drowning in a sea of nostalgia, George summed up his whole existence in just thirty-five minutes, and sang nine songs in what we now know he intended to be his farewell performance.

The show is in some ways reminiscent of the later *Elvis 68 Special*, and the autobiographical recitals which Marlene Dietrich had just begin presenting around the world. The backdrop is simple but effective: the door, surrounded by lights and surmounted with the massive "Mr Formby" logo, through which George enters in silhouette to sing several songs and tell a few anecdotes, before transferring to the intimacy of a mock sitting-room, then lastly the all-important street scene complete with lamp post.

George ambles on, looking a little plumper and sounding breathless, instantly creating an ambience of radiant sincerity:

> *No girls, no dancers, no acrobats, no conjurers, not even a guest star. Just me and the uke. But I'm going to tell you a few home truths I've never told in public before...*

And he does. Coughing every now and then, he recalls his first film, and its world premiere—at Burslem, near Stoke-on-Trent:

> *Oo, and it was a lousy picture! It was so dark in places you had to strike matches to see it. The courting couples liked it, though!*

He cheerfully speaks of his roots:

> *Of course, most people know that I was born in Wigan. And don't say, "It serves you right!" because I'm very proud of Wigan. Every time I drive through it in the car I raise my hand and say, "Thanks very much, Wigan!"*

George bemoans his lack of education and urges youngsters watching him not to follow his example. Then before singing "Goodnight Little Fellow Goodnight", he ruefully confesses that this particular number always makes him feel sad, because he has never been blessed with children of his own. He dismissed his first stage appearance: "Three minutes, died the death of a dog!" Then he jokes about his inability to write music or tune his ukes, and about failing his wartime medical:

> *That was the biggest laugh I ever got in my life. When I stripped off, I never knew I'd flat feet. And the doctor looked at me: he gave me a shilling, and he gave me a card which said I was Grade Four. I didn't even get in the first three!*

With the utmost sincerity, he praises Beryl...

> *I married her, and that was when my luck turned...I shall always be grateful to Beryl for doing all the business for me. Of course it'd take me a month to tell you all the things Beryl's done for me. Some other time, probably.*

...but most especially his father, wiping away a tear whilst in the background we hear Formby Sr's 1907 recording of "Standing At The Corner Of The Street".

> *I think he went the way he wanted to do...in harness. He was a great fella, you know...he certainly was a great star. I don't think I'll ever be as good as him.*

And finally he defines his impression of stardom:

> *People say to me, "How did you become a star?" Huh, that's a daft question! I mean, what do WE do? We don't do anything. We don't BECOME stars. You people make us stars. We wouldn't be any good without you. And our present stars today, if they believe anything different, they're crazy! I shall always be grateful to the public for what they've done for me...*

Beryl watched the programme with Harry Scott and his wife, on a bedside television set in her room. Scott cloyingly recalled an improbable scenario, how Beryl had treated the occasion like a gala premiere, taking half an hour to put on her make-up, saying, "I must make myself up nice for George," then selecting her best pink satin bed-jacket and most expensive jewels:

> *Gone, at least for the time being, were those heavy shadows under Beryl's eyes. Gone too was the pallor.....*

the transformation, the excitement bubbling away like champagne, and the light sparkling in her eyes made me forget for a moment or two that she was so tragically ill. The scene was George's. The star was Beryl, for I will never forget the gentle smile on her face as she shared with her husband his quips and his seriously...She was always George's severest critic, but back in those eyes that refused to mirror the pain of her suffering came from the unswerving admiration, understanding and love she had always had for George.

Again, one finds it impossible to imagine that Beryl could have shown such demonstrativeness for a husband who, only weeks before, had told her to her face that he had a mistress. Equally, George seems to have made a Herculean effort *not* to be at Fairhaven when the end came. For the last three years he had refused to do pantomime, claiming that he was following his doctor's instructions and that the medium would prove far too strenuous for his own failing health. During his last Blackpool season, he had been offered his usual £1,000 a week, plus a cut of the profits, for a "stress-free" pantomime season in Liverpool, within easy driving distance of his home...only to turn this down and *accept* the one in Bristol for just £600 a week. It was here, during rehearsals on 21 December—minutes after singing the ironically inappropriate "Why Don't Women Like Me?" to Yana, who was standing in the wings—that he received a call from Fairhaven, informing him that Beryl had lapsed into a coma from which she would never emerge.

The *Aladdin* premiere went ahead, even though two hours before curtain-up George had received a second call, from Beryl's doctor, stating that she might not make it through the night. After the performance, he spent several minutes signing autographs in his dressing room. Instead of attending the party in the theatre's Green Room, he climbed into his car—despite being urged not to do so by Yana, who was terrified that the stress of driving over such a long distance, so soon after his performance, might trigger another coronary—and headed *not* for his own home, but to the Warrington home of Fred and Jessica Bailey, two old friends who owned a grocer's shop in the town. It was here, at just after two in the morning—Christmas Day—that he was informed that Beryl had passed away half an hour earlier.

George's reaction to his wife's death may be gathered from the business-like expediency with which he, who had hardly ever had to organise anything in his life, consciously mapped out the next few days. The news was included in radio and television bulletins throughout Christmas Day, and the next morning Harry Scott and George's London agent, Henry Foster, spent several hours calling friends and colleagues. Beryl's funeral, astonishingly, had been arranged to take place the next day and emerged that she, an agnostic, had requested not only that there should be no religious service and no spot should mark her final resting place.

George would not agree to the former, but he saw to the latter by having Beryl cremated, and insisted that her ashes be scattered "with everybody else's" in the rose garden at Lytham St Annes Park Crematorium. George's wreath was simply inscribed, "Goodbye, pal".

Just one hour after leaving the crematorium, George returned to Bristol for the next afternoon's matinee of *Aladdin*. "He's missed four performances already," Henry Foster told the *Daily Express*'s show business editor, Michael Walsh. "He can't afford to miss any more!" George himself was asked by Walsh, who called him that evening at the theatre, why there had been no show business personalities at Beryl's funeral. His excuse was a muttered, "Because there were no newspapers to publish that she'd died—and because they all had commitments up and down the country." This of course was untrue. Such was the dislike that this woman had inspired amongst virtually everyone who had come into contact with George that not one of these people had wished to be accused of hypocrisy by attending her funeral—or by sending flowers.

George soldiered on with *Aladdin* until 14 January, when he was forced to pull out of the production with a heavy cold which, he was warned, could easily develop into pneumonia. He left Bristol—and Yana—early the next morning and drove the five hours back to Fairhaven, where he immediately contacted Pat Howson. Two days later, when his condition remained unchanged, she called his doctor and he was admitted to Blackpool's Victoria Hospital, where he stayed until the end of the month. He was so desperately ill that at one stage the hospital priest, Father Lakeham, thought of administering Last Rites.

George's first visitors, once he had started to rally a little, were two small boys who had walked all the way from Preston, they said, to bring him chocolates. He was touched by the gesture. What he never knew was that the boys had stolen the money for the gift from a charity collection-box. Not only this, when the pair were brought before the Juvenile Panel a few days later, they were further charged with breaking into a number of shops and warehouses, and sent to a remand home.

During George's hospitalisation, Pat visited him every day, and the switchboard was instructed not to put any calls through to his room from Yana. The singer confessed to friends that her romance with George had been but a "sugar-daddy fill-in" during the temporary rift with her female lover, and that she did not wish to be held responsible for him "fucking himself towards another heart attack". She was now also saying that George had proposed to her in Bristol, and that he was about to take steps to remove all memories of his late wife from his life by putting his house on the market and getting rid of Beryl's things.   She added that George had "cursed himself for being too good a Catholic", in that he had never tried to escape his living hell of the last two years by leaving Beryl, an atheist who had always mocked his faith. Much more seriously, she told one friend that George had got her pregnant, though never let on what had happened to the baby. This of course because the story was completely untrue, though a few eyebrows were raised at the end of 1960 when a photograph appeared—thought to have been taken at a christening, where Yana is seen holding the baby, with a very proud-looking George standing behind her.

The marriage proposal could have been pure invention, though the rest of Yana's statement was only too true. George discharged himself from the hospital, telling the nurse, "I'm off home, lass, for a decent cup of tea!", so that he could organise the sale of Beryldene. The next day, accompanied by Pat, he began searching for somewhere else to live. He settled on Clock House, a run-down property in Lea Town, near Preston—not far from the Howsons—and immediately brought in a team of builders to get the place renovated.

On 13 February, almost certainly on the rebound after dumping Yana, George called his journalist friend Brian Hargreaves, and announced that he was going to marry Pat Howson:

> *I was too shy to ask Pat herself, so I popped the question to her dad instead. A chap like me needs company. I don't think it's strange me proposing like this, and don't think the public will begrudge me a little happiness late in life. I'm hopeless in the house and I can't leave everything to my valet, Harry Scott. And Pat and me are already the best of friends!*

The engagement was announced next morning, St Valentine's Day, and Pat's thirty-sixth birthday—when pictures of the happy couple appeared on the front pages of most of the national newspapers. George had not had the time to buy his fiancée a ring, so he had given the one which had belonged to his grandmother. The wedding, he said, would take place in May, and would be followed by a Mediterranean cruise. "It's a fairytale come true," he told the *Daily Mirror*'s Arthur Brooks. "I really *do* feel like singing 'Happy Go Lucky Me'!"

Yana appears to have taken rejection badly, in spite of having been reunited with her lover. According to Harry Scott, the phone at Beryldene had not stopped ringing that morning. He recalled, "In replying to one of the many calls I heard George say, quite distinctly and with an unusually firm voice, 'Well, you've had your chance, now you've had your chips!'"

In choosing Pat Howson for his future bride, George was clutching at straws. Beryl had kept him on a leash for so long that he had hardly ever enjoyed *any* kind of female company, even platonically, for as long as he could remember—towards the end she had even been jealous of his affection for the moribund Sylvia—so George was in no position to discern between the gentler refinements of courtship and the slobberings of lust. The latter was probably the only thing that had attracted him to Yana, and would have been out of the question with the young schoolma'am from a decent family which upheld all the moral sensibilities of the Catholic church...and who almost certainly would not have made herself available for what George referred to as "hanky-panky" until after they were married.

George's greatest enemy, more than the wife he had come to loath in later years, was the commodity he knew he had so little of—time. He had dismissed his entire family—but most especially his mother—as "bloody scroungers", and as he had explained to Brian Hargreaves, he appeared to have developed a paranoia that his fortune would very soon end up in undeserving hands. And who else was there to lean upon but this wholly unselfish woman to whom he had confided so many of his most pressing problems—the only person apart from the two boy fans, when he had truly thought himself at death's door?

Pat was sitting next to George a few days later when he offloaded his ultimate *mea culpa* on the *Daily Express*'s Michael Walsh. For the first time, the *public* learned that his marriage to Beryl had been a charade—adding that her atheism had clashed with his faith, and that each time he had wanted to go to church there had been a tremendous row. He concluded:

> *For the last fifteen years we did not live as man and wife. We tried to keep drink away from her, but the damage was done. The public had built up a certain picture of us and I had no wish to spoil the illusion of that. My life with Beryl was hell.*

The excitement caused by his engagement, followed by the repercussions of this last confession, proved too much for George. On 22 February he suffered a heart attack whilst having dinner with the Howsons at their Penwortham home. The fact that a doctor lived only three doors away and that he was able to administer emergency treatment whilst an ambulance was on its way saved George's life, but only just. This time he was given Last Rites, and his solicitor, John Crowther, was summoned to his bedside at Preston's St Joseph's RC Hospital.

George's main concern was that his house at Fairhaven be sold as quickly as possible, even at a loss, before he died. He had no intention, he vowed, of leaving this world whilst even the slightest vestige of Beryl's existence remained in his life. Pat, however, instructed Crowther *not* to inform anyone that the Great

Formby was dying, as George wanted him to do. As a result, a simple statement was issued to the press: "Mr Formby is poorly, but he is more in need of a long rest than anything. There is nothing to worry about."

It did not take George's estranged family, nor Harry Scott, very long to work out that the end was fast approaching, and as had happened with Yana, the nursing staff at the hospital received strict instructions to keep these people away from him. George told John Crowther, who would soon prove just as grasping as they were, "They're nothing but a load of money-grabbers. If it's left to them they'll pinch my shroud before my body's cold. I want nothing to do with any of them."

On Saturday morning, three days after George's heart attack, and still clinging to a decidedly flimsy precognitive dream—the fact that all will turn out well in the end, as long as this is what one wishes—Pat, assisted by the matron, the Reverent Mother Ignatius, gave a press-conference at the hospital, and the reporters who turned up agreed unanimously that this warm-hearted young woman was anything but a gold-digger, as the Booths had branded her, as she cheerfully announced:

> *I'm happier about his condition today than at any time since he came in here. George is very cheerful. He's now sitting up and enjoy radio or TV if he so wishes. He's not likely to leave hospital in the immediate future—we expect him to be here for another two weeks at least. After that we'll be going somewhere where it's reasonably peaceful. And after our wedding in May—no exact details, yet, I'm afraid—we'll probably be going for a long sea cruise. George has been told that he must rest for nine months.*

The end came peacefully, nine days later, during the afternoon of

Monday 6 March 1961. Pat was at his bedside, holding his hand. That morning bought her wedding-ring...we now know that the couple had decided to bring the ceremony forward to 8 March, so that it could take place before news of it leaked out to George's family. A hospital spokesman described his final moments:

> *Mr Formby had asked to be married on the Wednesday and the hospital priest, Father Lakeham, had agreed to conduct the bedside ceremony. Mr Formby had especially demanded that no one else be told. It was whilst the couple were discussing this—Mr Formby's voice was raised and angry—that he suddenly began coughing. Then his head fell forwards. Father Lakeham, attending a patient nearby, was summoned at once, whilst Reverend Mother Ignatius and the [chest] specialist, Doctor Geake, attempted but failed to revive him. A moment later, Father Lakeham administered the Last Rights.*

It seems sad but apt that a man who had spent the better part of his life sheltered from a rapacious family by a wife they had hated—because she had seen them for what they were, and kept them at bay—should have died whilst criticising them, and in such a hurry to divorce himself from them, financially, by wedding the woman he loved. Had he lived two more days, the wedding would have taken place and saved Pat from a great deal of strife. A few years later she confessed in a radio interview:

> *All he ever wanted was for us to be happy. I can understand why the people jumped to all the wrong conclusions, but I never understood why they never gave us the benefit of the doubt. Ours could have been a nice story. Strange circumstances do occur with people, but we were just the victims of circumstance.*

The obituaries were legion, though George was perhaps best summed up by his friend, the *Blackpool Gazette*'s Brian Hargreaves:

> *The sudden death of George Formby is the more tragic because most people had the idea that he was over the worst. But the heart is a strange and unpredictable organ, and in the spite of all possible medical care he went out like a candle in a sudden wind. So the last chord is strummed, and the last song sung. Blackpool, Lancashire and Britain as a whole are sad at the passing of a native comedian who came up the hard way and, in spite of his success and wealth, never had an easy life. Yet he was still, in essence, an unspoilt Lancashire lad.*

Summer 1959: Beryl launches *Beryl II* at Windboats and quips as she smashes the champagne bottle, "I hope *I'm* nt paying for this!" (Jack Littlewood)

The party after the launch. Beryl was excluded and according to the director of Windboats, this was the first and last time George paid for a round of drinks.
(Jack Littlewood)

George and Beryl, just weeks before she died.

June 1960: in *The Time Of Your Life* with Yana and Italian tenor Tony Dalli (RC).

A photograph which is not what it seems! Despite the rumours, the baby was neither George's nor Yana's.

George with Pat Howson, February 1961, a few days before he died (GFS).

George's final television appearance on *The Friday Show*, December 1960 (GFS).

Epilogue:
"A Set Of Scroungers"

"The tragedy is that a man who gave so much pleasure to others was not allowed the time to taste a little himself." David Nathan, film critic, *Daily Herald*.

For those who generally cared about George, mourning him was marred by an exceptionally greedy family squabbling over his not inconsiderable fortune. Just two hours after he died, his mother—now eighty-two and almost blind—called the *Blackpool Gazette* from her Liverpool home and announced, "I don't care what *she* says. *We'll* be bringing George home here tomorrow, and he'll be buried in the family grave at Warrington."

This attack on Pat Howson was wholly unnecessary, and of course an exercise in supremacy on Eliza's part. George had always expressed a wish to be buried with his father, and Pat had known this. What she did not expect, either, was a call from this nasty old woman warning her to stay away from George's funeral.

Pat ignored the threat, assuming that Eliza's grief had affected her sensibility. When she turned up at the Booth house, in Sefton Park, she realised that Eliza had meant every word. The undertaker, Bruce Williams (aka George's songwriter, Eddie Latta) had been given explicit instructions not to allow "George's floosy" to ride in any of the limousines paid for by the family. She subsequently travelled in her parents' car, a dozen vehicles behind the main cortege. She was also requested—very loudly, by George's sister, Ethel—not to sit on the same side as the family in the church. What the Booths could not prevent was Pat's cross of deep red roses—placed next to the family's one of pink and white carnations on top of George's simple oak coffin. It was inscribed, "Now and always—Pat."

George's funeral, on 10 March 1961, remains the largest there has ever been in Britain for a show business personality. Over 150,000 people lined the two-mile route from the chapel of rest to St Charles' Roman Catholic Church, where the Requiem Mass was officiated by Monsignor Francis Chaloner. Traffic was reduced to a virtual standstill as the cortege set off on the twenty-mile journey to Warrington. Eliza Booth was so overcome with emotion—most agreed put on, just for show—that she had to be supported much of the time by her sons, Ted and Frank, who had seen little if anything of George in recent years. Most eyes were focused not on them—or Pat, who had been rudely shoved to the back of the crowd clustered around the graveside—but on George's sixteen-year-old Lakeland terrier, Willie Waterbucket, who had accompanied his master on his final journey sitting on Harry Scott's knee, and who whined inconsolably whilst the coffin was being lowered into the ground.

The entertainment world was represented by Ronnie Hilton, Jimmy Clitheroe, and Billy Matchett, who was there on behalf of the Grand Order of Water Rats. Eric Dobell represented the Variety Artists' Federation, the body which had caused George and Beryl so much anguish during the war. There were wreathes from Yana, Beryl Reid, Irene Handl, Arthur Askey, Joseph Locke, Gracie Fields, Tommy Trinder and a host of others.

Just forty minutes after George had been laid to rest, the Booths—having ensured that Pat had been on her way back to Preston—convened a meeting with George's solicitor, John Crowther, in a Warrington café, and demanded to know the contents of his will. Shortly afterwards, having learned that, aside from a £5,000 bequest to Harry Scott, Pat Howson had been named George's sole beneficiary—but not yet wishing for this to be made public—Ted Booth, who henceforth would style himself Ted Formby—issued a statement via the *Blackpool Gazette*:

> *We cannot officially say what is in the will until I get a copy from the solicitor tomorrow. But if the will is disadvantageous to our family, we shall certainly contest it. My main consideration is that Mother should be well provided for. We did hear that George had revoked his first will not very long before he died. George was a very sick man...*

This closing phrase, "George was a very sick man"—which of course intimated that he had been suffering from considerably much more than mere physical illness—would be bandied about courtrooms and solicitors' offices for several years.

On the evening of Saturday 11 March, the day after George's funeral, Pat and Father Lakeham, the priest who had been present at his deathbed, organised a remembrance for his soul at Preston's St Wilfrid's Catholic Church...and despite their appalling treatment of her, George's family were invited. None of them turned up. That morning, the contents of Beryl's will had been published and it was revealed that John Crowther had been holding on to this information since two weeks *before* George's death. It now appeared that the £25,000 left by George's wife would be going straight to Pat Howson.

Matters were further complicated when Crowther revealed that George had made *three* wills I as many months:

> *WILL No. 1: Dated 19 December 1960, the same day as Beryl's and five days before she died, wherein the couple bequeathed their entire estate to each other.*

> *WILL No. 2: Dated 18 January 1961, wherein George bequeathed £5,000 each to Eliza Booth and Harry Scott*

(aka Harold Scothron), £1,000 to Lily Ashton (Beryl's last private nurse), and the "residue" to his three sisters.

WILL No. 3: Dated 23 February 1961,wherein George bequeathed £5,000 to Harry Scott, and the "residue" to Ada Patricia Howson.

Two days later on Monday morning, Eliza, accompanied by her daughters Ethel, Louis and Mary, went to see her lawyer, John Cowper, and announced that she would be contesting George's third will. She added that she was doing so very reluctantly, having been outraged because her son had snubbed his sisters—indeed, he had been snubbing them for years, for the only time they had ever tried to contact him had been when they had been "on the cadge". Ethel told Cowper that, as the family's spokeswoman, she too was "devastated" that George had shown such disdain towards the woman who had brought him into the world. Nothing whatsoever was mentioned about George's brothers. Within the hour, Cowper had applied for a caveat to be filed with the London High Court which would prevent probate from being released from George's estate until an agreement had been reached between Pat Howson and the Booths. Both parties were given until 25 August to settle their differences and prevent the matter from being brought before a judge.

Pat tried her utmost to placate the angry relatives, though she was neither legally nor morally obliged to do so. She attempted to call Eliza to arrange an informal meeting, only to be rewarded with a torrent of abuse. Her solicitor then advised the Booths that though she was not obliged to do so, his client would be willing to pay Eliza the £5,000 which George had obviously intended her to have at the time he had signed his second will, in addition to which *she* would personally ensure that his sisters would be generously provided for by giving them £2,000 each.

Eliza neither accepted not rejected Pat's offer, but when John Cowper's caveat expired on 25 August she applied for a seven day extension. "I need time to think the matter over," she told the press. This was refused by Pat, who gave a statement by way of the same reporter—George's pal, Brian Hargreaves:

> *This family have already had three months to consider my offer, and seeing as they don't appear to be able to make up their minds, the offer's been withdrawn. I've done my best to avoid a lot of trouble, and this is something of a bombshell. I suppose that it will mean court action and no doubt some unpleasantness, but otherwise I'm not in the least worried.*

Upon hearing this, Eliza clearly set her sights on grabbing the lot, and vowed to sue George's fiancée for every penny he had left her, even when told that it might take another year for the case to reach the courts. The fact that she could well be dead by this time did not perturb her in the least, she declared, because her daughters would still "fight that fucking little floosy schoolma'am with their last breath".

The sale of George's effects, ordered by John Crowther in his capacity as the executor of his estate, opened at Fairhaven on 20 June 1961, and went on for three days. A huge marquee was erected in the garden and a catalogue was printed detailing 1,007 items, much of this household furnishings and bric-a-brac of little value save that it had formerly belonged to George Formby. One lot comprised "a walking stick, toilet-brush and holder, two truncheons and a shillelagh", another an empty oil drum upon which he had carved his initials, and a wine bin filled with coal which fetched £200. There was a huge collection of jewellery, glassware, china and furs which had belonged to Beryl and over a thousand articles of clothing, some still in their wrappers, several original paintings, and George's most recent Bentley which only had 2,200 miles on the clock.

For many, the most important—and touching—items to come under the hammer were fifteen of George's ukuleles, several of which had been autographed by him and labelled with song-titles he had recorded with them, such as the "Mr Wu" and the "Windows". Two were purchased on behalf of George's brother, Frank, by his wife, who outbid the skiffle singer Lonnie Donegan. "They need to be cherished by us, his loved ones," she told the *Blackpool Gazette*. What she did not add was that George had not spoken to her or her husband—an unshady character with a long criminal record—for over twenty years, and that like most of his family they had ever been welcomed at the various Beryldenes.

Prior to the auction, Beryldene was thrown open to the public, and amongst the first to arrive were George's sisters, accompanied by Harry Scott, each of whom asked for "a little something to remember him by". Pat told them, sharply and quite rightly, that if anything caught their eye they would be at liberty to put in a bid the same as anyone else. Ethel would eventually pay £380 for a Jacobean dining-suite and a bedroom suite, telling the press, "We had to borrow the money from friends, but we wanted to keep *some* of George's things in the family." Scott bought Beryl's television—and the bed she had died in.

Another interested party, of little consequence at the time but immensely so, today, was the George Formby Society—formed just two weeks previously by a fan, Bill Logan, who had travelled down from Carlisle hoping to buy ukuleles, photographs and other memorabilia so that his 50-strong group might perpetuate their idol's memory. Logan purchased six ukes, a gold-topped walking cane, and several other items.

The house itself was sold for £9,000—less than George had paid for it to Joseph Locke—to a female buyer, who asked not to be named, but who was later revealed to be a Mrs Murray. George's yacht, *Lady Beryl II*, was sold back to Windboats, in Norfolk, for £5,500—which was the same amount that an Isle of Man hotelier paid for his Bentley. In all, the sale raised £22,430. Pat had not, however, allowed John Crowther to sell everything. £20,000 worth of Beryl's jewellery and George's four favourite ukuleles were set aside to be sold separately because, she claimed, George had wanted her to have them. She kept the ukes, but sold the jewellery at Sotheby's and placed the money in a "kitty" which she had opened to pay for the court case.

The hearing opened on 13 May 1963 at the London High Court, and was presided over by Justice Ormrod. Eliza and her daughters—described by one newspaper as "acting and looking like a quarter of rowdy old washerwomen"—had purposely dressed down to invoke pity from the judge and the press, in an attempt to object to George's third will and hammer home the fact, not at all true, that *they* were struggling to survive whilst "Lady Muck" was now in possession of the fortune which was rightly theirs. In doing so, they would only gain themselves reputations for being not merely greedy, but downright nasty towards their kinsman's memory. John Cowper, their lawyer, told the court:

> *The substance of my clients' plea is that the testator, Mr Formby, was not of sound mind, memory or understanding at the time he executed his will. The previous day Mr Formby had suffered a coronary thrombosis. He was treated with drugs and therefore in consequence unable to understand the nature of the act of making a will or the extent of his property, or the claims upon his testamentary bounty to which he ought to give effect. Therefore the will of 18 January must stand.*

Of course, had George left *everything* to his mother and family, instead of to Pat, the Booths would now not be declaring him mentally ill from beyond the grave. John Crowther, George's solicitor and now Pat's representative, opposed this statement when he took the stand and pronounced, whilst glaring at Eliza:

> *I myself was present when he signed his third will. Mr Formby was bright, cheerful and alert. There is no doubt in my mind that he knew what he was doing. I'm Mr Formby's sole executor, I receive no benefit under this will, but I still intend to prove its validity by way of my counsel, Mr James Fitzhugh.*

Fitzhugh's testimony was even more hard-hitting. Asked to take Eliza's age and infirmity into consideration, he ignored the court's instructions in this respect. To his way of thinking—not just in his capacity as counsel, but as George's friend—if Eliza could desecrate her son's memory by implying that he had been mentally ill, she would have to withstand the circumstances:

> *It is of my opinion that the third will should stand. When the second will was made, Mr Crowther suggested to Mr Formby that the mother should share residue with the sisters, but Mr Formby replied that he had well-provided for her and had bought her a block of flats. About this time, Mr Formby was trying to persuade Miss Howson to marry him. He even took her to a doctor, who felt able to tell Miss Howson that she would not be marrying an invalid. Mr Formby told Mr Crowther that she intended to marry Miss Howson soon, even if he was still in hospital and wanted to leave everything to her. After some hesitation Mr Formby said, "Let Harry have his £5,000—if he's still in my employment." But he said he*

> had provided for his mother in her lifetime, and that he did not want his sisters to have anything. He made certain disparaging remarks—describing the family as a set of scroungers. Mr Crowther then asked if Miss Howson should receive the money only if they married. Mr Formby's response to this was most emphatic. If he were to die tomorrow, he wanted Pat to have everything. She had brought him more happiness than he had ever known before.

Fitzhugh's diatribe upset Eliza and her daughters so much that Justice Ormrod was forced to adjourn the hearing for an hour whilst they were "treated for shock". Many of the press simply dismissed this as play-acting and a call for sympathy, particularly when Eliza used the period to tell reporters that George had never bought her anything in his life, let alone a block of flats—these, she declared, she had purchased herself with money from her husband's estate, though she had conveniently lost the documents to prove this. She had made the whole thing up, which was why her lawyer avoided this point when the hearing resumed, though he did ask the court to question what James Fitzhugh had meant by the term "well-provided for"—arguing that upon his rise to fame during the early Twenties, George had begun paying his mother a weekly allowance of 50 shillings, and that she had still been receiving the same amount at the time of his death. Fitzhugh's response was that George *would* have increased his mother's allowance had it not been for her "persistent greed and insistence that she had brought him into the world, so he should continue paying her for the privilege". Almost certainly, Beryl had been unaware of this, otherwise these payments would have stopped. Fitzhugh again used the term, "set of scroungers", the headline which was splashed across the *Daily Mail* the next day. To add weight to his argument, he held aloft a bundle of letters, for once written in George's handwriting and not Beryl's—and concluded:

> *I am not suggesting for one moment that these letters show that the description of scroungers is applied to Mr Formby's family. What they do show is that some members of the family sought help from him and that he had a certain resentment that greater demands were made upon him than ought to have been...*

Upon hearing this, Justice Ormrod ordered that the proceedings should be adjourned yet again owing to "the distressed state of Mrs Booth". Before the hearing resumed the next morning, however, Eliza agreed to a private meeting in the judge's chambers with Pat Howson and John Crowther, during which the pair proposed a compromise. Should the Booths publicly renounce their earlier statement that George had not been of sound mind when signing his final will, Pat would grant Eliza a non-negotiable, one-off payment of £5,000—the amount George had left her in his earlier will—and she would pay her daughters £2,000 each, itself a considerable gesture, she concluded, bearing in mind that George had not wanted them to have anything at all. Pat also agreed that the legal costs for both parties would be paid out of the Formby estate.

Eliza accepted the deal without hesitation, but her daughters initially elected to continue with their action against Pat. Justice Ormrod, however, instructed them that this was a "take it or leave it" offer, that Pat's conduct and attitude throughout the hearing had been "right and proper" whilst theirs had been anything but, and that if they did decide to pursue the case, they would be liable to pay for their own costs—indeed, that a further hearing might order them to reimburse the Formby estate with the costs of this one. As with Eliza, all three accepted the deal.

Outside the court, Eliza and her daughters—still looking like bag-ladies—posed for the press, whilst one photographer yelled, "Which one of you is Ena Sharples?", referring to the *Coronation Street* battleaxe. All four declined to give interviews. Pat, linking arms with Sister Marie Burnard, a nun from the hospital where George had died, offered a brief statement to a reporter from the *Daily Mail,* telling him how she had been impressed by the previous day's headline, adding:

> *I'm not sure what I'm going to do with my life. I'll probably go back to teaching. I certainly shall never marry. I'll never find anyone like George. Everyone loved him. He was the most wonderful man I've ever met.*

Pat also defended her decision to sell more of Beryl's jewellery—a heart-shaped diamond brooch, and a ruby and diamond bracelet which went under the hammer at Sotheby's for £15,000, money which she had immediately handed over to her lawyer:

> *I still haven't received the whole of my inheritance, and the jewellery was of no use to anyone lying in a bank vault. This is the best way to find the cash to meet the fantastic costs of the lawsuit over George's will. It's what he would have wanted me to do.*

For another two years, George's mother and sisters—knowing that *they* would not be contributing to the legal costs—fought to have Justice Ormrod's decision over-ruled, and the matter was only conclusively settled, in Pat's favour, in September 1965 upon the intervention of the Solicitor-General, Sir Dingle Foot.

After this spiteful, unnecessary business, whilst the Booths continued in their attempts to impress a disbelieving world how much they had loved George, adding that he had also them which of course was utter tosh—Pat Howson retired gracefully to her house in Preston, emerging only rarely from her enforced solitude for the odd media interview. On 10 March 1969, on the eve of a television tribute broadcast by Granada, she stringently denied the latest rumour cooked up by George's sister, Ethel—that only had she been sleeping with George whilst Beryl had been alive, she had been doing so since the age of fifteen. She fumed to the *Blackpool Gazette*:

> *George didn't even like this particular sister. And if she adored him the way she says she did, then she ought to be ashamed of herself for trying to blacken his name in such a despicable manner. George told me that she had always been such a disgusting woman. Now can you see why he didn't want any of them to have his money?*

In the actual television programme, Pat paid the ultimate tribute to the man she loved. When asked by the presenter, Brian McGregor, *what* it was about George that she had fallen in love with, she replied:

> *First of all, it was tremendous sympathy. But above all it was his wonderful warmth, his tremendous humility, and his honesty. I don't just mean being humble. He must have known of his own greatness, but he did not spout about it. He just took himself for granted and he was so wonderful in his relations with other people...I have no regrets. Materially, I would have been saved a great deal of trouble if we had been married, but that is the only regret. I have no personal regrets at all.*

On 22 November 1971, Pat Howson died of cancer, aged just forty-six, in a Lytham nursing-home. Almost at once, a legal row blew up over *her* will—instigated by her own father and Ethel Booth, who told the *Daily Mail*'s Sydney Brennan, "George's money had a jinx on it, I'm sure of that. If the fortune is restored to its rightful place, back to our family, this jinx will be lifted."

In fact, there was not a great deal of George's bequest lest to be argued over. The bulk of the original £135,000 had been swallowed up in legal costs and death duties, and Pat had bequeathed the remaining £20,000 to two close friends, Marjory Butler and Mary Rawcliffe, who both lived locally. The royalty rights from George's songs—which he and Beryl had purloined from their composers—were to be shared amongst these same friends, and the Prioress Carmelite Convent, near Wigan. Effectively, anyone wishing to contest this aspect of Pat's will would, her solicitor declared, be running the risk of putting personal greed before the needs of the Catholic Church, who had cared so much about her. Shortly before her death, Pat had announced that she intended returning to this devotion by becoming a nun.

Fred Howson was so convinced that he would succeed where others had failed that he pleaded his case through the newspapers, and announced how he would spent his inheritance. "I'll get myself a small bungalow, then delight in buying things for the poor and the needy who have had a tough life but never grumbled," he told the *Sunday Express*.

In recent years, Howson had really fallen on hard times. His marriage had collapsed on account of his womanising, his daughter had disowned him, and soon after George's death he had moved out of the family home and into digs. His wife had died in 1970, and by this time he had been eking out an existence on £6 a week in State benefits and living in a filthy caravan, parked in a field near Garstang. His and Ethel's pleas fell on deaf ears, and Pat's will was not over-ruled.

Eliza Booth would plead abject poverty, for another ten years.

In 1979, she invited a *Sunday Mirror* journalist to her terraced house in Warrington—she had moved their eight years previously, she said, after selling her block of flats because she could not afford to keep them on, though she did not say what she had done with the money. Her plight was highlighted under the heading: "ELIZA HAVE-LITTLE: FORMBY'S MOTHER FACES HARD TIMES". Now aged ninety-nine and totally blind, Eliza was living in near-squalor with another daughter, Louisa. Their home was infested with vermin, squatters had moved in next door, and for months the pair had been pestered by vandals. These deplorable living conditions had however been self-inflicted, for it subsequently emerged that Eliza had rejected numerous offers from Warrington's council to be rehoused. This puerile, reprehensible woman lived on until the age of 102, dying in August 1981.

Louisa Formby—*all* of his siblings tried but failed majestically to monopolise on his name—had followed George on to the stage, forming a fairly successful tap-dancing act with her brother, Frank, before the war, and then a comedy due with Bob Hall. Off and on, Frank worked as a solo performer, imitating his brother and reworking some of his songs, but he never amounted to much and died completely forgotten.

The retainers—friends and foes alike—are all gone, along with all of George's family and his co-stars. Each played a part in his success, or failed to contribute to the besmirchment of his memory and good name. Imitators, at best mediocre in comparison to the supreme artiste that he was, fail to capture his magic and will always be relegated to walking I the shadow of his sun. Thora Hird, who *almost* appeared in one of his films, hit the nail on the head by hailing him, "A legend sent by God!"

Legends, of course, never die and George Formby's name and his unique legacy live on.

"George Formby—a legend sent by God!"

Appendix I:
George Formby Discography

The following represents George Formby's recorded output between 1924 and 1960 on 78rpm shellac singles, and on 33rpm and 45rpm vinyl. Alternative and reject takes, more numerous at the beginning of his career, are not included unless they were not released on 78rpm. The original recordings are as they were issued in the UK—the frequently differing B-sides which accompanied overseas A-sides are not included. More details of these, along with the lyricists and composers, can be found in Brendan Ryan's exhaustive, *George Formby: A Catalogue of His Work*, published in 1986 by the George Formby Society. All of these recordings were released during his lifetime.

1924 (HMV)

BB 4164: Rolling Around Piccadilly (Audition) Unreleased.

1926 (EDISON-BELL WINNER) All Formby Sr Songs.

4409 John Willie Come On/I Was Always A Willing Young Lad

4418 John Willie's Jazz-Band (I) / Since I Parted My Hair In The Middle

4437 The Man Was A Stranger To Me/Rolling Around Piccadilly

1929 (DOMINION)

C 347 All Going Back/ In The Congo

1932 (DECCA)

Matrix T620-1 Our House Is Haunted/ I Told My Baby With My Ukulele (Auditions)

Matrix GB 5028/ 5029 Yo, Yo Men Of England. Parts 1 & 2

F3079 Do De O Do/Chinese (Laundry) Blues

F3219 I Told My Baby With My Ukulele/ If You Don't Want The Goods Don't Maul 'Em

F3222 The Old Kitchen Kettle/ The Baked Potato Man (instr)

F3259 John Willie At The Licence Office Parts 1 & 2 (with Beryl Formby)

F3377 I Could Make A Living At That/ Let's All Go To Reno

1933 (DECCA)

F3254 Why Don't Woman Like Me/ Running Round The Fountains In Trafalgar Square

F3458 Sitting On The Ice In The Ice Rink/ Levi's Monkey Mike

F3615 With My Little Ukulele In My Hand (I)**/ As The Hours And The Days…

F3615 Sunbathing In The Park/As The Hours And The Days (** deemed offensive: the A-Side replaced with "Sunbathing In The Park")

F3666 She's Never Been Seen Since Then/Swimmin' With The Women

F3752 My Ukulele("cleaned-up" version of "With My Little Ukulele In My Had") / I Went All Hot And Cold

F3800 The Wedding Of Mr Wu/ Baby

1934 (DECCA)
F3950 Believe It Or Not/ In A Little Wigan Garden

F5183 You Can't Keep A Growing Lad Down/ It's No Use Looking At Me

F5232 John Willie's Jazz-Band (II)/ There's Nothing Proud About Me

F5287 The Best Of Schemes/ Madame Moscovitch

F5303 John Willie Goes Carolling (I & II)

1935 (DECCA)

F5569 Fanlight Fanny/ Share And Share Alike

F5699 The Fiddler Kept On Fiddling/ I Do Do Things I Do

1935 (REGAL ZONOPHONE)

MR1932 Riding In The TT Races/ The Isle Of Man

MR1952 Pleasure Cruise/ The Wash House At The Back/ I'm Going To Stick To My Mother/ I Promised To Be Home By Nine O'Clock/ Isn't Love A Very Funny Thing/ There's No Harm In A Kiss

1936 (REGAL ZONOPHONE)

MR2033 A Farmer's Boy/ Radio Bungalow Town

MR2060 Gallant Dick Turpin. Sketch, both sides, with Beryl Formby & Co. Includes the ditty, "Gallant Dick Turpentine"

MR2083 *George Formby Medley*: Sitting On The Ice In The Ice Rink; Do De O Do; Chinese Laundry Blues; Madame Moscovitch; My Ukulele; Fanlight Fanny

MR2162 Ring Your Little Bell/ *Quick Fire Medley*: It Ain't Nobody's Business What I Do; Goody-Goody; I Like Bananas

MR2199 When I'm Cleaning Windows (banned version)/ Keep Your Seats Please

MR 2232 Sitting On The Sands All Night/ Five And Twenty Years

MR2270 I'm A Froggie/ The Ghost (updated version of the 1922 song, "Our House Is Haunted")

MR2295 Bunkum's Travelling Show/ Dare Devil Dick/ Riding Around On A Rainbow/ Your Way Is My Way

1937 (REGAL ZONOPHONE)

MR 2368 Hindoo Man/ My Little Goat And Me

MR 2399 The Window Cleaner (No 2)/ The Lancashire Toreador

MR2430 When We Feather Our Nest/ You're A Li-a-ty

MR2431 Oh, Dear Mother/ With My Little Stick Of Blackpool Rock

MR2469 Trailing Around In A Trailer/ Said The Little Brown Hen

MR2490 Leaning On A Lamp Post (I)/ Hit-Tiddley-Hi-Ti Island

MR2506 Somebody's Wedding Day/ Easy Going Chap

MR2570 Biceps, Muscle And Brawn/ Keep Fit

MR2571 I Don't Like/ My Plus-Fours

MR2616 Remember Me/ Maybe I'll Find Somebody Else (sung by the boxer Tommy Farr, with Formby spoken intro and ukulele solo)

MR2628 You Can't Stop Me From Dreaming/ She Can't Say No

IR-51 [Matrix: 4448-1] Keep Your Seats Please**

IR-52 [Matrix: 4657-1] Keep Fit** (** These were film-trailers issued to cinemas for promotional purposes and not issued commercially. Formby speaks about the film, followed by a musical extract.

Unknown: I'm As Happy As A Sandboy (from the film *Feather Your Nest*, but not recorded)

1938 (REGAL ZONOPHONE)

MR2684 Does Your Dreamboat Tell You That? (sung with Beryl Formby)/ Like The Big Pots Do

MR2709 Have You Heard This One/ Wunga Bunga Boo

MR2735 Springtime's Here Again/ The Joo Jah Tree

MR2752 Mother What'll I Do Now/ Noughts And Crosses

MR2753 I Blew A Little Blast On My Whistle/ In My Little Snapshot Album

MR2890 Our Sergeant Major/ Rhythm Of The Alphabet

MR2891 It's In The Air/ They Can't Fool Me

MR2925 I Wonder Who's Who's Under Her Balcony Now/ Tan-Tan-Tivvy-Tally-Ho

MR2947 Sitting Pretty With My Fingers Crossed/ Kiss Your Mansy-Pansy

MR 2969 FrigidAir Fanny/My Little Wooden Tool Shed In The Garden

1939 (REGAL ZONOPHONE)

MR3022 It's Turned Out Nice Again/ Hilly Billy Willie

MR3026 Swinging Along Singing A Song/A Lad From Lancashire

MR3039 Hitting The High Spots Now/ I Can Tell It By My Horoscope

MR3081 It's A Grand And Healthy Life/ I'm The Husband Of The Wife Of Mr Wu

MR3103 *Swing It George Medley*: Some Of These Days; Hard-Hearted Hannah; Sweet Georgia Brown/Sweet Sue; Dinah; Tiger Rag

MR3121 Dan The Dairy Man/The Blue-Eyed Blonde Next Door

MR3147 With My Little Stick Of Rock */Lancashire Hot Pot Singers
*replaced the suppressed "Low Down Lazy Turk". See G-23917 below.

MR3160 Goodnight, Little Fellow, Goodnight/Pardon Me

MR3161 I'm Making Headway Now/I Couldn't Let The Stable Down

MR3301 Grandad's Flannelette Nightshirt/Mr Wu's A Window Cleaner Now

G-23917 Low Down Lazy Turk */ Lancashire Hot Pot Swingers.
*Suppressed in Britain, released only in Australasia.

1940 (REGAL ZONOPHONE)
MR3316 Count Your Blessings And Smile/Oh, Don't The Wind Blow Cold

MR3324 I Always Get To Bed By Half-Past Nine/You've Got Something There

MR3325 Down The Old Coal Hole/On The Wigan Boat Express

MR3358 I'm The Ukulele Man/ On The Beat

MR3394 Bless 'Em All (I)/Letting The New Year In

MR3411 Guarding The Home Of The Home Guards/ Letting The New Year In

Matrix TT-2623 *George Formby Entertains The Troops*: Dick Whittington Sketch (with Beryl Formby); With My Little Stick Of Blackpool Rock; Imagine Me In The Maginot Line; When I'm Cleaning Windows; Chinese Laundry Blues (recorded live in France, 23-3-1940).

1941 (REGAL ZONOPHONE)

MR3441 Bless 'Em All (2)/Thanks Mr Roosevelt

MR3463 I Did What I Could With My Gas Mask/ You'll Be Far Better Off In A Home

MR3472 Delivering The Morning Milk/It Might Have Been A Great Deal Worse

MR3482 *Formby Favourites For The Forces*: Our Sergeant Major; The Lancashire Toreador; It's A Grand And Healthy Life; With My Little Stick Of Blackpool Rock; I'm The Husband Of The Wife Of Mr Wu; When I'm Cleaning Windows

MR3512 You're Everything To Me (with Beryl Formby & John Firman)/ The Emperor Of Lancashire

MR3520 Aunty Maggie's Remedy (I)/ You Can't Go Wrong In These (with Beryl Formby)

MR3521 The Left-Hand Side Of Egypt/Who Are You A-Shoving Of?

MR3550 *George Formby Crazy Record*: Alexander's Ragtime Band; La Donna E Mobile; She'll Be Coming Round The Mountain; The Old (New) Sow. With Beryl Formby & John Firman

MR3553 Swing Mama/I Played On My Spanish Guitar

MR3567 I'd Do It With A Smile/The Barmaid At The Rose And Crown

1942 [REGAL ZONOPHONE]

MR3599 *Formby Film Favourites*: When We Feather Our Nest; Our Sergeant Major; The Isle Of Man; Hitting The High Spots Now

MR3619 Katy Did, Katy Didn't/ Frank On His Tank

MR3624 Smile All The Time/ Out In The Middle East

MR3640 Mr Wu Is Now An Air-Raid Warden/ Got To Get Your Photo To The Press

MR3645 Talking To The Moon About You/Delivering The Morning Milk

MR3648 Andy The Handy Man/They Laughed When I Started To Play

MR3654 Thirty Thirsty Sailors/Hold Your Hats On (sung by soldiers in the film, *Troopship*.

MR3663 Cookhouse Serenade/You Can't Love Two Girls At The Same Time

Matrix CAR6348-1 Sally The Salvage Queen

1943 (REGAL ZONOPHONE)

MR3672 The Baby Show/When The Waterworks Caught Fire

MR3682 Spotting On The Top Of Blackpool Tower/ Sentimental Lou

MR3689 Get Cracking/Home Guard Blues

MR3694 Under The Blasted Oak/Oh You Have No Idea

MR3705 *American Medley*: My Old Kentucky Home; Camptown Races; She'll Be Coming Round The Mountain; Old Folks At Home; Oh Susannah; Over There/*British Medley*: Hearts Of Oak; Men Of Harlech; John Peel; On Ilkley Moor; Loch Lomond; Come Landlord Fill The Flowing Bowl; Auld Lang Syne

MR3710 Bunty's Such A Big Now/On The HMS Cowheel

1944 [REGAL ZONOPHONE)

MR3720 Bell-Bottom George/If I Had A Girl Like You

MR3733 Swim Little Fish/It Serves You Right

MR3736 The V-Sign Song/The Old Cane-Bottom Chair

1945 [REGAL ZONOPHONE]

MR3475 Our Fanny's Gone All Yankee/ Unconditional Surrender

MR3750 Mr Wu In The Air-Force/Blackpool Prom

MR3760 The Daring Young Man/I'd Like To Dream Like That

MR3761 She's Got Two Of Everything/Up In The Air And Down In The Dumps

1946 [COLUMBIA]

FB3251 You Don't Need A Licence For That/The Mad March Hare

FB3262 We've Been A Long Time Gone/It Could Be

Matrix CAX9466-2 Get Cracking (Live recording at the Leicester Square theatre, 16/4/46, subsequently released on Columbia DOX 823)

1950 [DECCA]

F9356 Come Hither With Your Zither/Aunty Maggie's Remedy (Version Two, minus two verses contained in Version One)

F9444 Leaning On A Lamp Post (II)/When I'm Cleaning Windows (II)

1951 [HIS MASTER'S VOICE]

B-10179 I'm Saving Up For Sally/The Pleasure Cruise

B-10180 Ordinary People/Zip Goes A Million

1960 [PYE]

7N-15269 Happy-Go-Lucky Me/Banjo Boy

MISCELLANEOUS 1953-69
Between these dates George Formby sang the following, not previously recorded or in the stated versions, on radio (R) or television (T):

Sweet Georgia Brown (R), *In Town Tonight*, BBC, 5/10/53

Leaning On A Lamp Post (T) with Terry-Thomas, *Top Of The Town*, BBC, 9/1/55

Sara Maraise (R): *In Town Tonight*, BBC, 16/4/55

Ordinary People (T) with Petula Clark, *The George Formby Show*, BBC, 15/5/57

MEDLEY: Some Of These Days; Dinah: Sweet Georgia Brown (T) with The Deep River Boys, *Formby Favourites*, BBC, 6/9/58

Hello Canada (T), *Atlantic Showboat*, BBC, 13/12/58

'Tain't No Sin To Take Off Your Skin; Piccolo Pete, *Stepping Out With Formby*, BBC, 25/4/59

MEDLEY: Living Doll; Scotland The Brave; Ma, He's Making Eyes At Me (T) with Morton Fraser & The Harmonica Rascals, *Showtime*, BBC, 29/11/59

THE "MISSING SONGS"
Around 100 George Formby songs were recorded on acetate between November 1935 and June 1945, few of which have been commercially released. Most are by the regular teams of Gifford and Cliffe, Eddie Latta and Formby himself, and Jack Cottrell. Some are in the EMI archives, others may be lost. In alphabetical order they are as follows:

All The Girls Serving On The Jury
Another Lucky Day
Antonio My Romeo
At Dusk
Because Of You
The Bell Tolled Out
The Bomb-Proof Shelter In The Garden
Bottle-Nosed Bertha From Bow
The Butcher's Meet
Bye And Bye
The Canal Boat Queen
Casey's Charabanc
A Couple O' Pounds Of Tripe
The Colonials Are Calling Me

The Coronation March
Cucumber Time At Kew
Down On Our Little Farm
Draw My Cigar
Drinkin'
Every Bit Of Help
Every Little Corner Of My Irish Home
George's Christmas Box
Give Me A Cosy Parlour
The Green Green Grass Grew All Around
Hello Canada!
He Said He Would Remember
Hey, It's A Wonderful Day!
How I Play The Ukulele
Hurrah For The Rolling Sea!
I Ate One Two
I Could Do With A Day In Bed
I Couldn't Let The Boy Scouts Down
I Couldn't Miss A Chance Like That
I'm A G-Man
I'm A Sailor
I'm Daft When I'm In Love
I'm Going to Take Up Flying
I'm Leaving The Women Alone
I'm Leslie The Wrecker of Women
I May Not Be Your First Love
I Must Have A Change With My Meals
In 1944
In My Little Store Of Melody
I Remember
I Said "Ee, You're Welcome!"
It's All Through Mr Wu
It's No Laughing Matter
It's Only A Question Of Time
I Was Waggling My Magic Wand
I Was Touching My Lucky Charm

I Was Touching My Wishbone
Jolly-Polly Oliver
The Lancashire Scotch Brigade
Let George Do It
Let's All Go To A Holiday Camp
The Liverpool Song
Living On Our Avenue
Love On Wheels
Make A Start
Making The Most Of My Time
The Meditating Hindoo Man
Murphy's Museum
My Little Boomerang
My Oasis Of Love
My Perso-nality
My Ukulele Sweetheart
No One Understands
Now-Now, Come-Come!
Only Half A Day-Trip
O Pola-Nocola
The Pie-can Eleven
The Plumber's Song
The Private, The Corp And The Sarge
Robbing Hood
Rollin' Into France
Shake Yourself A Sunshine Cocktail
Seringatapan
Seven O'Clock
The Sheik Of Araby
Shout At Auntie Lily
Sixpence Ha'penny
Somebody's Son
There'll Be No Performance Tonight
Thirty-Bob A Week
Those Were The Days
The Triumph Of Alceste

The Wart On Grandad's Nose
We Can't Make William Tell
When It's Cucumber Time
Who Told You That
The Wigan Butcher
The World Would Be Mine Once Again
You Never Can Tell With Me
You're A Great Big Beautiful Boy
You've Got To Make A Start Some Time

VINYL RE-ISSUES OF 78RPM RECORDINGS
Recordings issued during Formby's lifetime.
45rpm Extended Play (All 1959)

George Formby & His Ukulele Vol 1: Sitting On The Ice In The Ice Rink; Levi's Monkey Mike; Chinese Laundry Blues; Do De O Do
    DECCA EP-DFE 6144

George Formby & His Ukulele Vol 2: Leaning On A Lamp Post; When I'm Cleaning Windows; Auntie Maggie's Remedy; Come Hither With Your Zither
    DECCA EP-DFE 6328

George Formby & His Ukulele Vol 3: She's Never Been Seen Since Then; Swimmin' With The Women; It's No Use Looking At Me; You Can't Keep A Growing Lad Down
    DECCA EP-DFE 6355

The Ukulele Man Vol 1: Mr Wu's A Window Cleaner Now; Hi-Tiddley-Hi-Ti Island; When I'm Cleaning Windows; Leaning On A Lamp Post
    COLUMBIA EP-SEG7550

The Ukulele Man Vol 2: I'm The Husband Of The Wife Of Mr Wu; Grandad's Flannelette Nightshirt; Under The Blasted Oak; Oh, You Have No Idea
    COLUMBIA EP-SEG7661

Stepping Out With George: Our Sergeant Major; Frigid Air Fanny; With My Little Stick Of Blackpool Rock; Oh, Dear Mother
   COLUMBIA EP-SEG 7936

Stepping Out With George Again: She's Got Two Of Everything; When The Waterworks Caught Fire; The Blue-Eyed Blonde Next Door; Like The Big Pots Do
   COLUMBIA EP-SEG 7964

33 rpm Album (1961)

George Formby Souvenir: When I'm Cleaning Windows; Why Don't Women Like Me; Fanlight Fanny; Auntie Maggie's Remedy; I Told My Baby With My Ukulele; Believe It Or Not; Chinese Laundry Blues; My Ukulele; There's Nothing Proud About Me; As The Hours Roll By; Madame Moscovitch; Leaning On A Lamp Post
   DECCA ACL 1062

Appendix II:
George Formby Filmography

NO FOOL LIKE AN OLD FOOL [1915] BARKER FILMS. 5 reels. No other details.

BY THE SHORTEST OF HEADS [1915] BARKER FILMS. 5 reels. Director: Bert Haldane. Script: Percy Manton, Jack Hulcup. With Sidney Blackmer, Valerie Hobson, Moore Marriott, Jack Hulcup, Jack Tessier, Percy Manton, George Formby.

BOOTS! BOOTS! [1934] BLAKELEY PRODUCTIONS
Director: Bert Tracey. Script: Jack Cottrell, George Formby. Photography: Roy Fogwell. Music: Harry Hudson. With Beryl Formby, Tonie Ford, Arthur King, Lillian Keyes, Donald Reid, Constance Fletcher, Myfanwy Southern, Wallace Roscoe. A scene featuring Betty Driver was cut from the finished print. George played John Willie, aka "Boots". 50 mins. **Songs**: Baby; Why Don't Women Like Me; Sitting On the Ice In The Ice Rink; I Could Make A Good Living At That; Chinese Laundry Blues (instrumental only).

OFF THE DOLE [1935] BLAKELEY PRODUCTIONS
Director: Arthur Mertz. Script: Arthur Mertz, John Blakeley. Photography: Sidney Leach. With Beryl Formby, Dan Young, Clifford McLaglen, Wally Patch, Tully Comber, James Plant, Constance Shotter, Stan Pell, Daisy Maynard, Stan Little, Lew Martin. George played John Willie. 69 mins. **Songs**: With My Little Ukulele In My Hand; If You Don't Want the Goods Don't Maul 'Em; I Promised To Be Home By Nine O'Clock; I'm Going To Stick To My Mother; Isn't Love A Very Funny Thing; Surely There's No Harm In A Kiss; The Nearer The Bone The Sweeter The Meat (sung by Dan Young).

GEORGE FORMBY CAVALCADE [1935] BLAKELEY PRODUCTIONS. The songs from Formby's first two films. 26 mins.

NO LIMIT [1935] ATP/EALING
Director: Monty Banks. Script: Tom Geraghty, Fred Thompson. Photography: Roy Fogwell. With Florence Desmond, Edward Rigby, Bert Tyldesley, Jack Hobbs, Peter Gawthorne, Alf Goddard, Florence Gregson, Beatrix Fielden Kaye, Howard Douglas, Evelyn Roberts. George played George Shuttleworth. 77 mins. **Songs**: Riding In The TT Races; Riding Around On A Rainbow; In A Little Wigan Garden; Your Way Is My Way.

KEEP YOUR SEATS PLEASE [1936] ATP/EALING
Director: Monty Banks. Script: Tom Geraghty, Ian Hay, Anthony Kimmins. Based on the play, *Twelve Chairs*, by Eugene Petrov and Elie Ilf. With Florence Desmond, Alastair Sim, Gus McNaughton, Harry Tate, Fiona Stuart, Hal Gordon, Mike Johnson, Enid Stamp-Taylor, Tom Payne, Feldon Kaye, Clifford Heatherley. George played George. 82 mins. **Songs**: Keep Your Seats Please; Standing Of The Tip Of My Toes; Goodnight Binkie; When I'm Cleaning Windows.

FEATHER YOUR NEST [1937] ATP/EALING
Director: William Beaudine. Script: Austin Melford, Val Valentine. Photography: Ronald Neame. Original titles: *He Never Touched Me!; Marriage By Instalments*. With Polly Ward, Enid Stamp-Taylor, Val Rossing, Davy Burnaby, Jimmy Godden, Ethel Coleridge, Jack Barty, Tom Payne, Frederick Burtwell. George played Willie Piper. 88 mins. **Songs**: When We Feather Our Nest; I'm As Happy As A Sandboy; Leaning On A Lamp Post.

KEEP FIT [1937] ATP/EALING
Director: Anthony Kimmins. Script: Anthony Kimmins, Austin Melford. Photography: Ronald Neame. With Kay Walsh, Guy Middleton, George Benson, Gus McNaughton, Evelyn Roberts, Edmund Breon, C Denier Warren, Hal Gordon, Leo Franklyn, Hal Walters, Aubrey Mallalieu, George played George Green. 82 mins. **Songs**: Keep Fit; Biceps, Muscle And Brawn; I Don't Like.

CHRISTMAS GREETINGS OF 1937 ATP/EALING
Formby was one of numerous participants in this 8 minutes trailer.

I SEE ICE [1938] ATP/EALING
Director: Anthony Kimmins. Script: Anthony Kimmins, George Bright. Photography: Gordon Dimes, Ronald Neame. With Kay Walsh, Cyril Ritchard, Garry Marsh, Betty Stockfield, Gavin Gordon, Ernest Sefton, Frederick Burtwell, Archibald Batty, Frank Leighton. George played George Bright. 82 mins. **Songs**: Mother What'll I Do Now; Noughts And Crosses; In My Little Snapshot Album.

CHRISTMAS GREETINGS OF 1938 ATP/EALING
Formby was one of numerous participants in this 10 minutes trailer.

IT'S IN THE AIR [1938] ATP/EALING
Director & Script: Anthony Kimmins. Photography: Ronald Neame. With Polly Ward, Garry Marsh, Julien Mitchell, Jack Hobbs, C Denier Warren, Esme Cannon, Hal Gordon, Jack Melford, Scruffy. George played George Brown. 84 mins. **Songs**: It's In The Air; Our Sergeant Major; They Can't Fool Me.

TROUBLE BREWING [1939] ATP/EALING
Director: Anthony Kimmins. Script: Anthony Kimmins, Michael Hogan, Angus McPhail. Photography: Ronald Neame. Based on the novel by Joan Butler. With Googie Withers, Gus McNaughton, Martita Hunt, Garry Marsh, Josh Ambler, Ronald Shiner, Basil Radford, Esme Cannon. George played George Gullip. 85 mins. **Songs**: I Can Tell It By My Horoscope; Hitting The High Spots Now; Fanlight Fanny.

COME ON GEORGE! [1939] ATP/EALING
Director: Anthony Kimmins. Script: Anthony Kimmins, Val Valentine, Leslie Arliss. Photography: Ronald Neame. Music: Ernest Irving. With Pat Kirkwood, Meriel Forbes, Ronald Stagg, George Carney, Ronald Shiner, Cyril Raymond, George Hayes, Hal Gordon. George played George. 86 mins. **Songs**: I Couldn't Let The Stable Down; I'm Making Headway Now; Goodnight, Little Fellow, Goodnight. Pardon Me.

LET GEORGE DO IT [1940]ATP/EALING
Director: Marcel Varnel. Script: John Dighton, Austin Melford, Angus McPhail, Basil Dearden. Photography: Ronald Neame. Music: Ernest Irving, Harry Bidgood. With Phyllis Calvert, Garry Marsh, Coral Brown, Romney Brent, Diana Beaumont, Torin Thatcher, Hal Gordon, Donald Calthrop, Bernard Lee, Percy Walsh, Ronald Shiner, Gavin Gordon. George played George Hepplewhite. 78 mins. **Songs**: Grandad's Flannelette Nightshirt; Oh, Don't The Wind Blow Cold; Count Your Blessings And Smile; Mr Wu's A Window Cleaner Now.

SPARE A COPPER [1940] ATP/EALING
Director: John Paddy Carstairs. Script: Roger MacDougal, Austin Melford, Basil Dearden. Photography: Bryan Langley. With Dorothy Hyson, Bernard Lee, Beryl Reid, Elliot Makeham, Ellen Pollock. George played George Carter. 77 minutes. **Songs**: I'm The Ukulele Man; On The Beat; I Wish I Was Back On The Farm; I'm Shy.

TURNED OUT NICE AGAIN [1941] ATP/EALING
Director: Marcel Varnel. Script: Austin Melford, Basil Dearden, John Dighton. Based on the play, *As You Are*, by Hugh Mills and Wells Root. Photography: Gordon Dines. With Peggy Bryan, Elliot Mason, Edward Chapman, Mackenzie Ward, O B Clarence, Wilfred Hyde White, John Salew, Michael Rennie, Hay Petrie, Ronald Ward. George played George Pearson. 77 mins. **Songs**: Auntie Maggie's Remedy; You Can't Go Wrong In These; The Emperor Of Lancashire; You're Everything To Me.

SOUTH AMERICAN GEORGE [1941] COLUMBIA
Director: Marcel Varnel. Script: Leslie Arliss, Norman Lee, Austin Melford. Photography: Arthur Crabtree. Music: Harry Bidgood. Tenor voices: Giovanni Martinelli (*La Traviata*), Webster Booth *(Lucia di Lammermoor)*. With Linden Travers, Jacques Brown, Ronald Shiner, Enid Stamp-Taylor, Felix Aylmer, Beatrice Varley, Alf Goddard, Herbert Lomas, Gus McNaughton, Marie Villiers, Muriel George, Eric Clavering. George played George Butters and Gilli Vannetti. 88 mins. **Songs**: The Barmaid At The Rose And Crown; Swing Mama; I Played On My Spanish Guitar; La Donna E Mobile; I'd Do It With A Smile.

MUCH TOO SHY [1942] COLUMBIA
Director: Marcel Varnel. Script: Ronald Frankau. Photography: Arthur Crabtree. Music: Harry Bidgood. With Jimmy Clitheroe, Eileen Bennett, Kathleen Harrison, Hilda Bayley, Joss Ambler, Brefi O'Rourke, Peter Gawthorne, Charles Hawtrey, Gus McNaughton, Eric Clavering, Valentine Dyall, Frederick Burtwell, Gibb McLaughlin, D J Williams, Percy Walsh, May Norton, Wally Patch, Jack Vyvvyan, André Sacré, Marjorie Pointer. George played George Andy. 88 mins. **Songs**: Andy The Handy Man; They Laughed When I Started To Play, Talking To The Moon About You, Delivering The Morning Milk.

GET CRACKING [1943] COLUMBIA
Director: Marcel Varnel. Script: L Du Garde Peach, Edward Drynhurst, Michael Vaughan, John L Arthur. Photography: Stephen Dale. Special Effects: Fred Ford. With Dinah Sheridan, Everett Manley, Ronald Shiner, Edward Rigby, Frank Pettingell, Mike Johnson, Wall Patch, Irene Handl, Vera Frances. George played George Singleton. 92 mins. **Songs**: Under The Blasted Oak; Home Guard Blues; When The Lads Of The Village Get Cracking.

BELL-BOTTOM GEORGE [1943/4] COLUMBIA
Director: Marcel Varnel. Script: Peter Fraser, Edward Dryhurst, Peter Cresswell, Richard Fisher, John L Arthur. Photography: Roy Fogwell. With Anne Firth, Charles Farrell, Peter Murray Hill, Reginald Purdell, Elliot Makeham, Manning Whiley, Jane Welsh, Dennis Wynham, Hugh Dempsey, Charles Hawtrey, Peter Gawthorne. George played George Blake. 94 mins. **Songs**: Swim Little Fish; It Serves You Right; If I Had A Girl Like You; Bell-Bottom George.

HE SNOOPS TO CONQUER [1945] COLUMBIA
Director: Marcel Varnel. Script: Howard Irving-Young, Norman Lee, Stephen Black, Langford Reed, Michael Vaughan. Photography: Roy Fogwell. With Robsertson Hare, Elizabeth Allen, Claude Bailey, James Harcourt, Gordon McLeod, Vincent Holman, Aubrey Mallalieu, William Rodwell. George played George Gribble. 97 mins. **Songs**: Hill Billy Willie; Got To Get Your Photo In The Press; Unconditional Surrender.

I DIDN'T DO IT! [1945] COLUMBIA
Director: Marcel Varnel. Script: Howard Irving-Young, Norman Lee, Stephen Black, Peter Fraser, Michael Vaughan. Photography: Roy Fogwell. Music: Harry Biggood. With Carl Jaffé, Billy Caryl, Jack Daly, Marjorie Brown, Hilda Mundy, Gaston Palmer, Wally Patch, Ian Fleming, The Boswell Twins, Vincent Holman, Georgina Cookson, Dennis Wyndham, Gordon McLeod. George played George Trotter. 93 mins. **Songs**: She's Got Two Of Everything; I'd Like A Dream Like That; The Daring Young Man.

GEORGE IN CIVVY STREET [1946] COLUMBIA
Director: Marcel Varnel. Script: Peter Fraser, Ted Kavanaugh, Max Kester, Gale Pedrick. Photography: Philip Grindrod. Music: Johnny Claes & His Band. With Rosalyn Boulter, Ronald Shiner, Ian Fleming, Frank Drew, Philippa Hiatt, Wally Patch, Mike Johnson, Enid Cruickshank, Robert Ginns, Moore Raymond, John E Coyle, Roddy Hughes, Daphne Elphinstone. George played George Harper. 76 mins. **Songs**: The Mad March Hare; We've Been A Long Time Gone; You Don't Need A Licence For That; It Could Be; I Was Christened With A Horse-Shoe; You Don't Need Them (sung by Daphne Elpinstone).

FAREWELL SHOW [1960, restored 1994. MASTERSOUND]
George Formby's legendary *Friday Show*, which serves as his epitaph. The opening caption reads: *In December 1960, one of the world's greatest stars said his farewell in a musical concert which revealed many surprising details of his life. The business deals, the first films, his poor education, the famous father, the regrets of his private life, and those exciting wartime years. Supported by a full orchestra and ten hit songs, this is a recording to enjoy and treasure. Ten weeks later, the cheerful Emperor of Lancashire lost his long battle against ill-health.* **Songs**: With My Little Stick Of Blackpool Rock; It Serves You Right; George Was A Miner (Down The Old Coal Hole); Swim Little Fish; Guarding The Home Of The Home Guard; Goodnight Little Fellow Goodnight; Sitting On The Ice In The ice Rink; When I'm Cleaning Windows; Chinese Laundry Blues; Leaning On A Lamp Post. 36 mins.

Appendix III:
George Formby Stage Plays

ZIP GOES A MILLION! 20/10/1951 Palace Theatre, London.
An Emile Littler Concept/Presentation. Libretto: Eric Maschwitz. Music: George Posford. Producer: Charles Hickman. Musical Direction: Debroy Summers. Based on *Brewster's Millions* by George Barr-McCutcheon and Winchell Smith. Previewed in Coverntry and Manchester in September 1951. Formby left the production in April 1952. Cast: George Formby, Ward Donovan, Barbara Perry, Wallace Eaton, Sarah Gregory, Ian Stuart, Wilfred Kirkness, John Marquand.
Songs: Zip Goes A Million; Riding Into Town; Raratonga; I'm Saving Up For Sally; The Story Of Chiquita; The Thing About You; It Takes No Time To Fall In Love; Nothing Breaks But The Heart; Thou Art For me; I Owe You; Big Business; Ordinary People; Running Away To Land; Garter Girl; The Pleasures of A Pleasure Cruise.

TOO YOUNG TO MARRY 1954-56. Touring
An Emile Littler Concept/Presentation. Libretto: Martin Flavin, revamped by Emile Littler. Director: Maxwell Wray. Cast: George Formby, Arthur Hoskins, Eric Yorke, Shaun O'Riordan, Sydney Arnold.
Song: If You Don't Want The Goods Don't Maul 'Em.

BESIDE THE SEASIDE: A HOLDAY ROMP! March-May 1958.
Script: Leslie Sands. Presented by Derek Salberg. Director: Maxwell Wray. Cast: George Formby, Barbara Mitchell, Nancy Roberts, Doreen Andrew, Michael Lomax, Rosemary Towler, Anne Jameson, Susan Neil, Denis Spenser.
Songs: Leaning On A Lamp Post; Swimmin' With The Women.

Appendix IV:
George Formby: Immediate Family

Eliza Ann Hoy (1879-1981) married George Formby Sr (James Lawler Booth, 1875-1921).

Children:

1. Louisa (1900)
2. Beatrice (1901-2)
3. Edith Lillian (1903)
4. George Hoy (1904-61)
5. Unknown (1905)
6. Louisa (1906—?)
7. Unknown (1909)
8. Frances (1908-9)
9. Ella (1910-98)
10. Mary (1912-87)
11. Frank Allen (1913-83)
12. Ethel (1915-98)
13. Edward (1918-2007

Bibliography & Primary & Secondary Sources

BEVAN, Irene: *Interviews with David Bret*, 1993-5.
BOOTH, Eliza: *Interviews with David Sharpe*, 1974.
BRET, David: *Gracie Fields, The Authorised Biography* (Robson, 1995).
COTTRELL, Dorothy: *Interview with David Bret*, 1998.
DANCE MUSIC POLICY COMPANY: *Minutes* (unpublished, 1944).
DUNN, J H: *Letters from Palestine* (unpublished, 1943).
ELLIS, Sqd-Leader Frank: *Letters from North Africa* (unpublished, 1943).
FISHER, John: *George Formby* (Woburn-Futura, 1975).
FORMBY, Beryl: *War Diary* (unpublished, 1940).
FORMBY, George: *In The Days Of My Youth* (unpublished, 1936).
FORMBY, George: *Interviews with Brian Hargreaves* (unpublished, 1956-61).
HIGH COURT OF JUSTICE: *Probate, Divorce & Admiralty Papers, 1961-6.*
HOWSON, Fred: *Interview* (*Sunday Express,* 1971).
HOWSON, Patricia: *Interviews* (published/unpublished, 1961-6).
KIRKWOOD, Pat: *Interview with David Bret*, 1998.
RANDALL, Alan & SEATON, Ray: *George Formby* (W H Allen, 1974).
SHERIDAN, Dinah: *Interviews with David Bret*, 1998-9.
SMITH, Phyllis (Sylvia): *Journals* (unpublished, 1936-44).
SMITH, Phyllis (Sylvia): *Interviews with Beryl Formby* (unpublished, 1956-60).

Publications:
GREAT BRITAIN: *Daily Telegraph; The Stage; The Independent; Blackpool Evening Gazette; Tatler; The Times; The Daily Mail; Sunday Express; Daily Herald; Daily Express; Daily Mirror; Variety; Sunday*

Mirror; People; Pictorial; Daily Film Renter; The Guardian; Sunday Times; The Daily Worker; Today's Cinema; The Vellum; Picturegoer; Film Weekly; Kinematograph Weekly.

AUSTRALIA: *Adelaide Advertiser; Sydney Current Affairs Bulletin; Sydney Morning Herald.*

CANADA: *The Hamilton Spectator; Toronto Globe & Mail; Toronto Star; Vancouver Sun.*

SOUTH AFRICA: *Cape Times; Johannesburg Sunday Times; Durban & Natal Mercury; Pretoria News.*

SOUTHERN RHODESIA (Zimbabwe): *Bulawayo Sunday News; Bulawayo Chronicle.*

JOURNALISTS & CONTRIBUTORS: Chris Arnot; Michael Berry; Sydney Brennan; Arthur Brooks; Peter Clayton; Hubert Cole; Kevin Daly; Russell Davies; Jane Fickling; Clifford Greenwood; John Gale; Brian Hargreaves; Ed Hocura; Fred Bruce Lockhart; Kerstin McClure; Morrissey; David Nathan; Harry Scott; David Sharpe; Hannen Swaffer; Leonard Wallace; Michael Walsh; Cecil Wilson.

David Bret has also written...

"Our George": A Two-Act Play

c/w "Our Annie's Funeral"

Printed in Great Britain
by Amazon